A BUCKEYE IN THE LAND OF GOLD

The Letters and Journal of
William Dennison Bickham

BICKHAM'S GOLD COUNTRY: 1850-1851

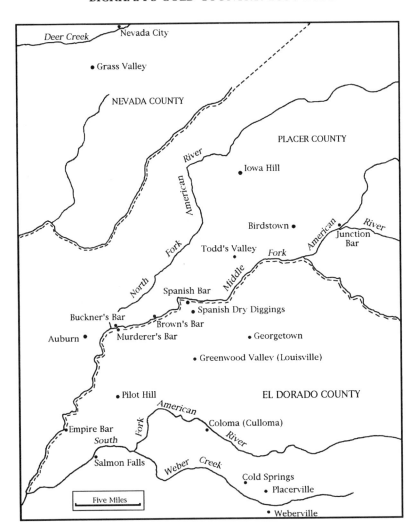

A BUCKEYE
IN THE
LAND OF GOLD
The Letters and Journal of
William Dennison Bickham

Edited by
RANDALL E. HAM

THE ARTHUR H. CLARK COMPANY
Spokane, Washington
1996

Arthur H. Clark Company
P.O. Box 14707
Spokane, WA 99214

LIBRARY OF CONGRESS CATALOG CARD NUMBER 96-33028
ISBN-0-87062-263-3

Library of Congress Cataloging-in-Publication Data

Bickham, William Dennison, 1827-1894.
    A Buckeye in the land of gold: the letters and journal of William
Dennison Bickham / edited by Randall E. Ham.
    p. 286   cm. —(American trail series; 19)
Includes bibliographical references and index.
ISBN 0-87062-263-3 (cloth: alk. paper)
    1. Bickham, William Dennison, 1827-1894—Correspondence.
2. Bickham, William Dennison, 1827-1894—Diaries.   3. California-
Gold discoveries.   4. Gold mines and mining—California—History—
19th century.   5. San Francisco (Calif.)—Social life and customs.
6. Customs administration—Californ' —San Francisco—History—
19th century.   7. Pioneers—California—Correspondence. 8. Pioneers—
California—Diaries.   I. Ham, Randall E., 1946-   II. Title.   III. Series.
F865.B52
979.4'04'092—dc20   96-33028
                                                                              CIP

TO LINDA

Contents

Illustrations

Acknowledgments

In preparing the diary and letters of William Dennison Bickham for publication I benefited from the help of many persons and institutions.

My thanks go first of all to the late Professor James D. Hart of the Bancroft Library, Berkeley, California, for permission to publish the journal which forms the major part of my work. The Bancroft Library has likewise been a great source of background information regarding California during Bickham's sojourn.

Two Ohio repositories: the Western Reserve Historical Society Library in Cleveland, and the Dayton and Montgomery County Library, contain collections of Bickham family papers, which provided me with invaluable information on Bickham's family background and his life before and after his California sojourn. Special thanks are due to Nancy Horlaker of the Dayton and Montgomery County Library. Background information on Bickham and his Ohio friends was also to be found in three other Ohio repositories: the Cincinnati Historical Society Library, the Cincinnati and Hamilton County Library, and the Ohio State Historical Library in Columbus.

Thanks are also due to the staffs of the California State Library, Sacramento; the Sutro Library, San Francisco; the San Francisco room of the San Francisco Public Library; the California Historical Society Library, San Francisco; the Mechanics Mercantile Library, San Francisco; the library of the Society of California Pioneers, San Francisco; the Stanford University Library; the Henry E. Huntington Library, San Marino, California; the University of California Main Library, Berkeley; and the Missouri Historical Society Library in St. Louis, Missouri.

Finally, I must thank my wife, Linda, for the patience which she has shown in the face of the disruptions sometimes caused by my research and writing schedule.

Editorial Practices and Abbreviations

In editing these documents for publication, I have retained the spelling and capitalization of the originals, but have modernized the punctuation. I have broken up some lengthy paragraphs and have occasionally combined very short ones. Some minor grammatical errors have been corrected without comment, and words or letters which appear to have been unintentionally left out have been added between brackets. Where Bickham has occasionally provided an incorrect date in the journal, I have added the correct date in brackets. Bickham's marginal notes have been labeled as such and bracketed. Words which Bickham crossed out in the original have been left out of this text, with the exception of one lengthy phrase, which has been bracketed.

In the interest of space, this work has been abridged for publication by about one fifth, without, I hope, sacrificing its value. Several digressive sections, including Bickham's speculations on the origin of gold deposits, a list of the duties of customs inspectors, and short essays on religion in California, seccession, and political economy, have been deleted, as have several lengthy quotations from contemporary newspapers. A number of florid or repetitive passages have likewise been shortened or removed, as have some brief references to persons not involved in Bickham's California life, or to events which he did not witness or comment on at length. Deletions are indicated by ellipses.

Most persons mentioned by Bickham are identified in the notes, as are a number of places, historical events, ships, and literary references. Sources are cited in each note except in cases where the subject of the note is widely known or described in a number of readily available sources.

The bibliography contains full names, titles, and dates of publication of works cited in this volume, with the exception of city directories. As I have cited an unusually large number of city directories, I have, in order to keep the bibliography from becoming excessively long, listed them by city and date only. An exception has been made in the case of some of the earlier San Francisco directories, which I have cited more frequently. The full titles of most of the cited city directories are provided in the following two volumes: Dorothy N. Spear, *Bibliography of American Directories through 1860,* Worcester, Massachusetts, 1961; and *City Directories of the United States, 1860-1901,* Woodbridge, Connecticut and Reading, England, 1983. Cited manuscripts have been listed by repository. Abbreviations used in the notes and bibliography are listed below on this page.

The text of both letters and journal have been divided into chapters for greater convenience in reading and notation.

ABBREVIATIONS

BL	Bancroft Library, Berkely, California.
CHSQ	*California Historical Society Quarterly.*
CSL	California State Library, Sacramento.
DAB	*Dictionary of American Biography.*
DMCL	Dayton and Montgomery County Library.
DNB	*Dictionary of National Biography.*
MHS	Missouri Historical Society, St. Louis, Missouri.
WRHS	Western Reserve Historical Society, Cleveland, Ohio.
Alta	*Daily Alta California.*
Union	*Sacramento Daily Union.*
Bulletin	*San Francisco Daily Evening Bulletin.*
Herald	*San Francisco Daily Herald.*
Call	*San Francisco Call.*
Republican	*St. Louis Missouri Republican.*

Introduction

For William Dennison Bickham, editor and proprietor of the *Dayton Daily Journal*, the trip to Colorado was a return to his past. The stocky, fifty-year-old journalist had, it was true, never before visited the Rockies, but now, in June, 1879, as he, a member of a party of Ohio journalists, toured this remote mining region, Bickham was repeatedly reminded of his far longer and more adventurous journey, almost thirty years before, to the still more remote region of Gold Rush California. The "long lines of expectant men in single file at the post office windows" in Denver took Bickham back to "the early days in San Francisco, when waiting for a letter was an event in a man's life—sometimes a sad one."[1] The remains of miners' excavations and lodgings served him as a series of "pictures hung long ago in memory's misty gallery," when "toil and disappointment" had been his "portion too, in just such scenes."[2] "My own little cabin on the mountainside," he wrote, "a celebration of many delightful reveries and inspiring visions, was ever present in fancy, while passing these scenes, so like those in which I once toiled."[3] Georgetown Gorge resembled "the river diggings of California," although he considered the latter more "romantic." "Nature," he wrote, "is kinder [in California], for with equal majesty in the mountains, it softens ruggedness with forests whose splendor is unparalleled elsewhere."[4] Standing on the summit of Pike's Peak, his memories grew more romantic still:

---

[1] Bickham, *Ohio to Rocky Mountains*, 70.
[2] Ibid., 146.
[3] Ibid., 147.
[4] Ibid., 146.

A gold hunter in my careless youth, tramping in reckless rapture over the stately peaks of gold-ribbed California, dallying in gay and hopeful fancy with an imaginary sweetheart, or dreaming of that evanescent vision of nights on summits that coquetted with Orion, seeking wild adventures and the most savage haunts of nature for their own delights, and camping under the moon, courting companionship with the wildest solitudes...[5]

For Bickham as for many gold-seekers, the journey to California was the great adventure of his youth, the final burst of freedom before surrendering to the duties of family and career. The Gold Rush was also, as Bickham was well aware, a climactic moment in the history of his country, marking the completion of the Anglo-American advance from sea to sea. California had scarcely been conquered from Mexico when the gold discovery transformed this pastoral backwater into a vigorous, rapidly growing American state. Bickham, like most of his Anglo-American contemporaries, had no doubt that it was the Manifest Destiny of the "Universal Yankee Nation" to dominate North America, and he was proud to belong to this nation. For both these reasons, personal and patriotic, Bickham, like many other Argonauts, regarded his journey to California and his adventures there as worthy of recording.

Bickham's account of his California adventure survives in two forms. His journey to San Francisco and his first months in the mines are recounted in a series of letters to the *Cincinnati Gazette*, while his experiences as a miner during the winter and spring of 1851, and as a San Francisco customs inspector during the summer and autumn of that year, are described in a journal which he intended to send to his sisters. Despite the gap of four months between the last of these letters and the beginning of the journal, letters and journal together provide a detailed and intimate record of one man's experience in Gold Rush California.[6]

While many Gold Rush letters and journals are terse and uninformative, the best of them serve as windows through which a by-gone era may be viewed. It is to this category that Bickham's writings belong. His

---

[5]Ibid., 117-18.
[6]Bickham kept an earlier journal during his voyage to California, but it has been lost. He continued to send dispatches to the *Cincinnati Gazette* from the summer of 1851 through 1853, but these contain few autobiographical details.

style, like that of many nineteenth century writers, is sometimes excessively flowery for twentieth century tastes, but this defect is amply compensated for by Bickham's ability to bring to life the events, places and people about which he wrote, and by his treatment of topics neglected by most other Gold Rush diarists and letter-writers. His near fatal landing on the Santa Cruz coast, the fire of June 22, 1851, in San Francisco, and the hanging of Whittaker and McKenzie are among the more dramatic events recorded by Bickham, but he no less vividly conveys, often with considerable humor, the sights, sounds, and tempo of daily life in both the mining camps and San Francisco. He brings to life such figures as the courtly Dr. Flewellan, the saloon keeper/politician E. C. Cromwell, and the jolly mountain man, Jean Baptiste Charbonneau. Women are by no means neglected, and the Amazonian Mrs. Tubbs, the hoydenish Sally Mayfield, and the graceful Josefa Ainsa are among the memorable female characters in the journal. He highlights such little-known topics as the friction between the Missouri "Jumpers" and the "Gentleman Miners," the presence of Mormon families in the Northern Mines, and the lives and duties of San Francisco customs inspectors. An active member of the Whig Party, Bickham records many phases of the electoral process from a local party meeting in Murderer's Bar to the statewide election of September 1851. An avid reader, whose literary tastes ranged from the works of Aristotle to pulp fiction, Bickham provides information on the type of literature popular with middle-class gold seekers, and his comments on such authors as Dumas and Lamartine, while not always profound, are generally interesting. More than most gold-seekers, he reflects on such ironies of California life as the contrast between its excitement and fast pace, and its underlying loneliness.

Perhaps most appealing of all is the portrait he provides of himself. More reflective than many diarists, he reveals himself in a variety of changing moods: depression and stubborn optimism, longing for his family and keen interest in his surroundings; enjoyment of solitude and reading, and equally strong enjoyment of congenial company, particularly that of attractive young women. Bickham's candor may not, of course, be total. If, for example, his relations with women ever progressed beyond the flirtations he describes, he would have hesitated to include this fact in a journal intended for his family's viewing. Bickham's letters and journals remain, nonetheless, a vivid self-portrait by an intelligent and lively gold-seeker, more articulate than most of his fellows, but not untypical in his moods, aspirations and experiences, living through one of the most dramatic eras in the history of the American West.

Prologue

William Dennison Bickham was born on March 30, 1827, in the suburb of Riverside, some five miles down the Ohio River from the rapidly growing river port and pork-packing center of Cincinnati. The "Queen City of the West" had, only seventeen years before, been a village of some 2,500 people, most of whom were housed in frame or log cabins. According to businessman Stephen S. L'Hommedieu, who arrived in Cincinnati by keelboat as a boy in 1810, the "graveyard, court house, jail and public post" were all located on the same village square, where "friendly Indians would occasionally have war-dances, much to the amusement of the villagers, after which the hat would be handed around for the benefit, it may be, of the papooses"[1] The arrival of the first steamboat in 1811 marked the beginning of Cincinnati's growth. By 1830, three years after Bickham's birth, the population had increased to almost 25,000, and by 1850, the year of his departure for California, it had reached 115,000, including many Irish and German immigrants.[2] Charles Dickens, who visited Cincinnati in 1842, described it as "a beautiful city, cheerful, thriving, animated" with "clean houses of red and white,... well-paved roads and footways of bright tile."[3] British traveler Isabella Bird, who passed through the Queen City during the following decade, commented on the colorful mix of people, the vigorous manufacturing, well-stocked stores and burgeoning cultural life, as well as on the "lean, gaunt and vicious looking swine" that thronged the streets of "Porkopolis."[4] This vital, expanding city formed the backdrop for most of Bickham's

---

[1] Greve, *Centennial History,* Vol. I, 418-19.
[2] Ibid., Vol. I, 684.
[3] Dickens, *American Notes,* 162.
[4] Bird, *Englishwoman in America,* 117-22.

early life, and he was proud of being a Queen City man. Not until he reached California would he witness more explosive urban growth.

Bickham's father, William Ard Bickham, a native of Pennsylvania, had arrived in Cincinnati in 1819, and by 1825 was established as grocer and produce merchant. By 1840 he had become head of a line of steamers shipping freight down the Ohio and Mississippi rivers, and he invested the profits of this enterprise in real estate and railroads.[5] As a person the elder William Bickham remains somewhat shadowy. According to his grandson, Daniel D. Bickham, none of William Ard's "sons or daughters ever mentioned or discussed their father in the presence of the writer of this. Nor did his wife ever speak of him. He must," concluded Daniel, "have been a stern man."[6] The younger William Bickham, claimed Daniel, always regretted his father's failure "to make a pal of him and show him the raw side of life."[7] In his California journal, written several years after his father's death, William Dennison referred to him only once, but this reference indicates that his memories of William Ard were not altogether negative. "I am," he wrote, "always gratified when I meet with old acquaintances and friends of my father; the pleasant remembrances of the past are brought before me so vividly."[8]

It was Bickham's mother who aroused the greatest affection in her eldest son, and more details of her life have been preserved. Eliza Dennison was descended from a family of Scotch-Irish Protestants who arrived in New England in the early 1600s. Members of both sides of her family served in the Revolution, the War of 1812, and the Civil War. Eliza was born in 1802 in Genessee Falls, New York, where her parents had migrated from New England, and, according to her grandson, Daniel, she was "educated as a Yankee and became a Yankee schoolteacher."[9] In 1818 Eliza and her family joined a party of settlers traveling down the Ohio River by flatboat. They landed at North Bend, Ohio, where she met William Ard Bickham whom she married in 1826. The following year their eldest son, William Dennison, was born, to be joined

---

[5]Cincinnati City Directories, 1825, 1836-7, 1840, 1846; DMCL Bickham Collection, Biographical Notes; *Cincinnati Tri-Weekly Gazette,* September 23, 1845.

[6]DMCL Bickham Collection, Biographical Notes.

[7]Ibid., WDB-Personal, 10.

[8]See below 155.

[9]DMCL Bickham Collection, WDB-Personal, 2; Biographical Notes.

in the succeeding decade by four sisters and two brothers. Eliza long outlived her husband, and died at age ninety-one, a year before her eldest son.[10] She aroused great respect in her grandson, Daniel, who characterized her as "Spartan" and praised her courage and "mental equipment."[11] She was, he claimed, "a strong minded Christian Godfearing mother who grooved the whole [family] to her bidding as to morals and living around the [Bickham] home."[12]

The home in which William Dennison Bickham was born and raised was a two-story frame house situated on a four acre plat sloping down to the Ohio River. It was, according to Daniel, one of the first frame houses built along that river.[13] Describing it at a later date, Bickham wrote:

> Our home, not strictly luxurious, sufficed for present enjoyment. Its lovely garden, its handsome groves of fruit and umbrageous trees, the lofty hills of Old Kentucky in the Southern distance, the richly cultivated vineyards flourishing in the Ohio hills; fine villas on the graceful hill-slopes, and the noble river winding its silver stream in picturesque beauty through the clefted hills formed a landscape that any heart might love.[14]

At an early age William was enrolled at a country school some three miles down the river from his home. According to Daniel, the schoolboy, William, "was husky and redheaded, soon developing strength and scrappiness." As eldest son he had the job of escorting his younger siblings to the school which they all attended. He became "protector of his sisters and other girls over that long trip," and "was the hero of many a fray."[15]

At age fifteen, Bickham, in his own words, "exchanged the homely country academy with its moss-covered eves for the walls of College," first attending nearby Cincinnati College, later transferring to Bethany College in what is now West Virginia.[16] Bethany had been founded in 1840 by Alexander Campbell, a leader of the Disciples of Christ, the religious sect to which Bickham's parents belonged, and it was doubtless

---

[10]Ibid., WDB-Personal, 3.

[11]Ibid., WDB-Sketch, 2.

[12]Ibid.

[13]Ibid., WDB-Sketch, 1.

[14]WRHS Bickham Family Papers, Container 1, folder 4: MSS biography of W. S. Bickham by his parents.

[15]DMCL Bickham Collection, WDB-Personal, 2.

[16]See below 74; *History of Montgomery County*, book 3: 191.

concern for his spiritual upbringing which led them to enroll him there. In Bickham's funeral service many years later, Reverend M. E. Wilson claimed that Bickham's "reverence for God and the Christian religion which he never lost," resulted from his "advantage of sitting at the feet of Alexander Campbell, and of hearing Christian truth from his lips."[17] Bickham's college days were not exclusively devoted to religion, however. According to one account, while at Bethany he "was such an irrepressible chap that the Faculty were compelled to rusticate him once in the course of his career in order to give the energy of character which still belongs to him free course to run and be glorified."[18]

In September 1845, Bickham's education was cut short by his father's sudden death at age 47.[19] Bickham, aged eighteen, was now officially head of his family and obligated to contribute to its support. Putting aside his studies, he commenced his life-long career in journalism, serving a two-year apprenticeship in the newsroom of the *Cincinnati Gazette*, where he acquired a knowledge of typesetting. His apprenticeship completed, he took employment with the *Courier* in Louisville, Kentucky, where he soon rose to the position of city and commercial editor.[20] In 1848, however, his family's deteriorating financial condition compelled him to interrupt his career and return to Cincinnati. Eliza Bickham had borrowed money on mortgage from a real estate dealer named Sedam, who had foreclosed a considerable portion of the mortgage. Bickham, according to Daniel, "took hold as fast as he could," and saved some of the family property, "picking up odd jobs" to support himself as he did so. "It is easy to picture," wrote Daniel, the demoralization felt by a "youngster ambitious to step out into his place in the world but stopped by the home obligations."[21]

In the autumn of 1848 Bickham's family obligations caused him to embark on the first great adventure of his life. Business connected with his father's estate compelled him to visit New Orleans, and he and his brother, John, elected to work their way downriver as flatboat hands for

---

[17]*DAB sub* "Campbell, Alexander"; DMCL Bickham Collection, WDB-Personal, 2; *Cincinnati Enquirer*, March 21, 1894.

[18]WRHS Bickham Family Papers, Container 2, Volume 2: newspaper clipping from *Wheeling Intelligencer*, June 20 [1876?].

[19]*Cincinnati Tri-weekly Gazette*, September 23, 1845.

[20]*History of Montgomery County*, Book 3: 191.

[21]DMCL Bickham Collection, WDB-Personal, 2; WDB-Sketch, 2.

"the munificent wages of $15 per month." Their choice of this arduous form of travel may have been due to scanty funds, but the desire for adventure, which would soon lead both William and John to California, may have also played a role. Flatboating, while neither as rough nor as dangerous as in the early decades of the century, still possessed much of the glamour of the Mike Fink era, and many Ohio Valley youths regarded a flatboat trip as a rite of manhood and a chance to "see the elephant." According to one account, the portion of the the Bickham brothers' trip from Cincinnati to Cairo, Illinois, "occupied twenty-nine days, during which the boat grounded on almost every bar of the river." The rest of the journey to and from New Orleans is not recorded, but the Bickhams, like most flatboatmen of their era, doubtless enjoyed the relative comfort of a steamboat on their upriver return.[22]

While Bickham struggled with career and family problems, an event occurred far to the west which would shape the next several years of his life. On January 24, 1848, in the newly conquered territory of Alta California, James Wilson Marshall discovered gold in a mill-race on the South Fork of the American River. By year's end word of the discovery had spread throughout the United States as well as to many other parts of the world, and thousands of gold seekers were preparing to journey to the new El Dorado. The Queen City was by no means immune from gold fever. In December 1848, the *Cincinnati Chronicle* announced that the "California gold mania has reached our city and is producing an extraordinary excitement... so great that the rapid approach of the cholera is unheeded in this seemingly rich enterprise."[23]

The following year saw the California Gold Rush in full swing. Several of Bickham's friends and acquaintances, as well as his brother, John, made their way by land and sea to the gold fields. Bickham at first resisted the gold fever, spending 1849 as a clerk in a financial establishment.[24] His duty to his family, whose financial condition may still have been uncertain, probably kept him at home, and he very likely needed time to raise sufficient funds to pay for his own journey. Romance may also have delayed his departure, for it was probably at this time that he

---

[22]*History of Montgomery County*, Book 3: 191; Allen, *Western Rivermen*, chapters 5 and 6 *passim.*

[23]Harlow, *Serene Cincinnatians*, 65.

[24]*History of Montgomery County*, Book 3:191; *Biographical Cyclopedia . . . of the State of Ohio*, 5: 1,243.

became enamored of the unnamed "sweetheart" whom he mentions in his journal.[25] By the beginning of 1850, however, he was ready to go. The family's financial situation may have sufficiently improved for him to be spared, and he was plainly hopeful, as were most Argonauts, that once in California he would acquire a fortune which would take care of his family's needs. He was, in addition, undoubtedly drawn by sheer desire for adventure. For Bickham, as for many of his contemporaries, the Gold Rush offered an opportunity to "see the elephant," to visit places and face challenges far removed from everyday life.

Three principal routes were available to Bickham. The first, the long sea voyage from the Atlantic ports around Cape Horn, was popular with residents of the East Coast, but less convenient for Midwesterners. The second, which had been used by several of Bickham's friends and by his brother, John, was the overland route from the Missouri frontier. The third, a seemingly more comfortable route, was by steamer from New Orleans to the Isthmus of Panama, across the Isthmus to Panama City, and from there by sea to San Francisco. It was this route that Bickham, who had probably learned from his brother of the hardships of the overland route, elected to take.

On March 2, 1850, Bickham, having bid good-bye to his family and sweetheart, departed from Cincinnati.[26] He had made up his mind to remain in California for four years, a decision to which he held.[27] There is no record of his journey downriver to New Orleans, but he undoubtedly traveled by steamboat.[28] Two weeks later, on March 15, he boarded the U.S. Mail steamship *Falcon* and began the first leg of his voyage. Four days afterwards, in the harbor of Havana, Cuba, he penned the first of a series of letters to the *Cincinnati Gazette,* beginning his account of his California adventure.

---

[25]See below 142. She may have been the "L.C.H." whose initials Bickham carved next to his own on an oak tree on February 4, 1851. (See below) Bickham hoped to marry his sweetheart upon his return to Ohio, but this wish was not fulfilled.

[26]See below 142.   [27]See below 123.

[28]Daniel Bickham, writing in the 1930s, claimed that William Bickham and his younger brother, John, flatboated to New Orleans before voyaging to Panama. Daniel was plainly confusing the 1848 flatboat trip with William's later journey to California. John had gone to California the previous year, and a flatboat journey would have taken longer than the two weeks which elapsed between William's departures from Cincinnati and from New Orleans. DMCL Bickham Collection, WDB-Sketch, 2.

CHAPTER ONE

Voyage to the Land of Gold

Havana, March 19, 1850
[*Cincinnati Daily Gazette*, April 2, 1850]:

GENTLEMEN:...On Friday the 15th day of March, 1850, I left the port of New Orleans on board the good steamship Falcon bound for Havana, where her passengers were to be transferred to the steamer Georgia. I had procured a steerage ticket at New Orleans, being determined to "rough it out" from the start. After getting under headway and being fully assured that we were off for California, I proceeded to make some inquiries concerning accommodations, number of passengers, &c. I found that we had just 420 passengers all told, and such a motley crew, perhaps you have not met this many a day. Nearly all nations were represented and *"Cincinnati"* in the bargain. Of the latter *nation* I found about forty, hale and hearty looking fellows as you would meet in a week's journey. Accommodations I found were to be scarce and fare rather *rare*. Of the former I can at present speak in terms of adulation, as I have during the last four nights, in company with others, slept on the soft side of a plank, with the blue Heavens for my cover, and I have yet to hear of any body complaining of his fellow "kicking the kiver off." Of the fare, it becomes me to say but little; our meat half cooked, and the gravy—shades of Epicurus!—such gravy. We are to have for dinner after leaving this port, a daily supply of tarpaulin soup and tarred rope pudding. I'm afraid to sleep on a bed just now, lest I may take cold. Truly some might be inclined to call these vessels *hard*-ships. But who cares, when "there's a better time coming."

Surely the proprietors of this line of steamers should be held up to the scorn of the people, for the gross imposition which they have been, and are in the habit of practicing upon their steerage passengers. They advertise that the same accommodations will be afforded that are given to the crew, mattresses, blankets, &c. Passengers get underway; they expect to find at least a clean ship, mattresses, knives to eat with, and cups to drink from. But wo unto the unlucky wight who bases his expectations upon Aspinwall's promises…[1] We had to buy our tin cups on board, paying 25 cts. each where 5 cts. would have sufficed on shore; and indeed making allowances for the querulous disposition of mankind generally, I must say that it is the unanimous opinion of all whom I have heard, that we have been basely imposed upon.

The officers of this vessel have paid but little attention to the steerage, taking no thought whether it were cleanly or filthy. To any of my Cincinnati friends who may hereafter "catch the fever," I most emphatically say, if you go as steerage passengers, buy tin-cups, spoons, knives, and forks, in fact all those little necessaries which you have occasion to use, for on ship board you will want them. If I were to start again, I would go by the "overland route," harder work doubtless, but more comfortable.

I was much amused on watching the effect of the rolling and pitching of the vessel, after we had embarked upon the rolling waters of the Gulf. Though momentarily in expectation of catching the sea-sickness, I could not refrain from laughing at those who were writhing under its effects. It was comically serious, and the poor fellows made it more so by their ejaculations. One fellow between the periods crying out, "New York," would gasp a moment and then cry out, "Who the d-l wouldn't sell a farm and go to California?" I saw between three and four hundred sick at one time; fortunately I escaped by exercising freely, climbing ropes and running around the decks.[2]

This is my first voyage at sea, and truly do I find many things to excite my wonderment; and also find in the survey of the illimitable expanse of ocean, that grandeur and sublimity which raises the soul to Heaven. The

---

[1] Bickham blames the wrong person. New York merchant William Henry Aspinwall was head of the Pacific Mail Steamship Company, which ran a line of steamers between Panama and California. The *Falcon* belonged to George Law's United States Mail Company which carried passengers and mail from New York and New Orleans to Chagres.

[2] According to fellow passenger Alfred S. Gould, some two thirds of the *Falcon's* passengers were seasick, himself among them. *Cincinnati Commercial,* April 2, 1850.

white cap waves rolling and pitching with angry impetuosity, the heaving of the waters, the roaring of the winds, all conspire to create an exultant feeling within, which I would in vain endeavor to express. The most gallant and beautiful sight I have yet witnessed was the appearance of a vessel under full sail bearing towards us immediately in the wind's eye. It is impossible to conceive of the beauty and gracefulness of the vessel as she breasted the white foaming sea. I was at the mast head, and as she passed she flung out the broad banner of Freedom to the breeze, and as the stars waved out over the sea I would have defied the grey headed sage of 80 winters to have refrained from the impulse to shout.

Yesterday morning we passed in to the mole under the frowning battlements of the "Moro Castle," bristling with bayonets, and after receiving the visits of the Quarantine and Custom House officers we hove anchor and "came to." "Then there was running to and fro," and such rushing as was made for the boats of the thieving Spaniards would astonish the good people of our own Queen City. Over board into the boats we went helter skelter, all eagerly bent on getting to land. We arrived safely to shore, and then gave the Spaniards a few lessons in finance. They wished to charge 50 cents each for riding 50 yards. They didn't begin to get it; since then they take us for 5c! what a fall was there!

I went to town with Mr. A. S. Gould,[3] who is with me, and finding another Cincinnati boy, we hired a "volante," (a one-horse vehicle made to carry two—the driver riding the animal) and took a drive out on the hills. To say that the scenery which met our view on every side was beautiful would be tame, 'twas ravishing: fruits, flowers, beautiful fields, gardens, splendid villas, the sea in the distance, and all this influenced by the contemplation that all these fair fields were once trodden by the feet of Christopher Columbus and his little band of gallant Cavaliers; these fair views were once the delight of the most wonderful man of the 15th century. I visited his tomb in the Cathedral, and as I stood uncovered before the marble tablet inscribed to his memory, I could not but bow in reverence to his name.

---

[3]Alfred S. Gould, (d. 1882) a native of Ireland and a Cincinnati resident, corresponded with the *Cincinnati Commercial* during and after his voyage to California, and his account of the journey supplements Bickham's. Gould was active in San Francisco journalism for many years, and worked for Bickham's *Evening Journal* in 1852. He spent the final decade of his life as a miner. 1852 California Census, San Francisco II, 247; San Francisco city directories 1850-82; *Call,* June 24, 1882.

I have taken considerable trouble to examine the military positions which guard this city, and am quite candid that the Yankee nation could walk in without any very great trouble. I surrounded one of the castles which commands the city, and thought of several very pretty little plans to gain possession. Take this city all in all, I like it very much; but I must say, I have a most utter contempt for its soldiers—little, shriveled, dried up, mokey looking chaps—why, one regiment of Buckeyes would whip five thousand of them with their phsts. This you will take with some grains of allowance, though I despise their appearance.

The weather here is most beautifully clear, and very hot at mid day. In the evening it is delightful to take a walk outside the walls, and imbibe the pure sea breezes. About an hour before sundown the Senoras and Senoritas ride out in volantes and air themselves. I went out last evening, and though I saw most tastefully dressed ladies, I saw not half the beauty that one would see in a ten minutes walk on Fourth street, in Cincinnati.

Business is quite brisk, and the harbor is full of shipping, with their flags of all hues and all nations. Three American steamers in port, the Falcon, Ohio, and Isabel. The Ohio arrived yesterday from Chagres, and reports cholera at Panama, and few passengers waiting exportation. I have this from a passenger. The Ohio, having left Chagres without health certificates, is placed under quarantine at this place.—She, however, is to leave for New York to-morrow.

You will excuse the haste with which this is written, as I have a poor opportunity for writing…Say that I am well; in better health, if possible, than I ever was, and as for regretting my trip—pooh. I would not come back without seeing California if any one were to offer me a small sized fortune…

BARQUE ANNE, Pacific Ocean, Lat. 23, Lon. 128,
Wednesday, May 15th, 1850
[*Cincinnati Daily Gazette,* August 4, 1850]:

GENTLEMEN: —My "Star of Empire" seems indeed to be "Westward ho!" for here am I on the face of the blue ocean, surrounded by a waste of waters, "west of all creation," and unable, on account of contrary winds, to reach my destination. I have been on board this vessel just 45 days, and have not been blessed with the sight of "terra firma" for more than 30 days, and presume from all appearances, that it will be 12 or 15 more ere my hearing shall be delighted with the cry of "land ho!" The life of a voyager on salt water may to some persons be most pleasing in theory, but when it is reduced to practice, and such practice as I have had, I opine it will be bereft of much of its romance. To give you an *inkling* of my experience for a few weeks past, it will be necessary to return for a moment to the point where I first fell in with the *real* "live elephant." I wrote you from Havana and you have doubtless heard of the arrival of the vessel which bore me from thence to Chagres, and how a few persons were imposed upon during that passage.[4]

Upon arriving in Chagres, I assisted in forming a company of ten young men, with whom I journeyed in a canoe from thence to Gorgona.[5] This passage was one which I shall not easily forget. The negroes whom we had hired to paddle our canoe proved lazy, as usual with their class, and we being impatient, went to work ourselves. We paddled all one night, until the water got too swift and shallow for this method of propulsion, and then several of us got overboard while others procured poles with which to push, and thus we worked until 6 P.M. of the 2nd day, when we arrived at Gorgona, having been in the water for 15 hours without *"a bite to eat."* At this place we got a good supper for 75c, and after making arrangements for the conveyance of our baggage to Panama, we spread our blankets upon the ground and slept.—At 8 A.M. we started "a-foot" for Panama, a distance variously estimated at from 27 to 35 miles. Two brothers named Liggett and myself preceded the party, having determined to sleep that night in Panama; the road, merely a

---

[4] The *Georgia,* the larger steamer to which the *Falcon's* passengers were scheduled to transfer, was already overcrowded with 900 passengers of its own. Despite protests to the American consul in Havana, the *Falcon's* passengers were compelled either to transfer to the *Georgia* or to return to New Orleans on the *Falcon.* All but twenty chose to continue on the *Georgia* to Chagres. The five-day voyage was, according to Bickham's fellow passengers, Thomas Spooner and Alfred Gould, even worse than that of the *Falcon,* with crowding, noise, little food, and that very poor, leading to clashes both among passengers and between passengers and crew. *Cincinnati Commercial* May 4, 1850; *Cincinnati Enquirer,* April 3, May 3, 1850.

[5] The village of Gorgona, thirty-nine and one half miles up the Chagres River from its mouth, was the head of navigation during the dry season from December through April. From there travelers continued overland to Panama City, twenty miles distant.

mule path, was the roughest I have ever seen, and the weather the warmest I had then experienced. At 5 o'clock, after a most toilsome travel, *"the three"* hove into Panama, the younger Liggett a few minutes ahead, the other Liggett and myself side by side. We had passed every one who had left Gorgona that day, whether riding or walking. The rest of our company came in after nightfall, sadly used up. I was never more fatigued; although the next day I could have started again.

You have had so many descriptions of that dreary, buzzard-infested, antiquated city, Panama, that mine may be dispensed with, and will only say of it, that the stranger who enters within its gates would do well to "keep his eye skinned" or he'll be skinned himself. The day after our arrival the company made arrangements with Messrs. Garrison & Fretz[6] for our transportation as steerage passengers upon the barque Anne, to San Francisco for $115. The sum of $25 each, extra, was to secure to us the "house on deck," and the privilege of being a "separate mess." Capt. Robinson, of Massachusetts, the owner of the vessel, assured us we should be "treated like gentlemen," and G.& F., his agents, said we should "live like fighting cocks." One of our number examined the vessel, and said she looked well, and the "bill of fare" exhibited to us *promised* fairly.

We were to start on the 1st of April for San Francisco, and accordingly we all assembled on board on that day, and started not for San Francisco, but to the Island of Toboga where the Captain said we were to get our supply of water, which G. & F. had said was already on board. We arrived at the Island of Toboga the same night, and the next day all went ashore to "stretch their limbs" for the last time during many days on the land. During my rambles among the mountains and groves of the island, I chanced to wander up the brook a short distance above the place from whence our ship's crew was obtaining water, and here I saw something which caused me to stop for a moment. Here were about one hundred of the native women engaged at washing clothes, some washing themselves, in the midst of the stream, the soapy water mingling with

---

[6]Former steamboat captains Cornelius Garrison and Ralph Fretz moved to Panama City in 1849 and formed a partnership, first operating a gambling casino, later branching into banking and shipping. They eventually moved to San Francisco where both became prominent bankers and where Garrison served as a reform mayor in 1853-54. Wiltsee, *Gold Rush Steamers*, 112-25; Lavender, *Nothing Seemed Impossible*, 21-26, 205-6; *DAB sub* "Garrison, Cornelius."

the dirt washed from the clothes, running down into our water casks, certainly not more than one hundred yards below. I turned to a companion, who was looking upon the scene with a lugubrious stare, and burst into a hearty laugh. Of course, Messrs. Editors, he laughed too, for it was a matter calculated to excite our risabilities(?) I thought that during the next sixty days I should be pretty well "soaped," and that if others could stand it, I could "shut my eyes to the evil." While thinking of this, however, I was admiring the beauty of the young Indian women who were before me, many of them with little more than nature's garb upon them. Their forms were arrowy straight and perfectly symmetrical, their features regular and countenances most expressive, in some of them very beautiful, and seemed perfectly aware of the fact by their proud Juno like bearing. I can safely say they were "killin purty" washerwomen.

The island was formerly a celebrated piratical haunt, and certainly offered in its mountainous recesses, and dense thickets, fine advantages for the secretion of spoils; and its fine harbor, hidden by numerous adjacent islands, offers the best security for vessels of pirates. It is now the shipping depot for supplies of water and fuel for vessels arriving at Panama. There is a small town of the same name fronting immediately upon the harbor, consisting of a few houses formed of the *"bamboo,"* and are covered with leaves. The inhabitants are the "natives," and are all Catholics. While I was there they were enjoying the holidays after "Lent," and many a poor game-cock offered up his life in conflict for their amusement. Their "bull-baiting" is somewhat different from those fights in which the "madadores" of old Spain once distinguished themselves, in nothing more than driving a bull into an enclosure and then plaguing him until he becomes exhausted in chasing them. Still it is quite amusing to see the natives engaged in the sport. Each night of the hollidays [sic] is celebrated by "fandangoes" and there the Indian beauties display the native graces of coquetry to perfection. The yankees have even settled in this wild spot, for I notice during my peregrinations the "Union Coffee House" in full blast. Our party at this place purchased about 500 oranges at one cent each, and also a number of pine apples; the latter were the most delicious fruit I have yet eaten. The island produces all the tropical fruits in great profusion, and it is only necessary to go a short distance from the sea shore to find oranges, pine-apples, bread-fruit, cocoa nuts, plantains, &c. in great abundance.[7]

Wednesday, April 3rd, we tripped anchor, and the Anne yielded gracefully to the breeze, and once more I was rejoiced to be on my winding way, and well, I know, did my companions echo the huzza which I gave as the white sails filled with the breeze, and the gurgling waters flashed before our prows. The first night we sailed 25 miles, and at sunrise we found ourselves becalmed, not a breath of wind stirring and a cloudless sky o'erhead, from which the sun poured down *directly* upon us his scorching heat. We lay thus becalmed, and almost in sight of Panama for some days, and during that time we had a gentle taste of "purgatory"—weather "hot as blazes," not a zephyr to fan our fevered brains, no awning to protect us from the sun; salt meat to eat, and thirst aggravated by it; and soapy water to drink. In addition to these evils we learned how "gentlemen were treated" on the Anne and how "fighting cocks live," as well as one other little item; viz.; that the Anne was built in 1807, instead of 8 or 10 years ago as we had been informed. This is all very fine to talk about, but when one comes to realize it, the poetry vanishes.

I will give you a fat "bill of fare" as we were in the habit of receiving it until a few days since. For breakfast we have a solution of a few grains of coffee and soapy water, made in a kettle not *very* clean; salt beef (or as we call it—"Salt Hoss") or *pork,* which has such an unbearable stench that we invariably cast it overboard; (for a few days it was good) and mouldy sea-bread 18 months old, and moreover full of vermin—some of our *Grand-fathers* profess to believe that "skippery cheese" is superior to the *fresh* article, I can hardly think they would say as much of such *bread* as we have. Dinner—salt hoss or pork, and sea-biscuit. Supper— sea-biscuit and salt hoss with tea. Sunday morning we have, each, a small

---

[7]Taboga Island, approximately two miles long and one mile wide, is situated eleven miles south of Panama City. It was used by 17th century buccaneers for careening and watering their vessels and as a base for raids against Spanish settlements and shipping. During the early 1850s Taboga served as a coal and supply base for the Pacific Mail Steamship Company, and was used by most ships as a watering place, Panama City having a limited water supply. According to Mrs. D. B. Bates, who visited Taboga in early 1851, "nearly all the washing" was brought to the island from Panama City "and here cleansed by native women and spread upon the bushes to dry." Many California-bound travelers found Taboga a pleasanter place to sojourn than Panama City. Gerhard, *Pirates of the Pacific,* 53, 140, 150-51, 160, 182; J. H. Kemble, *Panama Route,* 133; Bates, *Incidents on Land and Water,* 83.

slice of boiled Ham. Thursdays and Sundays, the dinner table is garnished with fresh bread, made of sour flour, and a kind of pudding, made
of flour and water and boiled in a bag, which is called "duff," I call it
dough—occasionally we have a few yams, a vegetable which tastes like
boiled snow, pea-soup, or squashes—our meat is all freshened and boiled
in *salt* water. We had until two weeks ago, when the supply failed, for
each mess of 12 men a half gallon of molasses per diem, to sweeten our
coffee and tea and eat with our bread. We could eat the "duff" and sour
bread with molasses on account of its being fresh, consequently when
Thursday and Sunday came round, we had quite a feast. Sunday was a
day of regular rejoicing on account of the *ham* and *dough, all* on the same
day. Twice or thrice a week comprised nearly all the eating some of us
did.

This was suffered for some days, say 18, when becoming quite desperate from hunger, I went to the sailing master, whom we had supposed
had direction of all, and demanded better food and more of it. For two
or three days after we got along tolerably well, but soon affairs got worse
then ever. I went again, again our mess fared better, but as before it
slacked off and got so bad that I went to Mr. Sailing Master Swift of N.
O. and wished to know whether it were himself or Capt. Robinson that
I must appeal to for redress. Being informed that it was the Captain, I
went in the name of the company and demanded peremptorily that we
should have that for which we had contracted. Here we joined issue, he
arguing one way, I another, and finally concluded the argument by saying "our mess" would have it anyhow. A short time after we were told
that a sack of flour should be placed at our disposal if any of us could
make bread; one of our number happened to know how, and agreed to
the proposition. It was necessary to get the flour into our apartment
secretly, to prevent other passengers from finding it out until we had it
safe; accordingly at midnight, we got into the hold and *raised* the flour.
The next day quite an excitement was raised when our baker held up his
loaf, but our mouths were filled. I assure you that matters had come to a
crisis, and if we had not received the flour, the cry of "bread, bread,"
would have terminated in something else.

Before we received our sack of flour, the "Upper Saloon" mess, sitting
around their *"grub,"* with miserable fare, and allowanced at that, certainly

presented a most interesting tableaux. Some of us would bite at a biscuit, and make some remark, another would turn over the *bone* and pick it with a lugubrious stare of countenance, and then all would join in a simultaneous yell of laughter, as one would mention "other days," and the next moment some anathema would be hurled upon the Captain...You would certainly laugh most heartily at the picture we present, laughing, joking, singing, &c. over our fare. We go upon the principle that "there's a better time coming." A. S. Gould, of Cincinnati, was added to our company at Panama, and since our departure, our mess is known as the "Upper Elevens." Gould looks almost starved, and to tell the truth, I could eat at this moment, "a *small* beefsteak." But it is melancholy to think of such a luxury, so I will drown such thoughts by turning to "Salt Hoss." The long and short of the story is, we have been subject to a foul imposition, and we warn all who may hereafter adventure to California, *via* the Isthmus, to steer clear of Garrison & Fretz of Panama, and if they ship on a sailor, to examine the ship's stock of provisions before purchasing tickets.

One of the great difficulties with which a voyager has to contend, is the weariness which is sure to take possession of him, unless he is one who may content himself with books and the contemplation of the beauties and sublimities to be seen upon the ocean. Every man may for a few days find plenty to keep his mind active in viewing the new and strange scenes to be met with upon the "great waters," but with the generality of mankind, this pleasure which one feels in watching the sparkling of the blue waters in the light of the sun, the rolling and heaving and dashing of the snow-crested wave, the phosphorescent sparkling of ocean in the night, the beauty of a southern midnight sky lighted with its million stars, the roaring of the winds in the gale, the bounding and leaping of the vessel from billow to billow, the innumerable varieties of the dwellers of the sea which present themselves to the view, soon lose the charm of novelty, and he wishes for something else to chase away the tedium vitae which renders his situation so unpleasant. For a few days, after our departure from Toboga, everything wore an animated appearance on the venerable "Anne." One hundred passengers, all "land lubbers," and a majority of them from the back woods, were constantly engaged in watching for sharks, whales, and other little fishes, and immediately upon the discovery of anything, all hands rushed to see. Those who could contemplate the ocean by day, and the heavens by night with feelings other than those of curiosity, had a far superior and more lasting enjoyment; but ocean soon became familiar, and ennui seized upon the greater portion of the passengers, and this particularly during days of calm. I had taken care to provide myself with books, and experienced none of those feelings of discontent which were and are so prevalent. One would naturally be impatient to arrive at the end of the voyage, but with employment, impatience could not assume a very troublesome form. Thus I contented myself during days of calm, and *now,* while we are running off our course, by reading and writing in my journal during the day,[8] and at night, by leaning over the bow of the vessel and watching the white foam sparkling with diamond fire as it rolls away from the vessel as she rushes through the waters, or in romantic spirit look into that most beautiful of all heavens, the southern sky, and think of home and friends or raise up castles "which vanish into airy nothing," time flies swiftly and agreeably.

The universal sentiment of discontent which prevailed during the period in which we were becalmed, naturally created a desire in those subject to the feelings, to endeavor to find amusement. Various were the expedients adopted; some would fish when they could, others would play cards, checkers, back-gammon, &c. and at night all hands would assemble on the quarter-deck, and have a dance. All the tricks in the catalogue were practiced upon each other, and finally one man broached the idea of starting a newspaper. This famous idea was made public one Sunday, and a meeting of the passengers immediately took place upon the quarter-deck. I was busily engaged in writing a letter, when a committee waited upon me, and "announced my election to the Editorial Chair of the 'Weekly Anne Gazette.' Whew! thinks I, here's a *rise!* I made my bow, and in a few words accepted the post, though "of course" pleaded my *fears* concerning my "want of ability, &c." A. S. Gould was elected Local Itemizer. The object of the paper, "the amusement and association of the passengers of the Anne," to be "neutral in Politics and Religion, &c." The paper was to be published every Sabbath, and to be

---

[8]This journal is not among the surviving Bickham family papers, but Bickham transcribed an entry from it into his shipboard newspaper, the "Weekly Anne Gazette."

read to the passengers assembled on the quarter-deck. Here was something calculated to keep me busy, as I certainly experienced during the first week. I wrote my address "To our Patrons" and a paper reflecting upon the Captain, &c., and with "Local Items," contributions, &c., had sufficient to make up a paper of 12 pages closely written packet post. The Gazette being full of little squibs and jests at the expense of different parties on the vessel, created considerable amusement, and as the play-bills announced the affair, "took like hot cakes." As the man says, "I feel my oats, since I've become one of the fraternity."[9]

But ours has not only been a voyage of prolific amusement among ourselves, and imposition on the part of the agents and owners of the vessel. To us has been allotted the sad duty of inhuming in the deep blue waters of the ocean two of our comrades who left Panama full of life and hope, but alas soon went to "that bourne from whence no traveler returns." John B. Scott of Guernsey co., Ohio, aged 16 years, died April 16th of Bilious Diarrhaea, and Samuel Hopper of same place, aged 30 years, died April 17th, of Bilious Fever. Their bodies were enveloped in blankets, a sack of sand attached to their feet, and after the reading of the Episcopal Burial Service by the Captain, they were launched into the bosom of the deep, and disappeared forever from our view. The father of the former, and brother of the latter, were with them to soothe their last moments, and Mr. J. R. Swift of New Orleans, the navigator of our vessel, was unceasing in his attentions throughout their illness. I have witnessed death and the funeral service upon the land, and have thought it solemn enough; but never again do I wish to witness the awful ceremony of a burial at sea.

The nearest approach to the Equator which we have made on this journey was on Thursday, April 18th, at which time we were in latitude 4 18, longitude 87 07. We lay becalmed during the whole day, and the heat was most intense. At nights the rain came down in such torrents, that I almost thought the flood gates of heaven were opened. A wind

---

[9] A copy of the "Weekly Anne Gazette" survives among the Bickham papers in Dayton, Ohio. It contains an editorial by Bickham entitled "Emigration to California," an entry from his lost journal of the voyage, and various "local items" and jokes contributed by Bickham and Gould. One of Bickham's wittier entries is the following riddle: "Why was the Bean Soup which was served out to us for dinner Tuesday last like a pleasant kind of a riding vehicle much in vogue in the United States? Because it 'was buggy.'" DMCL Bickham Collection, "Weekly Anne Gazette."

sprang up and blew almost a gale, but died away again before morning. After many anxious days we reached the Trade Winds, for which we had been looking most anxiously. Since then we have been sailing merrily, though rather off course...

SAN FRANCISCO, June 8, 1850
[*Cincinnati Daily Gazette* August 17, 1850]

GENTLEMEN: -...At the time I wrote last, I stated that I expected to reach San Francisco in a few days, though at that time we were troubled with adverse winds. After that date we continued to sail close under the wind to the W. N. W. until we reached Longitude 131 deg. 30 sec., we then tacked round, and on the 30th of May found ourselves in sight of land, in a dead calm within one degree of this city. All that day and the next we lay be-calmed, watching with interest the sportings of sperm whales with which the Sea seemed literally filled. Some of the huge monsters came to blow within 50 yards of the vessel and gave us fair opportunities for observing their huge proportions. Still we were exceedingly impatient, as our provisions were nearly exhausted, and those we had of the most *nauseous* description save a very small quantity of flour.

Sunday morning our flag of distress was hoisted that it might attract the notice of a vessel which we saw in the distance, but, it proving of no avail, some of the passengers, A. S. Gould and myself among the number, concluded to request the Captain to send us ashore that we might walk to the city. He acquiesced, and at 1 o'clock, thirteen passengers with four sailors, got into the ship's boat and started for the land, distant 10 miles. The boat was very small, and certainly should not have carried more than 10 men, instead of 17, but as the Captain said she was safe we started, and [not] until we got too far to return did we perceive the danger. The proposition was made by several whom we knew to be arrant cowards to return, but was immediately cried down. As we neared the beach we became aware of the fact that the surf was rolling tremendously and as we looked we found that we had but a narrow place between the breakers to land, and, moreover, we found that a heavy belt of sea weed was to be passed. I was sitting in the stern of the boat and making sport of the fears of a poor fellow who appeared to be desperately alarmed, when Mr. Carey, of Ripley, O., who had been a whaler, whispered to me that it was really alarming. I immediately whispered to a friend sitting before me, that in case of an accident he must immediately strike out from the boat in order to get out of the reach of the man at whom we had been laughing. Many did not see the danger, their backs being towards the stern.

We passed the sea weed, had ridden several huge rollers gracefully as a swan, and had reached a point 75 yards from the shore, when I saw a roller coming which I felt must overwhelm us. I glanced forward to see what the sailors would do that I might shape my course by that pursued by experienced seamen, then to the rear, and far above our heads, beheld the angry waters coming down upon our devoted heads. In an instant the stern portion of the bottom of the boat was dashed out as though it had been so much paper, and I found myself struggling beneath the waters. I raised for a moment to the surface and gasped for breath, throwing out the salt water which had strangled me, and closing my mouth in an instant, was again hurled by the succeeding wave sheer down to the bottom. I raised again, and in the instant beheld, some rods distant, the wrecked boat with several of our friends grasping her sides. Among the rest, Gould, who looked the very image of despair. The third time I was hurled beneath the surface I grasped a stone that I might hold myself down until the next roller should pass, but the stone, proving too light, came up with me. The next time I was fortunate enough to find another and a larger, and as I felt the waters rush over me I raised and struck for the beach, as the next one came I dived under, and in a few desperate strokes my feet were on firm ground. I fell to my knees and crawled to the edge of the water and for a few moments was almost insensible. The steersman had let the oar fall on my head as the water struck the boat and it almost stunned me.

As soon as possible I proceeded to assist my suffering comrades on the boat, and with the aid of the sailors and B. Read, of Guernsey Co., O., we recovered several who were fast drifting beyond all human aid. The man of whom we had made sport before the accident had given up in despair, when three of us succeeded in reaching him and pulled him ashore. I never saw a more grateful man than him. Most strange to relate we all escaped though some of us severely bruised. The tremendous force of the waters, and the tide setting in is all that saved us. Some men whom we afterwards met said that that coast was at all times dangerous on account of the surf and that day surf was remarkably high. Some four or five hundred dollars were lost, beside 4 rifles and various other articles such as pistols, coats, &c. I had a heavy California suit, four large pockets filled with bread, a bag of bullets, my pistol and bowie knife, and after all reached terra-firma. I need not say that we all rejoiced in our safety.[10]

We clambered to the top of the cliffs under which we had been wrecked, and stretched ourselves in a row that we might be counted on the vessel. Even my drowning could not prevent an ejaculation of admiration escaping my lips as I looked upon the enchanting prospect by which I was surrounded. Before me, for miles upon miles, as far as the eye could perceive, more than a mile in depth, and then hedged in by green grassy mountains, was spread a beautiful prairie decorated with an innumerable variety of the richest flowers, and herbage. Indeed there seemed a wilderness of flowers, and I could not but think nature had been most lavish in her gifts of beauty on those shores, hitherto described as so bleak and desolate. On these plains were grazing in peacefulness, hundreds of cattle and horses, teeming with health and flesh.

We had been on the prairie but a short time, when a Mr. Williams, a gentleman engaged here in getting out lumber for San Francisco,[11] rode up and upon hearing our story, kindly invited us to his house, though at the same time informing us that our better plan would be to proceed to what is known as the "Russian Farm," and get our suppers and then proceed to Santa Cruz. We followed his advice and finding the Old Russian at home,[12] we made known our wants, and in a short time were

---

[10]A. S. Gould, in his shorter account of the boat wreck, wrote, "I found I was severely bruised, my ankle was out of joint, and my legs both badly sprained. My letters of introduction, together with several entrusted to my care in Cincinnati, my revolver and some three hundred dollars, were all lost. Another person lost, I think, twenty-five sovereigns. But discouraging as these losses are, we all consider ourselves fortunate in the extreme that we saved our lives." *Cincinnati Commercial,* August 15, 1850.

[11]Probably James Williams, who came to California with the Chiles-Walker party in 1843 and settled in Santa Cruz as a blacksmith and lumberman. Bancroft, *California,* 5: 775-76.

[12]The "Old Russian" was José Antonio Bolcoff (1789-1861) a sailor and shoemaker from Kamchatka who, in 1815, deserted his ship in Monterey and became California's first Russian settler. He located in Santa Cruz where he served on three occasions as *alcalde* of the Villa of Branciforte. In 1841 Bolcoff was granted the vast Refugio Rancho west of Santa Cruz where he fed Bickham's party. Although he mined a sizable amount of gold in 1848, Bolcoff's later business activities were unsuccessful, and he died in poverty in 1866. Bancroft, *California,* 2: 723; *Alta,* March 19, 1866.

engaged in the discussion of one [of] the most delectable suppers, as I then thought, I had ever eaten. Perhaps the fact of 63 days starvation and a drowning had its effect. Certain it is that 17 hungry men did justice to the fare, and that the host only charged us 70 cents each. He is one of the richest men in the country, possessing 9 miles square of the richest land, 700 horses and 500 cattle. His gardens resembled those of our own country in appearance and his orchard is certainly deserving of much credit on account of the tact and care bestowed upon it. All his grounds are irrigated, and the soil is very black, richer indeed than our boasted Miami bottoms, being a sandy loam and easily cultivated. We endeavored to buy horses of him, but he would hear of nothing under $200 each for them. We thought this rather high, and paying his bill, we bade him and his handsome daughter, with whom I endeavored to chat a little Spanish, adios, and started for Santa Cruz. We arrived about 9 P.M., and put up at a house kept by an American, and who treated us with true hospitality. That night there was a fandango in town, which some of our party visited and saw some of the Spanish lassies. I was much too fatigued, even had I wished to go.

Monday morning before starting across the mountains, I walked around the town and noted the various improvements taking place, and I must own I was much surprised at the number of American buildings already erected, which I saw, and the preparations being made for improvement. The town was formerly the Catholic Mission Station, and was walled in by houses made of unburnt brick, having in its centre a large church composed of the same rough materials. It is situated on the Pacific ocean, and on the San Lorenzo river, not far from its mouth, in the midst of a splendid grazing district, and lands which, if cultivated, would yield with astonishing abundance. The mountains nearby are covered with splendid timber, a description of pine, here called redwood, growing very straight to a tremendous height. Speculation in town lots is as much the rage here as in the Queen City. Our landlord owns most the whole place. They have a city council and government, and I noticed in my peregrinations that "the council had ordained that no hogs should be suffered to go at liberty under a penalty of $20 for each offence." Cincinnati is behind the times in some respects.[13] I was offered $12 per diem and my board by a citizen of this place to assist him in getting out lumber. As my baggage was to be at San Francisco, I was compelled to decline, although this was not my legitimate sphere of business. I would not wish to encourage any one by this statement to come out here, because this price for labor may not be sustained.

At 9 o'clock we started for Santa Clara, about fifty miles distant, beyond the Santa Cruz mountains. I found that my injuries received the day previously interfered with my walking, especially when I found in my path huge, precipitous mountains, sometimes requiring the aid of hands to climb. We had expected to find some houses on the route where we could get provisions, but in this we were disappointed, and accordingly at sundown we built a fire and laid down to sleep, weary almost to exhaustion, having traveled over twenty miles, surmounting most precipitous mountains. We had met several cattle drovers, who said it was exceedingly dangerous to sleep in the mountains, on account of the great numbers of grizzly bears prowling around at night. Those who saved their pistols prepared themselves to meet "bruin," should he make his appearance. We were so hungry we wished to see him, but we were not favored with a sight. The heavy dew which fell on us that night soaked almost as thoroughly as a rain storm, and we rested but little. At daylight we started again and after walking about six miles, we arrived at a saw-mill, having that morning passed through thick forests of splendid red-wood timber, some of it 20 feet through. A few yards further on we came to a farm house, and asked for breakfast, and in a few moments we were seated before a regular country table, with good fresh milk, coffee, butter, shortcake and delicious beef. Here one of our party was offered $200 per month and board to assist in building a saw-mill, but he refused; and after paying $1 each, we bade Mrs. Jones adieu,[14] and started for Santa Clara, 15 miles distant.

---

[13]Cincinnati during the 1840s and '50s was notorious for the large number of pigs which, according to one visitor, "walked about the streets as if they owned the town," and belonged "to no one in particular." Lyell, *Travels in North America,* 2: 61.

[14]Probably Mary, wife of Zachariah ("Buffalo") Jones, an emigrant of 1846, who owned a sawmill near present-day Los Gatos. Bancroft, *California,* 4: 695; Hoover and Rensch, *Historic Spots,* 455; 1852 California Census, Santa Clara County, 120.

About two miles from the saw-mill we began to ascend a steep and lofty mountain, and the last in our way, and after severe labor we accomplished our task. On the summit we rested, and as I glanced over the prospect beneath and before me, I could not but ask, what had I in comparison with this, when first I landed on the coast, to admire? An immense plain or prairie covered with yellow waving oats, appearing as if planted by human aid, large fields of clover, grass, and innumerable flowers, brooks and streams winding among groves of trees, and the "cattle on a thousand hills" grazing in peace and quietness, horses playing in the shade, were all spread before me in all the loveliness and wildness of nature... The view here presented to me was the most lovely my eyes have ever rested upon, and I have beheld some rich scenes. The feeling of enthusiasm in our party was as great as my own, and the universal sentiment was that if California presents at all times a picture of such exquisite loveliness, we would be content.

I descended the mountain and followed the narrow path of the plains, and constantly met with new objects of attraction. One great drawback, however, is the want of rain in the dry season. Yet, still this can be overcome by irrigation. The soil is of such a nature that it will produce when our Ohio lands would burn with heat. The mountains throughout our journey we found covered with wild oats, resembling the domestic oats in appearance, though neither so good or so heavy. I judge from this, that good seed from the States would produce the most happy results. Here the oats are cut in preference to hay. The clover is remarkably heavy, and bears a flower different from that which you have... I will send some of the seed to my mother.

At dinner time we stopped at the rancho of an old Spaniard of very aristocratic bearing, and got some beef from him, which we fastened upon sticks and broiled over the coals of a fire he had made for us. He had rather more conscience than the Russian or Mrs. Jones, charging us only 15 cents each. After dinner we arrived at the Santa Clara Mission, almost completely fagged, and convinced that we had seen the elephant. Here we were on the direct road to San Francisco, and learned that two lines of stage coaches passed daily, and that if we would send to Puebla[15] we could obtain tickets. We sent one of our number, and he telling them

---

[15]The Pueblo of San Jose, then the capital of California.

a tough story of our adventures, managed to get tickets at $10 each, the usual price being $16. Our messenger was a sailor. Eight of us were to go the following day, and the other nine the day succeeding. I was one of the party who laid over one day, and in the meantime learned many interesting particulars concerning the country. Every man you see here is in a great hurry. Those on horseback ride at Gilpin paces, those walking have their coat-tails streaming out behind them, and the stages whiz along like meteors. I had the honor of riding in the first regular coach on her first trip in California, and I do assure you I went as fast as four good horses could run on a perfectly level road, to within ten miles of San Francisco, when the road became hilly and sandy. There are public houses at each depot for changing horses, and their charges are not very light. For instance: a glass of milk 25c, eggs 25c each, turnips $1.25 each, &c. I made quite a speculation, in a small way, during the trip down, getting an equivalent of $2 for a clay pipe worth half a cent in the States.

It would be vain for me to attempt to give you a description of San Francisco, for the very simple reason that I do not think it can be described. It is unlike anything of which you ever dreamed, and has not its comparison in existence. The spirit of go-ahead-ativeness is certainly manifested to a most astonishing degree. Houses 100 feet square, three stories high, burned by the late fire,[16] in two weeks were rebuilt and occupied; good houses at that. The majority of the buildings are frame, though there are many fine brick warehouses. The custom house is an excellent building, and is well finished.

The hills around the city are covered with grotesque looking shanties and tents, the camps of emigrants stopping here, and many of them have the features of squalid poverty. The public houses, with exception of the St. Francis Hotel, are gambling saloons, and any hour of the day or night you may see hundreds engaged in playing at tables surrounded by the most abandoned of both sexes. All the games of chance that you have ever heard of are here in a flourishing condition. Some fools bet as high as a panful of dust at a time. There are now in the harbor of San Francisco three Pacific steamers and over 500 other vessels, besides innumerable yawl boats for the taking of passengers to and from the vessels

---

[16]The fire of May 4, 1850, the second in a series of six major fires which devastated Gold Rush San Francisco.

arriving and departing. There are several lines of steamers running daily to Sacramento and Stockton, and are crowded every trip at $25 to the former place, and $20 to the latter. Innumerable sailing crafts ply between this port and the other two, at much cheaper rates...

The steamer Sarah Sands was compelled, on account of the filling of her boilers with kelp and the incrustation of salt, to discharge most of her passengers 200 miles below here, some few weeks ago. The passengers had to cope with many hardships before arriving, but with the exception of one emigrant who accidentally shot himself when but a few miles from here...[unfinished sentence in original]. The Sands did not arrive until yesterday, and suit was instantly brought against her by the passengers.[17] The sailors of the Anne, the barque on which I sailed, have brought suit against her, and I intend doing so in a day or two.[18] The steamer Chesapeake, which left Panama in January, has not yet arrived. Some of her passengers are awaiting her arrival in order to sue for damages.[19] Never in the annals of time has such imposition been practiced, as that daily practiced by American citizens on their own countrymen emigrating to this country. They seem to lose every spark of honor and principle, and become almost devils incarnate...

The city council rejected an ordinance to the effect that each one should have a salary of $6,000 per annum, Mayor, Treasurer, &c.,

---

[17]The *Sarah Sands*, a 1,400 ton iron screw steamer, built in Liverpool in 1847, was chartered by the Empire City Line in 1850 and sent to San Francisco. She had a slow passage to Panama City, and the captain, in his haste to reach San Francisco, neglected to careen the ship or to take on an adequate supply of coal. When the absence of coal, plus heavy northwest winds, forced him to put in at San Simeon Bay on the central California coast and send for help, several of the passengers elected to make their way to San Francisco by land. After another steamer arrived with more fuel, the *Sarah Sands* arrived in San Francisco on June 7, sixty-four days after leaving Panama, the longest steamer passage on record. J. H. Kemble, *Panama Route*, 246; Wiltsee, *Gold Rush Steamers*, 35-39.

[18]The *Anne* reached San Francisco on June 3, four days after dropping off Bickham and his associates. BL: C-A 169, Part II, reel 11.

[19]The *Chesapeake*, a 392 ton steamer, left New York in August 1849, carrying about one hundred and forty passengers. By April 1850, she was off the coast of Baja California, short of provisions and fuel, with a leaky boiler. The majority of her passengers left the ship in the neighborhood of Cabo San Quintin, and walked some two hundred miles to San Diego from where several of them were conveyed to San Francisco by the steamer *Oregon*. The *Chesapeake* herself, with her remaining twenty-six passengers, reached San Francisco on August 7, after a 364 day voyage. *Sacramento Transcript*, May 23, 1850; *Alta*, May 20, 1850; BL: C-A 169, Part II, reel 11; Rasmussen, *Passenger Lists*, 1: 27, 130; Wiltsee, *Gold Rush Steamers*, 44.

$10,000, and it raised quite an excitement. Shouldn't wonder. But, Mr. Editor, this is a singular place, and the best way for a man to get along is to look upon everyone he meets as a rascal until he finds him honest. Boarding is very high here, $3 to $4 a day being the very least. The water has been so high at the Sacramento mines, where I intend going, that little has been done this season. It is now receding. The country is now very sickly. The southern mines yield very well.

I do not feel prepared to advance an opinion with regard to young men leaving home and coming here, as I have not been here long enough to judge. The hardships they will be sure to undergo are very great, but they would be rather a glory, were they to be fortunate. You hear much of the misery of this country, yet I think the reports no worse than what you may see in your own city in actual existence. There are many worthless drunken fellows here; so are there in other places. I will say this much, that a man who comes here must be prepared to meet every temptation, and laugh it to scorn, and bid defiance; for just so sure as he is not determined, just so surely will he fall. I must say, and without profanity, that this is an almost perfect h-l of a place.

San Francisco deserves all that is said of its climate, being certainly one of the most disagreeable places imaginable. Very cold at night and in the morning, and dust flying thickly all day long. At present the bilious diarrhoea prevails to a great extent. The disease is attributed to the water. But as my letter has already extended to an unwarrantable length, I must close, desiring you to present my respects to my friends, and assuring you that I am living in hope of a successful future.

CHAPTER TWO

First Months in the Mines

SACRAMENTO CITY, ALTA CALIFORNIA; Wednesday, June 12, 1850
[*Cincinnati Daily Gazette*, July 30, 1850]:

MESSRS. EDITORS:—...Monday evening, the 10th, I purchased a ticket on the steamer Gold Hunter, a regular packet plying between the ports of San Francisco and this city, for which I paid only $25, distance 150 miles, and at 4 o'clock was on route. At supper time, I seated myself at the table, supposing all to be correct, and was half finished partaking of a most excellent supper, when the clerk passed around, asking each passenger for $1.50, that being the extra charge. I thought it rather strange, as on our western steamers meals are understood to be in the bills. However, I paid my share, finished my supper, and walked around until bed time, and then went to the captain to get a state room. He very coolly remarked that they were *only $10 extra*. I asked him how much he charged for sleeping on the windlass, with a coil of rope for a pillow, assuring him that I was not used to luxuries. His answer was that if I could find a good place to lie down "he would charge nothing extra," and, taking him at his word, I procured my blankets and took a comfortable nap alongside the chimney. This is one of the ways of doing business in California, and as it is a tolerably fair sample, and quite the custom, I presume it is all right. There are three lines of steamers plying daily between the two cities, and their profits are immense. The tide of emigration is so great, that they can scarce accommodate those passing toward the mines.

We stopped a few moments at Bonicia, a town above the mouth of the Sacramento River, and which is to be the U. S. Naval Depot in California.[1] I discovered that the enterprise of the universal Yankee nation had fastened here, and that many good houses were in progress of erection, and that all kinds of business, from card playing to swapping horses, is transacted. The town was completely inundated by the last Spring's overflow, and I am informed that it does not present so fine an appearance as before that calamity. It is in contemplation to raise a levee to prevent a future overflow.

About half way between Bonicia and Sacramento City the river is so exceedingly crooked that it is a matter of great difficulty in low water for steamers to get through, the Gold Hunter being compelled to back out and make several attempts before she could make the proper channel. The valley of the Sacramento presented from the decks of the steamer a very fine appearance, being covered as far as the eye could see with a luxuriant growth of grass. The soil is said to be remarkably fertile, and only requires irrigation to make it one of the most productive valleys in the world. Many emigrants have lined their purses with gold dust by cutting the grass which grows so luxuriantly, and taking it to this city and selling it. In many places farms have been opened, and this year good crops will doubtless be produced, and the farmers be enriched thereby.

Yesterday morning at 8 o'clock we landed here, and since that time I have been engaged in making preparations for the mines, looking at the city, and wondering at many things which meet my view. The people of the Queen City have been in the habit of boasting of their enterprise, of the rapid growth of their city, of the speedy manner in which streets are laid out and tall rows of houses erected thereon, &c., &c., but I can assure you, Messrs. Editors, that they have never dreamed of building up a city in such an incredibly short space of time as has here sprung up. One year since, not ten houses were to be seen in this place; now Sacramento, a chartered city, boasts of its 15,000 inhabitants.

The houses are not mere huts as you would be likely to suppose, but are good, substantial buildings, and many of them brick. Main street and Pearl street of Cincinnati, in the busiest seasons of the year, present no

---

[1]Benicia was founded in 1847 on land donated by General M. G. Vallejo, after whose wife it was named. While it did not become the Bay Area's leading city as its founders had hoped, it served as the third state capital in 1853-54. The army, not the navy, established an ordnance supply depot at Benicia in August 1851.

greater scenes of activity than are here presented at all times. Hundreds of stores, having all manner of merchandise for sale, are constantly filled with customers; traders and miners with their teams throng the streets; small steamers ply constantly between the city and the Yuba river mines, all laden, the wagons with merchandise, and the steamers with both freight and passengers. The city is filled with Coffee Houses and Gambling establishments; in truth every Coffee House has its Faro and Monte Tables, and in addition to the usual inducements to enter their precincts, bands of music are employed to perform each night, having a fine orchestra box prepared exclusively for them.

"People must come to California if they wish to see every thing." Every hour I see something which reminds me of this remark. Last night while wandering around the city, I dropped into Lee's Coffee House, the principal gambling saloon of the city, and looking into the orchestra box, I beheld a woman "fiddling" away for dear life. She "drawed a bow" most exquisitely, and with all the grace of a Paganini, eliciting the praises of a large crowd of listeners. Curious employment for a woman, thought I, but then she receives $30.00 per night, and people who come to this country are not particular as to employment. This saloon is superior to anything of the kind I have seen save Parker's in San Francisco, and is yet in an unfinished state. There are some good Hotels, but their charges are enormous, and their fare only tolerable. One item of charge is $2 per night for sleeping on the floor, furnishing your own blankets.

The friends of emigrants at home would be amused on hearing of the occupations of young sprigs of nobility here. Some who carried a "stiff upper-lip" in Cincinnati, are ox drivers, mule drivers, &c. Some of them are engaged in building fences, and in sooth I cannot say what they are not doing. I know men who never shoved a plane before coming here, who make their $10 per day as journeymen carpenters; others who never opened Blackstone are practicing law; some lawyers are making brick, and some putting "bricks in their hat." It is certainly amusing. But times have sadly degenerated, and money is not so easily made as one year ago. It now requires more time and more labor to make money, yet still money can be made by persevering industry. I would not say to any man, "come to California," nor would I advise him against it, for I am not prepared to advance an opinion. Yet those with whom I have conversed tell me to advise my friends to stay at home. Perhaps the immense emigration of this year will have a serious effect upon the prospects of miners. The waters have been so high that the "diggings" could not be worked this spring, consequently but little gold has yet been taken out. There is undoubtedly much gold in the country, but the one and two hundred dollars a day licks are alarmingly scarce. From a half ounce to an ounce is considered good work; to be sure more is occasionally made, but I speak of the average daily labor...

I heard yesterday that my brother[2] is mining on the North fork of the middle fork of the American. To-day I "follow off a wagon" in search of him, and I learn that I am to have a "beautiful walk" of 76 miles—a portion of the distance over mountains almost perpendicular. Very good, I'm in for it now for certain. It appears the farther in I get, the more the plot thickens.

A party of emigrants, 40 in number, got in to-day from across the Plains, having left April 1st. The passage is a remarkably quick one.

To emigrants who may hereafter start for this country, I would say, *"bring nothing save what is absolutely necessary."* All extras will prove as so many incumbrances, and will have to be left behind when they start for the mines.

As all persons in this section of the world are hurried, it is unnecessary for me to offer any apologies, since I am now a Californian, and expect to be for the next four years. I yesterday received a "Gazette" of the 4th of April, for which you will please accept my thanks. My post-office is here, and any communications my friends may send will be received and perused with the greatest pleasure...

---

[2]William Bickham's brother, John C. Bickham, (1832-83) came overland to California in 1849. He remained in the mines after William had moved to San Francisco, and he was still in California in 1855. By the following year he had returned to Ohio, and during the later 1850s he worked as a brakeman on the Little Miami Railroad. John served as a wagoner during the Civil War, taking part in the Georgia and Carolina campaigns. During the late 1860s and early '70s he lived with his mother in Riverside, Ohio, and was employed as a watchman at the Theatre Comique. In the later 1870s he moved to Evansville, Indiana, where he spent his final years first as an engineer, and later as a janitor in the U.S. Custom House. *St. Joseph Gazette*, April 27, May 4, 1849; WRHS Bickham family papers, Container 1, folders 4, 7; Cincinnati city directories 1857, 1867-74; *Official Roster of the Soldiers of the State of Ohio in the War of the Rebellion*, 6: 415; "Old Woodward," 139; Evansville city directories, 1872-83.

NORTH FORK OF THE MIDDLE FORK OF THE AMERICAN RIVER, ALTA CALIFORNIA, July 19th, 1850.
[*Cincinnati Daily Gazette,* September 11, 1850]:

MESSRS. EDITORS:— At the time I last wrote you, I was engaged in making arrangements to follow an ox team destined to go towards the mines among the mountains, where I had learned my brother was engaged delving among the rocks and sands of a mountain stream for the *ore.* At that time I had experienced somewhat of hardships and toil, but had a very faint idea of the trials and troubles of a miner, and consequently could offer you nothing concerning the realities of such a life, save the ideas I had acquired through the partial hearsay stories of others. Still I had learned enough to satisfy me that as yet a portion of *"the elephant"* remained invisible to my eyes, and having a deal of curiosity in my composition, I determined upon following up "the animal," in order that I might discover what description of creature it really was. Accordingly on the afternoon of the day I wrote you, having disposed of my baggage, consisting of blankets, coat and sundry other articles, amounting perhaps to 40 lbs., I took up the line of march in the rear of a "prairie schooner," on that which I hoped to be the road to fortune. As you can imagine, this way of traveling on the road to fortune was perhaps about as rapid as is usual on this road, rather slowly, and as illustrative of this, I will merely remark that in the space of three hours the convoy "schooner," and self completed just two miles of our journey, and then came to anchor, and laid up at Sutter's Fort for the night. After preparing my supper, consisting of coffee, pork and bread, and satisfying the cravings of my stomach, I enveloped myself in my blankets, crawled under the wagon, and was soon lost in sleep, resting as comfortably on the earth as I could possibly have rested on the most downy couch.

I traveled three or four days, the greater portion of the time up to my eyes in dust—eating, sleeping, &c. as I have described, and finally arrived at the trading village of Culloma, on the south Fork of the American river, 50 miles from Sacramento City. To this place the road was through level and beautiful plains, covered with fine prairie grass, and ornamented with flowers and finely shaded oak trees, many places affording beautiful views, and the soil generally presenting an appearance which would prompt me to believe it to be productive were it in any other country than California.

The want of moisture here prevents such a belief, and consequently these fine plains are useful only as grazing lands for cattle. Every valley in which is a running stream has its claimants, and they universally have their houses of accommodation for travelers, and charge just as they think proper for "taking men in." I entered not a public house on the route which had not its monte table, nor indeed have I since my entry into this country. During the time which I was traveling the road was thronged with miners and teams, some going to the mines and some returning to the city for provisions, and the scene of activity presented reminds me much of the bustle and activity observable upon the principal thoroughfares leading into the good Queen City.

Culloma is another one of those mushroom towns with which California is filled, and which have sprung as if by magic within the last year. Its dwellings are mostly frame shanties and canvass tents, though here and there may be seen very respectable looking frame houses, two stories in height. It is filled with groceries from whence the miners in that vicinity obtain their supplies; and has its full complement of drinking and gambling houses, where the majority of the miners *deposite* their hard earnings for *safe keeping*. The inhabitants of this place have petitioned for a Post Office, and I presume their prayers will be answered ere long. A line of stages already ply daily between there and the city and I judge by the numerous travelers constantly passing and repassing that the business is profitable. The fare is $25 or 50 cents per mile.

At this place I parted company with the ox team and, placing my "kit" upon my shoulders in true military style, I started off for another walk of 50 miles, and, as I afterwards learned by dear experience, they were miles which would almost worry down the celebrated *steam leg*. Ascending the steep precipitous mountains one after another from noon till night, I found to be no joke, particularly when I thought of the 40 lbs. on my back, and that bothered me so much that I was constantly thinking of it. Going down the mountains was fully as bad as ascending, and perhaps the effect was worse, for my muscles were constantly stretched to the greatest possible tension, and the jarring sensation produced by coming down heavily laden was far from being agreeable.

My manner of descending one particular mountain reminded me much of the days of my urchinhood, when a fall of snow whitened the hills, and lads came forth in glee with their sleds. The declivity was so great that walking down was not to be thought of, consequently I procured a flat stone and, seating myself upon it, started down. I hardly knew where, but as the road was a little worn, I knew I should land somewhere, and, as the bushes along the sides of the path afforded opportunities for checking my speed, I feared not that I should meet with trouble. I had a merry ride for a few moments, when I came to a little jumping off place where I lost my "sled" and received a severe fall. After a long time I arrived at the bottom, and found myself among a number of miners' tents, the dwellers of which came out to see what was going on. I discovered to my surprise that I had lost my path and had descended the mountain in a place used for sliding down lumber and timber. The proper place for descending was several miles distant, and since I was down it only remained for me to find the way to the right road. This I accomplished by following the path pointed out by the miners, and I was soon ready to ascend another mountain.

After experiencing *considerable* toil and vexation of spirit for several days, I arrived at another trading post, known as Birdstown, near the boundary line of Eldorado county, and here had the good fortune to meet Truman Conclin, of Cincinnati,[3] and learned from him that I was within eight miles of my destination. I remained with him about two days, in the meantime gleaning facts concerning the life into which I was being ushered, also in gaining information concerning the prospects of miners in this section of the country. Eldorado county last fall was supposed to be the richest in the State, and consequently large numbers of emigrants were attracted to its mountain ravines and streams, to try their fortunes. In and about Birdstown, it has been computed, were during the spring at least 10,000 men, and I should judge from the number of deserted tents whitening the valleys and mountain sides near the streams, that there must have been near that population there congregated. Unfortunately for the great majority, the reputation which had gone forth of this place proved false, and in consequence nine-tenths of those who came there with bright hopes went away disappointed. Some were very fortunate, having secured the best claims and amassed fortunes, and are now delving with pick axe and shovel for more. A ravine known as the "Dutch Gulch," has proved immensely

---

[3]Truman Conklin, an Ohio native, returned home later that year. He practiced law in Cincinnati until his death, aged 53, in 1875. See below 113-14; 1860 Census: Cincinnati, 8th ward, 402; 1870 Census, Cincinnati, 8th ward, 207; Cincinnati directories 1856-76; *Cincinnati Enquirer,* Sept. 1, 1875.

rich, but only the lucky few have these drawn numbers. In this large population there was of course the usual number of black-legs and rascals, and as would be expected, they lined their pockets with the dust.

In April last, one of the most revolting murders on record took place there, or I may say two murders. Two gamblers named Helm and White quarreled; Helm sent for his brother, who was not far distant, and as the brother entered the door of the cabin where the two were quarreling, White shot his opponent through the neck, killing him instantly, and was himself the next moment stabbed to the heart by the surviving brother. Some one remarked, "Helm," or "Texas" as he was called—"you have killed him." "My God," exclaimed he, "he has killed my brother!" and then passed unmolested from the bloody scene. The two murdered men lie buried side by side upon a mound in the midst of the valley, and the brother who avenged the first murder is roaming at large. I expect to hear of his being murdered by the surviving brother of White, who is now in California, and is as desperate a gambler as lives.

There seems to be no restraint whatever upon the passion of men here for gambling, all giving way to it, without stint, men of all ages and all classes engaging indiscriminately. In one house two men dealing out Monte were pointed out to me as having been ministers when in the States. I have met during my travels a dozen of that ilk, and they seemed to think and act upon the principle that when "in Rome they must act like Romans." Gamblers are the aristocrats of California…

North Fork of the Middle Fork of the American River, Alta California, July 20th, 1850.
[*Cincinnati Daily Gazette,* September 12, 1850]:

Messrs. Editors: —At sunset on the 19th of June, I found myself weary and worn in the brush and rock habitation in which I am now seated, answering the numerous questions of my brother, as well as many inquiries of Cincinnatians who are engaged with him, of a description corresponding to such as, "Is the bridge between Cincinnati and Covington yet commenced?" "Is the work on the St. Louis and Cincinnati Railroad yet begun?" &c., the questioners not having heard from the Queen City for months, and having great faith in Cincinnati enterprise, deeming, of course, that these things and a hundred others must by this time be either finished or in process of construction.

The next day, upon looking round and taking a view of the place which was to be my residence for the summer, I could not help asking what had prompted men to seek for such a wild, forlorn-looking spot as this? At the same moment the answer, "that no one had tried here for gold," suggested itself, and I thought the selection a wise one. However, with all the wilderness and forlorn appearance of this "Cañon," there is much of beauty in it. The mountains hem us in on every side, looming up far, far above, covered with forests of tall pines, and here and there may be seen large rocks covered with moss; just at our feet and at the base of the mountains, a stream of crystal clearness rushes and foams o'er the rocks, and to our eyes seems to glitter with gold. The sun gilds the summits of the mountains, and is high up in the heavens long before he begins to brighten our homes, and we may with safety boast that we of the valley are always astir ere the sun-light glitters among us. But the contemplation of the situation of this camp, and the act of experiencing such daily labor as is our portion, and the fare with which we have to content ourselves, are entirely distinct and different affairs. It is *only* the *slight* difference of imagining one thing and relishing another.

The mining company consists of 16 young men, in which are Silas Smith,[4] H. Hubbell,[5] John Lauck,[6] David P. Marshall,[7] Wm. Crawford,[8]

---

[4]Silas Smith set out overland for California in 1849 as a member of the "Experiment Club." He and fellow Cincinnatian, William Poor, eventually separated from the rest of the party and crossed the Sierra with pack mules. He is probably the Silas F. Smith listed in the census as a 22 year old miner born in Maine, living in El Dorado County in October 1850. After returning to Cincinnati, Smith was employed for many years as a carriage maker. *Republican*, April 23, 1849; *Cincinnati Daily Times*, October 23, 1849; 1850 Census, El Dorado County, California, 381; Cincinnati city directories, 1857-90.

[5]William Henry Hubbell journeyed overland from Cincinnati to California in 1849. In November 1850, he was mining in Spanish Canyon, El Dorado County. During the Civil War, Hubbell served as a private in the Ohio Volunteer Infantry, taking part in the Virginia and Gettysburg campaigns. By 1867 he had returned to California and was living in Placer county. Haskins, *Argonauts of California*, 405; 1850 Census, El Dorado County, California, 404; *Official Roster of the Soldiers of the State of Ohio in the War of the Rebellion*, 9: 650; *Great Register of Placer County, 1867*.

[6]John Lauck, a Cincinnati comb maker, traveled overland to California in 1849. He was probably the J. B. Lauck listed in the 1860 census as a 36-year-old miner living in Siskiyou County, California. Cincinnati city directories 1849-50; *Republican*, April 23, 1849; 1860 Census, Siskiyou County, 37.

[7]David Pugh Marshall (b. 1822), a Cincinnati native, arrived in California in August 1849, became a grocer and served as a justice of the peace. From 1863 until his death in the mid-1890s, Marshall was employed by the San Francisco Gas Light Company as an inspector and foreman. *"Old Woodward,"* 229; Allen, *Society of California Pioneers Centennial Roster;* San Francisco City directories 1863-95.

[8]William Crawford is listed in the 1850 census as a 25-year-old miner, born in Ohio, living on the Middle Fork of the American River in January 1851. 1850 Census, El Dorado County, 467.

Thos. Morrow,[9] Pius Chambers,[10] Jno. Wooley,[11] and John C. Bickham of Cincinnati, and others from different sections of the United States, some of whom have been here watching their claims and waiting since the month of April for the river to fall, that they might be able to work. They were compelled to watch, that interlopers might not appropriate the spot, and had been waiting here upon expense, and unable to work until about the middle of June, when they began the most arduous labor of digging a race and building a dam, in order to turn the stream from its bed, that they might work it. I arrived in the "nick of time" to see and experience HARD labor, and I must say that it almost makes me nervous to think of it. Digging canals in the States would be holiday amusement in comparison with that at which we are engaged. I never wish to see a boulder stone after I leave California, and I presume that there are hundreds of others who will echo that wish.

I might make use of all the language contained in Webster's Dictionary and still be unable to give you a true idea of race and dam building in this country. We have not, nor are we able to procure, machinery, consequently huge stones have to be lifted and carried away by main strength, and sometimes our thews and sinews seem almost ready to snap in twain; then again, such timber as we want is half way up the mountain, and has to be rolled down and carried to the proper place, and finally, after getting the timber ready, some portion of the party, to place the timbers, must get into the water reaching to the chin, and so cold that did it run by your city, the ice trade would be good for nought. One party goes in and remains 16 or 20 minutes, and comes out at the expiration of that time shivering and chattering like a man with the ague; the

---

[9]Thomas G. Morrow (b. 1824) a native of Ireland and a Cincinnati resident, came to California with the Cincinnati and California Joint Stock Company in 1849. For the next four years he mined near Hangtown and other parts of Northern California and, by his own account, "helped to bring the water from Mokelumne River to Mokelumne Hill." In 1854 he returned east to live with his parents in Baltimore, and he is listed in the 1866 Cincinnati directory as an "agent." CSL Pioneer Card File; *Republican,* April 23, 1849; Cincinnati city directory, 1866.

[10]Pennsylvania-born Pius Chambers came overland to California in 1849 as a member of the Cincinnati and California Joint Stock Company. After returning to Cincinnati he worked as a machinist and finisher. *Republican,* April 23, 1849; Cincinnati city directories 1856-73.

[11]John Wooley had been an exchange broker's clerk before coming to California. He may have been the John Wooley listed in the 1870 census as a U.S. government assessor residing in Cincinnati. Cincinnati city directories 1850-51; 1870 Census: Cincinnati, 11th Ward, 413.

next squad are occupied, and so on until all get a taste of the cold duck, and then—we revolve again. After standing in the water in the race knee deep for weeks, pitching and shoveling out gravel, unearthing or ungraveling huge boulders, carrying them out of the way, getting logs and building log walls in the race, then cutting and carrying timber, getting up to our chins in water almost as cold as ice, and fixing those timbers in the dam, bruising our limbs more or less, the work is still unfinished, for clay must be found to make all tight, and that unfortunately is 300 yards distant, and must be carried in hand barrows and buckets and tumbled into the proper place.

Well, Messrs. Editors, to-morrow night this work will be completed, and then we are ready to solve that important and mysterious problem, the characteristic question of the Cincinnati Merchant, *"will it pay?"* We think and hope it will, as in prospecting we have unearthed some of "the precious," as California miners say, when well pleased with anything, we think it will be *"oil."* But the *dam* thing is now finished, and the worst not yet told. In the bed of the stream are huge boulders to be removed before we can dig, and even then we will have to work in water because it will soak through the dam and banks. No water tight dam has yet been constructed in California, and I doubt whether one can be made. But if we get well paid we will "rock the cradle" and pay no attention to such trifles.

I have given you a correct picture thus far, of mining as carried on with us. It is a fair example of the river miner's life throughout the "diggings," and those who may read my hasty account must think it colored; if they try, they will find what I say to be "even so." What follows applies particularly to three camps on this stream, and each individual of each camp stands ready to avow that notwithstanding all have seen hard times, this circumstance is the *"sweetener."* After laboring hard all day, as I have described, we return to camp, prepare supper and set down to enjoy, day in and day out, bread, salt pork, and coffee. We vary the meals by having salt pork first, and through the rest in succession. Fortunately we have the very best water.

The manner in which we procure this hard fare is what we most dread. When a mess runs short of provisions, all the members rise early, and start up a steep mountain only two miles in length, then down the other side, two miles, a second one of equal dimensions is surmounted, and in addition just six hills for oft I have counted them, of which the hills about Cincinnati are fair samples, are to be climbed. We are now at Birdstown, eight miles from camp, at which place we buy our provisions, paying enormous prices, and then start home with them on our backs, each man packing, frequently 50 lbs, never less than 35. We have the advantage (?) of down hill going back, so far as the mountains are concerned, having two to descend, and only one to mount, but from that one "angels and ministers of grace defend us." ... When we get home we throw ourselves upon our blankets and there remain till daylight next morning. Sore toes are constantly complained of the day following this trip, going down hill generally, swing[ing] the feet forward into the boots, and wearing off the skin. This journey is made once in two weeks, and pity it were not less frequent...

I have been compelled to give you this lengthened description of my own adventures and experience in California thus far, that a true feature of what *every* mining adventurer who comes here must expect, indeed, I must say he will be very lucky if he fares as well as I have. I have had easy times, if you take into consideration the circumstances of a portion of the company with whom I am connected, having traveled over the mountains, far and near, with their blankets and a week's provision on their shoulders, sleeping on beds of snow, &c., in search of good claims. Those who are now at home and have any symptoms of the fever, had better look well ahead before they adventure, else they may leap from "frying pan to fire." I believe that any man may make a good living in California, and by digging—but I do most certainly think this thing of suddenly amassing fortunes is more frequently heard of than experienced. Some men in the States are fortunate in business, others not, so is it here—the proportion may be a little greater, but yet by no means is the proportion as much greater as has been represented. Undoubtably there will be more gold taken out of the ground this year than last, but it must be recollected that more than double the number of operators are engaged, and the proportion alluded to will be lessened. I have yet to see whether I will uphold or condemn the mines in toto. I don't expect any $100 per day strokes of fortune by any means; if I should be "in the vein" I shall be one of the lucky ones, "and there's an end on't."

The diggings which I have seen, and through which I have passed are all appropriated, or have been thoroughly worked, as far as it is possible to work them with the usual implements. I passed [not] a rivulet or ravine which had not at some time been turned over and over, and the spectacle presented to me was most curious. "Prospectors"—as they are called who are in search for better diggings—are constantly running all through the country over mountain and valley, carrying upon their backs pick, shovel, and pan, and digging holes in every spot which presents a favorable appearance. It may appear rather singular to those not conversant with the flats, that such an extent of country as that known as the mines, should so soon have been thoroughly examined and "prospected," yet such is the case. I have met with experienced miners just returned from "prospecting" tours, and in every case been informed that every favorable looking place had been tried before them, and even they had started out in the winter and journeyed over snow from three feet to twenty feet in depth. This prospecting business, however, I deem to be rather foolish, as more money could be amassed ultimately by remaining in common diggings, than is made by these searchers for "big lumps." The water in the mountain streams has been too high, up to this time for mining, and as yet operations are rather limited. I cannot give any information concerning the Yuba, San Joaquin and Feather River districts, as I am situated so far back in the mountains that news rarely reaches me, and it is only by chance that newspapers reach here at all; when they do they are thoroughly perused, advertisements and all.

Notwithstanding the great desire of our company to complete our dam and race they could not let pass the glorious anniversary of our country's Independence without a celebration... On the 23rd of June the gem of patriotism in our breasts budded into existence, and each member contributed his share to the general fund, for the purpose of providing a dinner for the occasion. An orator, reader of the Declaration of Independence and suitable committees were appointed, and three patriotic youths volunteered to go to Birdstown and "pack" over the "necessary articles." I can assure you that it was not a spirit "few" by which we were animated upon that occasion, for going over mountains and back with a load, a distance of 16 miles, to us is not very amusing, but we were animated by an ardent desire to commemorate the Day!

The dawn of the 4th was ussured in by a salute of fire arms from the camp, accompanied by cheers which reverberated and echoed among the rocks and mountain gorges in our neighborhood, and when the morning sun gilded the summits of the pines waving far, far above us, the busy hum of preparation might have been heard, and the blue smoke which curled from our fires told of the operations of the cooks.

The only place in the neighborhood suitable for our purpose was a level space of ground about 15 or 20 feet square, situated by the river side, at the foot of the mountain which towered in majesty above. On every side were large masses of rocks beaming as though they had been thrown together by some convulsion of nature, and imparting, by their irregular appearance, in connection with the surrounding mountains and pouring stream o'er hung by vines and shrubs and gnarled oaks, a scene of sublime wildness and beauty. Large stones seeming as if placed by nature in proper position for this occasion served as seats for the participants, and at the foot of a tall and graceful pine was a native seat covered with moss and partially surrounded by a natural arbor, somewhat more elevated than the others, and here the presiding officer at the proper time by virtue of his office placed himself.

At the appointed hour, 12 o'clock M., the little band of patriots, 15 souls all told, assembled together, and were called to order by your humble servant, who had the honor of being President upon the occasion. The Chairman, in a few remarks alluded to the circumstances which had brought the party together upon that day, and expressed his regrets at having been unable to procure the Declaration of Independence, and also he regretted extremely that Captain Jonathan R. Davis, of South Carolina,[12] the expected Orator of the Day, having met with severe injuries by falling from a precipice while hunting game for our dinner, would be unable to participate in the celebration. In conclusion, he expressed a hope that some gentleman would volunteer to act in that capacity in lieu of Capt. Davis. The difficulty was adjusted by a motion that the Chairman should assume the responsibility, and accordingly the aforesaid unfortunate made his first attempt in public.

---

[12]Jonathan R. Davis was later the subject of a mock-heroic ballad commemorating an occasion in December 1854, when Davis was reported to have single-handedly killed eleven bandits who had ambushed him and two fellow miners. Sioli, *El Dorado County*, 154-55; *Alta*, December 14, 1854.

The next in order, and to us poor starving mortals the most important part of the ceremonies, was the dinner, and to this we repaired with becoming dignity, and with firm resolutions to do justice to the occasion. Our table consisted of a large flat rock, selected from the multitude around on account of its superior position, size, adaptation to the purpose, and polish. A large oak spreading out its arms above, preventing the rays of the sun from penetrating, and the leaves fanning back and forth, created a gentle air which conduced to the general comfort. The furniture presented a bright and shining appearance, having been burnished with particular care, and I ventu[r]e to say that any thrifty housewife would have taken honor to herself at the parade on her kitchen shelfs of such a brilliant array of plates, tin pans, and tin cups...All were arranged in the best order, and on each plate was laid a tempting piece of beautiful white bread, and each cup was filled with cool delicious water dipped from the sparkling stream which flowed at our feet.

The attack was made upon our unfortunate ham which graced one side of the table, and soon the wide and deep gashes into its very heart showed the fury of the onset; and it was a ham too, not capable of sustaining, for any great length of time, a very serious attack. It was not one of your plump, round, rosy Duffield appeasing hams; it presented not the appearance of having once assisted in the locomotion of your luxurious, corn-eating Buckeye porkers, nor did it by its appearance indicate that the graceful and delicate trimming which characterizes the sweet savored ham of Porkopolis had conduced to its beauty or proportions, but it seemed of a form and nature peculiar to itself, boasting of hide, hoof and hair, and prompted me to believe from its thinness and form, anything but a ham. It would have been looked upon by the good people of your city, as a natural curiosity and a great admirer of proportion in this article would have been struck aghast at the very thought of calling this a *ham*. Yet verily this China ham was a goodly one, notwithstanding its attenuated form and queer appearance, and naught save the hoof and bone remained to tell of this oddest of luxuries.

Our next *layer* consisted of dried peach pies, of which we had a goodly supply, and you who are now in the full enjoyment of all the luxuries of a civilized life, smile not at the remark, that to us they seemed of most elegant flavor, and they likewise passed away, and are now spoken of only in connection with the past. But the *bonne bouche*, the tit bit of the occasion, which graced the middle of the table, looming up in pyramidical form and most elegant proportions, was "the observed of all observers." It rested on the firm rock, appearing as if conscious of its fate, but yet seemed a willing sacrifice. The "cobbler"—for it was a "cobbler," a "peach cobbler"—had been the "great talked of" for a number of days, and had been associated with our daily thoughts and nightly dreams, and the subject of immeassurable speculation with parties concerned. Plans for making it, the best modes for cooking, the most acceptable gravy, and countless suggestions were offered. It had in addition been the source of great tribulation and vexation of spirit to the three patriotic youth, H. Hubbell, D. P. Marshall and self, who had volunteered to transport to camp the ingredients and a large kettle for cooking it from Birdstown. The cooks had been in a rage, sweating and crying over a smoky fire, and had a family meeting when the bag was cut.

But here it now was, safe and sound, without a fracture, and appearing most attractive. Pius Chambers, by virtue of his office as first cook, assumed the right of dissecting it and with all the grace of an experienced Frenchman and pleasant smile playing on his countenance, carved off slice after slice, as each one's plate was extended. The gravy consisted of a "good deal" of brandy and sugar, a little flour and spices, and was poured over the slices as each one "jumped in." Many were the happy remarks attendant upon its destination, and the hearty laughs accompanying, doubtless assisted in the digestion thereof. The "Major" declared it was "Oil," and for my part I am willing to acknowledge that it went down slick. Each one had enough, consequently we had equal to two feasts on that day, for the adage, "*enough* is as good as a feast." The cooks were voted A No 1. They certainly did "lay themselves out," greatly to our satisfaction. A committee had prepared the 13 regular toasts for the occasion, and these were now drank with beaming *spirit*. After the regulars, the volunteers were in order, and these were mingled with songs, bon mots, &c., with short responses from the toasted, and when the sun was last passing from our view, and the shades of evening reminded us of the closing day, with three loud hip hip harras, we ended our most joyous and singular celebration.

I doubt whether as remarkable a celebration as was ours ever took place. One in which there was so much of the feeling of ardent patriotism, mingled with so much of what would to the eyes of persons in the States appear ridiculous. Such a rough and ragged looking set of tatterdemalions, congregated together in the States or appearing on any of the public highways would most probably frighten children to desperation, and cause horses to break away in wild dismay. Notwithstanding beneath these rough exteriors, warm, proud hearts were beating, and home and native land were in our thoughts.

A slight description of some of the *dramatis personae* might give you a tolerable idea of the whole party. Miners when starting from Sacramento for the diggings, generally leave all articles, save one suit, their blankets and kitchen furniture behind them, that they may not be encumbered with too much plunder; our party did thus when they started, and as they have been a long time in the mines, engaged at rough work, their solitary suit has of course become the worse for wear. On the field of operations to-day appeared one of our most important members, *sans-culotte,* sporting a pair of flaming red flannel drawers and shirt, his unmentionables being *non est inventus;* his pedal extremities were encased in what had once been a pair of shoes, but alas, they were sadly worn, and an opening at the toes presented the appearance of a mouth filled with glittering teeth, "grinning a horrid ghastly smile." On his caput was placed a sleepy looking hat, which appeared in its hapless and worn condition to have been his companion for many a weary year, serving to shield him from the sun by day, and answering as a nightcap in the "hour when church yards yawn." Another appeared in a tattered check shirt, with what for want of a name I shall denominate "trowsers," which were so much patched that I doubt much whether he could have said which piece belonged to the original garment. This gentleman sported one boot, into the top of which one leg of his unwhisperables was forced, and on the other foot was a worn out shoe, minus a string. A Panama hat with a rope for a band completed his attire. Another walked about independently, with a clean check shirt, a pair of buckskin tights, one leg of which was cut off half way between the ankle and the knee, the other dangled in strips around his foot; he also sported a pair of shoes the heels of which he had knocked off in sliding down hill when packing provisions. Others appeared in garments varied in hue as Joseph's coat, and one man had the unblushing impudence to appear in a "biled shirt," but soon the cries of "take it off, take it off," made him aware of the desperate position in which he was placed. One would have thought from the appearance of our party, that all had been turned loose in some old rag shop to search for old fashioned and unheard of patterns. In addition to the rags, the sun-burnt visages, the long hair and whiskered countenances lent their aid and gave the party in addition the appearance of a band of desperadoes. "Take it all and all" it was a celebration "the like of which I ne'er shall look upon again.".

The "diggins" about here are remarkably healthy, the mornings and evenings being delightfully pleasant, and the only thing one need fear is, that from eating so much salt provisions without vegetables, he is liable to take the scurvy. All are healthy with us, and I trust ere long that we shall have provisions brought where we can reach them...

Murderer's Bar, Middle Fork of the American, Alta California, Sept. 1st, 1850.
[*Cincinnati Daily Gazette*, November 11, 1850].

Messrs. Editors: —Early in the month of July I hailed you from among the tall mountains which confines the North Branch of this Fork, giving you at that time a slight idea of the troubles and trials as well as the hopes of a band of Mountain Miners. I stated at that time that we should in a few days be reveling in the bed of the stream which we were then engaged in sluicing and daming, the bottom of which we were so anxious to see, and moreover that we trusted the same would prove "*oil*," that when we went forth from thence we would be enabled to carry with us, the wherewithal to buy meat and drink, and serve ambitious yawning for a season. That it did prove "oil" when once we had attained our first wish, methinks you will not find one to deny, but alas for human flesh, it proved naught but "elbow oil." From the rising until the going down of the sun, none other save that of boulders presented itself, and with this we were forced to content ourselves. The Monday following the date of my letter, our dam was finished, the water rushing through our sluice at a rapid rate, and a bed of huge rocks lifted itself into the space. We partitioned our different claims, and with pick axe, crowbar,

shovel and rocker, commenced operations. The first day's labor produced none of the "ore," the second proved equally fruitless, the third
was of the same elk, and when the sun went down the majority of the
company gave up the search in dispair, and determined to go forth in
search of "new diggings." Our mess determined to persevere for a few
days, and accordingly went to work with vigor on the following day, but
still we were doomed to be unsuccessful. Layer after layer of boulders
weighing from a thousand pounds upwards presented themselves as we
sunk holes, and the water from the springs in the mountains came upon
us so copiously that two of our number were unable to keep it bailed out.

Saturday morning decided us with regard to these diggings. We had
no machinery with which to work, and this we were convinced was
absolutely necessary to accomplish anything, and furthermore it could
not be gotten to our stream without very heavy expense, therefore we
decided to leave our present diggings behind us. About a half a mile
below us at the same time were engaged a number of hardy, powerful
Germans, upon claims not so difficult to manage as ours, but they also
determined to remove, because of the severity of the labor, declaring that
"in three months they would be dead, if they did not depart." I imagine
that when Dutchmen yield to hard labor that it is time for those unused
to labor to desist operations for the same reason.

I was loth to leave the North Fork because I was firmly convinced,
and am now of the opinion that there were rich deposits of gold lying in
the stream, and in that portion which we sluiced. The nature of the place
gave the strongest indications, that is to say, if any faith can be placed in
the various theories advanced concerning gold, such as appearances of
volcanic eruptions, quartz, rock, &c. The sides of the mountains are covered with large masses of rock which appear to have been molten and
burned, and moreover on the northern side of the stream they are perfectly barren of verdure. Slate rock also abounds, and where this is found
the experienced miner generally looks for "rich diggings." Again,
notwithstanding my dislike at retreating from the old battle ground, I
was pleased at the idea of leaving behind me "those two" tremendous
mountains, which had been a source of so much tribulation, and still
more was I pleased at the idea of leaving behind me my abominable salt

pork diet. When we deserted the camp, we were compelled to leave behind everything save our blankets, three days provisions, a frying pan, coffee kettle, and a pick and shovel per man. In the El Dorado Cañon, four miles distant, we found but few persons, the diggings having failed. Birdstown, of which place I wrote you in my last, was almost entirely deserted. A few tents whitening the valley was all that remained to tell of the ten thousand adventurers who had early in the spring came here with golden hopes.

Our party now consisting of ten, directed their course to Murderer's Bar, the fame of its richness having spread abroad throughout the land. On our way thither we passed many who like ourselves had been disappointed and were in search of new diggings; we also met many who were going to places which had been but lately deserted. So we go in California, the "El Dorado of the World"...

On the 25th of July we arrived in the vicinity of Murderer's Bar, so called on account of the murder by the Indians, last winter, of several Oregon men who were here engaged in mining[13]—and pitched our camp, that is to say, spread our blankets under the shade of a pine tree. We crossed the river in the afternoon, and found the miners of the region in a state of great confusion concerning their "claims" or "leads." It appears that a party of Mormons, who last year had worked upon the Bar, upon returning this Spring, found it in the possession of a number of sailors who refused to give it up to the old claimants. A lawsuit ensued and the Court of Culloma gave decision in favor of plaintiffs. The sailors refused to abide by said decision and armed themselves, expressing their determination to resist the law to their utmost. The Sheriff summoned a posse and at the head of 100 men, demanded a surrender of the Bar. A long parlay ensued, and finally the sailors agreed to vacate the premises. The Sheriff gave possession to plaintiffs, dismissed his posse and returned to Culloma. No sooner had he departed, than the sailors returned to the Bar, armed to the teeth, and resumed operations. This state of affairs continued a few days, when the parties compromised, and

---

[13]According to Theodore Hittell, the Oregonians had attempted "to take improper liberties" with some Indian women, and killed their husbands when they dared to object. During the following two days the Indians took their revenge, killing all but two of the Oregonians. The name "Murderer's Bar" was given to the site where their remains were discovered in April 1849. Hittell, *California*, 3: 76-77; Sioli, *El Dorado County*, 182-84.

are now working in conjunction. The difference at one time bade fair to terminate in a bloody battle, and I fear there is yet trouble in store, for the fires are yet smoldering, and very little would fan them into flames.

The fame of these "diggins" has caused numbers to congregate here, and I discovered that naught but constant watching would secure diggings for my mess, consisting of W. H. Hubbell of Cincinnati, my brother, a young South American and myself. The laws established by miners here permitted a single individual to hold but one claim of 15 feet in width, to the middle of the river by purchase, and one by pre-emption; but I soon discovered that "sharpers" were as numerous here as in any other section of the world, and that they held in a *peculiar* manner much more than the laws permitted. To use a California expression, I "browsed" around for a time and met with the desired success, obtaining two claims. Thus much to show you to what shifts men in the diggings now have to resort to obtain "leads." They cannot now, as last year, strike their "pick" wherever they see proper, but they must first *pick* where they may strike. It is not so hard a matter to find where there is gold, the difficulty lies in finding the spot that is not *appropriated,* or if already appropriated, and not justly, how to obtain that spot. Upon obtaining leads, we proceeded to build ourselves a brush house, and since that day we have lived in the bush.

If this river and adjacent diggings could be placed before the eyes of the citizens of Cincinnati, merely for a moment, that they might have a peep, I will venture to say that their mouths would be filled, for a month or more, with remarks concerning "Anglo Saxon enterprise," "Western go-ahead-itiveness," "Yankee spirit," &c. Just above our camp is a fall in the river of about 25 feet, forming a miniature Niagara; below these falls the water is 25 and 30 feet deep. Early this spring some Vermonters and other "Down Easters" took up claims here, and posted up notices to the effect "that said individuals, having formed themselves into a company, &c., intend sluicing and daming said place as soon as the waters should recede, etc., etc." Now nobody, in my opinion, except a Yankee, would ever have thought of engaging in such an enterprise as this. The very idea of making a dam and race in such a place would be sufficient to startle ordinary men. The falls, the huge rocks, the depth and body of the water, all present apparently insurmountable difficulties; and in addition to this is the uncertainty of there being any gold after such work should have been completed, admitting that it can be accomplished. Notwithstanding all this, the company have toiled day after day for 6 weeks, hauling timber from the top of the mountain by hand, sawed their own lumber, and have now a complete aqueduct, ten feet wide and two deep, 400 in length, weather-boarded and canvassed inside, and their dam in a forward state. The dam is made of framed timbers, to be filled in with brush and clay, and outside of all this is to be placed a canvas covering to render it perfectly water tight. The water is to be raised 14 feet. The gentleman who planned the whole affair assures me that he has no doubt of its complete success. He intends making a water wheel, to run night and day, in order to pump out the deep holes I have already mentioned. I very much fear for the ultimate success of the project. Even should all be accomplished, it cannot be until very near the commencement of the rainy season. Certainly the company deserves a reward for their enterprise, and a compound interest for the $1000 per lead of 20 feet which it has cost them in money and labor.[14]

Connecting with the upper sluice above mentioned, is another of the same description of equal dimensions, made by a Missouri and Illinois company. Below them are two others, and at the foot of the last is another dam—built by the company in which I am concerned, entitled the Delancey [Dulany] Co. for the purpose of preventing the waste water above from troubling our "leads." All the above races connect with ours, and below us are several others. When all are finished there will be a continuous race of lumber and canvas of more than one mile in length...Now I suppose that it will be asked, "Are the individuals concerned in these works to be successful?" Each one hopes for himself, and I presume each one supposes himself to be deserving. One thing I will guarantee, that the gamblers, sailors, and sharpers will obtain "piles;" some good men will also make much by the operation, for their "leads" have been tested. I am ready for something or for nothing. I shall try for the former, and sincerely hope I may obtain enough, for mining is an abominable business.

---

[14]During July and August 1850, five mining companies in the vicinity of Murderer's Bar, numbering about 500 men among them, pooled their labor and resources to build this flume. It was completed by mid-September, but was destroyed by heavy rains. *Sacramento Transcript,* February 28, 1851; Sioli, *El Dorado County,* 83-4.

I will give you a few instances of "luck" in this neighborhood, that you may judge of the chances here for obtaining "ore." "The Bar" is situated where probably in former times was the bed of the river. It has been and is still so rich that I have known of instances where $100 of fine dust has been taken out in one panful of clay. From the top earth all "pays," and the deeper it is dug the richer it becomes. The sand on the top generally averages from 5 to 10 cents per panful. The bar has been turned upside down this season and still is not half worked. There are numerous holes 30 feet square and 20 deep, of which every particle of dirt taken therefrom has been washed. Last week in a half day 8 or 10 sailors, washing the top sand and earth with a "long Tom," took out $500, the next day $1000, and the next a like amount. Four men on Thursday took out with two cradles[15] five pounds, another person three and a half pounds, another, who the day before had paid $1000 for ten feet square, took out two and a half pounds. I could cite numerous instances of which I have heard; these I know personally. The dust is very fine generally, and mixed with black sand, which renders it troublesome to "pan out." You may see thus, Messrs. Editors, that here our footsteps are literally paved with gold. Particles of gold are found everywhere about. Buckner's Bar [is] on the opposite side of the river just above, and here is where I am located. It is fully as rich, it is supposed, as Murderer's Bar. When we get into the river I will know. Another indication I will give you of the prosperous times here. The population will amount to 500, and all seem to have sufficient of the "dust" to "pay their way." The traders are doing very well. Provisions cheap: Flour 20c per lb; Potatoes 30c per lb; Sugar 5c; Molasses $1 per bottle; Onions $1 per lb; Coffee had been $1.50, it is now $1; Beef 25c per lb. These constitute the chief articles of consumption; in fact, luxuries and all are comprised herein. Stoga shoes $6.00; Boots $18.00.

Sunday, two weeks since, a duel was fought a short distance from our

[15]The "cradle," or "rocker," a mining device introduced to California by Georgian miner Isaac Humphrey, was a three foot by one and one half foot box mounted on rockers with a perforated hopper on its upper end for sorting out larger rocks, a slanting apron, and near the box's open end a series of narrow wooden cleats along the bottom for catching gold as the pay dirt was washed through. It normally required three men, one to shovel dirt into the hopper, one to pour water over the dirt, and a third to rock the box. The "Long Tom," was an elongated stationary version of the rocker, in which a stream of water washed dirt down an eight by fourteen foot trough through a sieve into a lower trough with riffle bars.

camp between two individuals of this community. Cause: a dispute about a horse. The parties fought at a distance of 20 paces with pistols. Unfortunately neither of the parties were injured. This is the first occurrence on record of two jackasses fighting about a horse. But this is the way difficulties are settled here, consequently quarrels are rare.

On Saturday last I went to Sacramento city for letters, not having received any since my arrival in the country, and feeling alarmed at the reports which reached me concerning the cholera in Cincinnati.[16] ...Upon my arrival I found that the mail, which had but just arrived, was not yet distributed, and that owing to its great size would not be before Sunday evening. I contented myself until that time, when I entered in the line and waited two hours, and received one letter dated 6th May. The mail was larger by 25,000 letters than ever before.

Sacramento is still increasing with astonishing rapidity. Numbers of good brick houses are in process of erection. A brick Court House, to cost $300,000, is also being built. It is also in contemplation to surround the city with a levee, to prevent the encroachment of the Winter and Spring freshets. These public improvements are to be finished if the city is able, but of that there is some doubt, as the contractors for building the Court House have already gone by the board because of the want of funds. San Francisco is bankrupt. Speculators in Sac. City are failing daily...Business, however, seems remarkably active. The traders buying extensively, and the merchants receiving plenty of dust.

Emigrants from across the plains are flocking in daily, and look rather "down in the mouth" when they see things as they really are. One half of the emigration is supposed to be in. I have seen numbers who have just arrived, and they give sad accounts of their sufferings on the route. One company of eight men lost their lives by drowning on the Humboldt river. The first of the unfortunate men got into the stream beyond his depth—one of his comrades endeavored to save his life, and the rest followed successively, and all found a watery grave. Those who have arrived say their sufferings were severe, but their disappointment more so. Many

---

[16]The cholera epidemic of 1849, which devastated much of the United States, killed some 8,500 Cincinnatians, about one out of every fourteen. It recurred in 1850, threatening to depopulate the city and interfering with the census, and it returned again during the following two years. Greve, *Centennial History*, 1: 721.

came with the idea that gold could be picked up without any trouble. A little experience will teach them.

The California papers give most glowing accounts concerning the mines, taking care to leave the dark side of the picture. These bright accounts are most generally furnished by traders, who hope to gain by increase of population in their district, and the papers themselves are benefited by the same general increase of population in the country. As for my part, I place scarce any confidence in California newspapers. I have the best reasons for speaking thus of them; such as knowing men in different sections of the country, and meeting every day with those who have left places lauded to the skies. The Yuba and Feather river diggings are like all others—some extravagant rich "placers," and others, and by far the most extensive, so poor that the majority of miners are not averaging $1.50 per diem. Aye, men are absolutely working in this rich El Dorado for their board. In Sacramento city hundreds of men will work for $2 and $3 per day, and some for $1. In these diggings men are hired at $4 and $5 and their board; but wages are getting lower. What so many men will do next winter, I cannot tell. Hundreds who have just arrived would go immediately home if they were able. I know many who are striving for enough to carry them out of the country, saying they will be perfectly satisfied with that, and still their [*sic*] are many who will go home this Fall rich...

The health of the mines, as a general thing, is good. I don't know of a single case of sickness near here. Placerville is, I believe, the only place which is at all subject to sickness, and that place, I am informed, is very unhealthy, owing to the impurity of the water thereabout. Numbers are dying daily with the dysentery...

This season of the year is a most busy one with miners, for we, like the bee, must build our houses for Winter. The houses we *now* use are quite airy and roomy, and answer a very excellent purpose. Our house is made of one log and a few brush, and the boys occasionally have an original game of seven up on a log on Sunday, while I take items. I'm very well satisfied with California, and will be so long as she uses me no worse than she has. I fancy that that [*sic*] there is something in store for me here, and though the alley is a long one, I wish to make a "ten strike" or "cocked-hat."...

[Bickham left no detailed account of his activities during the remainder of 1850, but he occasionally refers to this period in his letters and journal. He appears to have remained in the area of Murderer's Bar until some time in October, at which time he and his brother, John, moved to the vicinity of Grass Valley and Nevada City, where they prospected with little success. By New Years Day, 1851, the day he began his journal, Bickham had returned to the Middle Fork of the American River, where he shared a cabin with a British sea captain].[17]

---

[17]See below 87, 89; *Cincinnati Daily Gazette*, September 13, 1851.

CHAPTER THREE

New Years Day, 1851

Summit of the Mountains, vicinity of the Junction of the North and Middle forks of the American.

January 1st, 1850 [1851].

What a bright and lovely New Year Morning, said I, as I stepped from the lowly door of my humble Log Cabin by the side of a rippling brook, meandering through the hills, coursing onward to the river. It was sunrise, and the bright reflection from the unclouded east upon the rocky breasts of mountains on the distant side of the roaring stream far beneath my feet presented a scene of wonderful beauty. No sound save that of the song of birds, the occasional sharp crack of the huntsman's rifle, and the waters of the Fork tumbling over the rocks disturbed the stillness of the hour. The blue smoke curled up in wreaths from the cabin's chimney, and mounted aloft until it vanished in the air; the stiffened earth covered with a mantle of white frost crumbled and crashed under my feet as I ventured forth on my morning walk, bucket in hand, towards the spring of cool, crystal-like water gushing forth from the hill-side among the moss-covered roots of one of those gnarled old oaken monarchs of the forest, whose wide spreading branches above seemed like giant arms stretched out as if to protect its lowly offspring at its base...I dipped fr[om] the fountain, and as I watched the pure stream flowing over the curious shapen pebbles, memories of the past came o'er me.

I thought of the days of gleeful boyhood, those sunshiny days when all is free from sorrow or care, and which return not again in life. The favorite playgrounds and urchin sports, the old schoolhouse; the scene of many a youthful triumph passed before me. I remembered the rows of benches, and the carved and whittled desks, where the handy jack knife had made deep and fanciful incisions, sometimes carving the name of a favorite lassie; the grim countenance and sharp eyes of the old school-master peering suspiciously and threateningly over his antique spectacles with heavy frames of silver, and then the birch rod & dreaded ferule which I used to eye askance when slyly pulling the hair of an unsuspecting schoolmate. I too remembered that eventful and—by so many schoolboys—dreaded examination week, its reviews, questions, and cross-questions; the exhibition day when young hearts beat with anxiety and hope for the meed of praise and reward of merit; and of the joyous exultation of the moment when our tyrant announced the commencement of the hollidays. I thought of the time when I exchanged the homely country academy with its moss-covered eves, for the walls of the College, and I thought of it with a sigh. I sighed with regret at opportunities lost, ne'er to be regained. But these memories gave place to memories of more recent times, the period when for youthful jollities and careless sports were exchanged for duties, toil, and trouble; and when first I knew the pleasures of society.

But more did memory dwell, as I sate beside the spring 'neath the old oak tree, upon the scenes and joys of my dear old home. Then indeed a sigh from the soul's depths found utterance, for the pleasant delights of home and society of dear friends were sadly wanting...I was lost in memory's sea, but not until I had thought of that pleasant old custom of the New Years day in my native city, so warmly welcomed by maid and youth, when old associations were again renewed, and friendly ties more strongly cemented; when the maiden[s] all wreathed and decked in smiles and loveliness meet youth with words of greeting. But the well remembered and hallowed old custom with me for a time is past; there's no donning of holliday suit in this wild, far distant land, no greeting of fair maiden. I must content myself with memories and fancy; fancy I how vain my task! No, I have it, I'll walk, I'll ramble the livelong day o'er hill and dale, through forests and over the mountains and valley, with none to accompany me; I'll commune with self, and the rocks, the streams, or the forest trees—and then I'll visit my old friend Dave Scott,[1] and with him take a New Year supper, and talk of other times and other lands.

Thus musing, I bade good morning to the silvered rock, and the bubbling fountain with its oaken canopy, and wandered to the cabin, the old cabin of six logs of trunks of pines on the sun side, and of six logs to the west; of five on the hill side, of ten toward the valley; of the rafters seven and seven, and roof of snowy canvass; the humble doorway, the little wing for the kitchen toward the spring, with its chimney and wide fireplace of stones, sticks and earth; and in the corner the tall oaken stump of a tree (which my messmate, an "old salt," calls the "main-mast") reaching through the covering. And in that cabin are slung, hammock like, our couches; one, the Captain's, slung "fore and aft" and mine (he says it is not "ship-shape") "thwart ships;" and "midships" stands the table of slabs, "fore and aft." There are the shelves, four in number, one on this side, one on that, and two in the corner on the left. These two in the corner compose the pantry and cupboard, and now are they garnished with bright tin plates and "pannakins," coffee and tea kettles, spoons, knives, and forks; and there's a nice roast of beef and white loaf of bread, and the pepper box, salt cup, coffee mill, and all the paraphernalia of the table. Beneath the shelves hang the luckless frying pan which answers to bake, boil, or fry, and oh! for the nice flap jacks which have come from its black depths! Then there's our stew pot, in which the Captain occasionally makes a "*Sea Pie*" for our dinner. Our shelf on the east side contains our limited stock of clothing, folded up in neat style, exhibiting in glowing colors our checked shirts and corduroy unwhisperables; and our last shelf contains a variety of articles, needles, thread, combs, hair brushes, &c. and my "*fuseé a piston*" with powder flask and

---

[1]David B. Scott, a native of Scotland, traveled overland to California in 1849, operated a shingle machine at what later became the town of Shingle Springs, and is listed in the 1850 census as a merchant living on the Middle Fork of the American River. Scott served as surveyor of Yuba County, California; Washoe County, Nevada; and Sonoma County, California. He was involved in the construction of logging railroads in the Sierra and was the chief engineer of the Marysville and Vallejo Railroad. 1850 Census, El Dorado County, California, 465; 1852 California Census, El Dorado County, 217; 1860 Census, Yuba County, California, 906; Sioli, *El Dorado County*, 200-201.

cap box; and last, though not by any means the least, my library, composed of a Bible, the gift of a friend,—Macaulay's Miscellaneous Essays,[2] which I also owe to the kindness of my most particular friend and associate; Milton, Beauties of Shakespeare,[3] Lallah Rookh,[4] and an old Law Book, while Irving's "Knickerbocker"[5] brings up the rear. The Captain acknowledges the possession of a few old Seafaring Novels and a work on Navigation. A few volumes of Romances by Scott, Bulwar, and Dumas sometimes garnish the Shelf, but now they are with some of my acquaintance.

But the Captain calls out "breakfast," and the fragrant odor of beefsteak calls me from my note book to refresh the inner man. Breakfast is simple and the hot cup of Coffee, white bread, and beef steak furnishes a repast [which], if not "fit for the Gods" is at least relished by the California Miner. My companion is seated on a box on one side of the table, I opposite him on a stool. He is communicative, I silent and thoughtful, for my mind is wandering to a far distant Home. Captain suddenly startles me with, "I say, Ship-mate, you're a rum 'un, I've been talking a half hour, and all you do is stare and nod your head. What tack are you on now?" I ask pardon, Captain, but I was ruminating!

I've laughed at this same old Captain till my heart has almost cracked. A regular "old Salt" and constantly crying out as if in command of a West Indiaman: "Bout Ship!" "Hew round there!" "Stir up the galley fire." And the old veteran of the Seas just put the *back logs before "to keep the small stake from falling overboard!"* Yet his conversation, though rough, is frequently most interesting, for he has seen much of the world. He don't like

---

[2]*Political and Miscellaneous Essays,* a collection of writings on political and literary topics by British historian and politician, Thomas Babington Macaulay, was published in Philadelphia in 1842. *DNB sub* "Macaulay, Thomas Babington, Baron Macaulay."

[3]*Beauties of Shakespeare,* printed by Dr. William Dodd in 1753, was the first published edition of Shakespeare's works. Adams, *Dictionary of English Literature,* 64; Dabble, *Oxford Companion to English Literature,* 279-80.

[4]*Lalla Rookh,* an "oriental romance" by Irish poet Thomas Moore, published in 1817, consists of four verse narratives strung together by a prose account of the journey of Indian princess, Lalla Rookh, to meet her intended husband.

[5]*A History of New York from the Beginnings of the World to the End of the Dutch dynasty by Diedrich Knickerbocker* (1809), Washington Irving's comic history of the Dutch New Netherlands, which Bickham had been reading on the bark, *Anne.* DMCL Bickham Family papers, "Weekly Anne Gazette."

California, but speaks of India in terms of rapture, and his sole ambition is to have a ship of his own, and sail to those fabulous climes.

The Captain announced his intention of "dismantling" the cabin and moving to Murderer's Bar, the "diggings" on the hill being very poor. Accordingly after breakfast he went in search of a horse with which to pack his "luggage." I started upon my walk in the direction of Greenwood Valley, from whence I intended to go to Spanish Bar, 18 miles from our Cabin...

I struck out in a South Easterly direction from the Cabin, winding along the side of a hillock until I reached its summit, and from thence rambled along the ridge of these mountains for a considerable distance. The ridges of these mountains are generally rough, or rather there are innumerable valleys through which fine wagon roads are made, — and countless hills. Thus generally when one says, "I kept along the ridge," it is meant that his travels have been among these small valleys and ravines, constantly ascending and descending these small hills. From the top of one of these I looked westward, down a large ravine, my eye catching in its scope a view of surrounding hillocks covered with waving forests, several small ravines, all verging to the main one and joining together in a beautiful spring, or pool, of clear water before making an abrupt descent and becoming lost in the parent ravine. Far below I could catch a faint gleam of the flashing waters of the river, shining between the branches of the trees as a puff of wind would sometimes separate them, and hear the sullen and hollow roar as they leaped from rock to rock, or rushed whirling over a fall. In the distance and northward, loomed up the frowning summits of the blue tower rock at Murderer's Bar, and I fancied I could hear the busy rocking, rocking, of the cradle, or the "pick-pick" of the Gold Hunter. But that old blue rock has witnessed the deed of blood! Alas poor Beck! and alas poor Walker, thy slayer! The 10th day of October (1850) was a sad, sad day for ye both![6]

---

[6]This tragedy resulted from a dispute over a mining claim between William H. "Black" Walker of Evansville, Indiana, and George W. Beck, a lawyer from Bourbon county, Kentucky. The two men scuffled and Beck pushed Walker into a pool of water. A gunfight ensued in which Walker, armed with a shotgun, mortally wounded Beck, armed with a Colt revolver. After standing his ground against an angry crowd, Walker was taken into custody by the El Dorado County sheriff. He received no punishment, but decided to sell his few goods and leave Murderer's Bar. Angel, *History of Placer County*, 89; *Sacramento Transcript*, October 17, 1850.

But away with such remembrances! What a lovely scene was this to day, and how still and solemn!

The Mountains in this neighborhood, to one unused to a Mountainous country, would seem gigantic, but they are anthills when compared with those on the N. Fork of the Middle Fork, and they in their turn become hillocks alongside the Sierra Nevadas. Yet the North Fork hills, beside being much greater in altitude, are characterized by more abrupt declivities, precipitous ascents, &c. Some of them afford some of the grandest views in nature, and withal some very terrible ones. One very general and pervading feature of these mountains is the dark forests of tall and beautifully proportioned pines, with a few scattered gnarled oaks, besides thickets of Chaparral and beautiful half shrub, half tree, groves of "Mancinitos." The sides of these mountains, where not too precipitous, rocky, or shaded, are decked, in spring and summer time, with many hued flowers, and seem like a tasteful garden. When the wind blows, a thousand fragrant odors impregnate the air, and the beautiful blossoms seem like so many banners set in motion by fairies or wood nymphs. These sylvan gardens are possessed of rare beauty, and tis delightful to inhale their fragrance.

The valleys between these "hills upon mountains," and the large flats occasionally to be met with, have rich soils, and they, too, become smiling gardens under a vernal sun, and furnish luxuriant pastures for stock, the grass springing up with the flowers spontaneously. These flats are generally appropriated by individuals for the purpose of making money, taking stock to pasture on their "Ranges" or "Ranchos." Some are turned into garden spots and become very valuable, more especially when on the public highway, they then being used as Ranchos & garden spots in conjunction with Public Houses.

From the ridge whence I look upon the River and Spring and old "Blue Rock," I turn and wander on my course. At the base of a rock which starts up before me like a huge tomb stone, I linger for a moment to cut from a Mancinito a fanciful looking walking stick, but I find it to be as yet *too much* twisted for beauty. I've surveyed every Mancinito thicket on my course during the past six months, hoping to find a straight and pretty cane, and have not yet succeeded. I will one day succeed in my desires. But time flies and so must I...

Ah, there's a "prospector" with pick, shovel, and pan, digging by the side of the rivulet. What success, my friend? "I shan't get much gold." So thought I. I wager a New Year's dinner that he's a man of the West. I guess it from his frank, independent demeanor. His eye is dark grey, piercing as an eagle's, hair long and dark, black as a raven's wing,—long grizzly beard, browned and weather beaten visage; stands full six feet in his stockings, and his stalwart frame and long sinewy arms betoken herculean strength. A backwoodsman; and his red shirt, buckskin breeches, slouching hat, long legged boots reaching to his thighs, and long knife in sheath betoken the experienced Miner. A mile farther and I meet a juvenile specimen of the Californian with a sack of provisions on his shoulders. The way to Greenwood, My Son? "Follow the trail to the highway!" Thank you, and again I trudge onward, my feet pattering the earth and my stick keeping time, eye peering abroad and taking surrounding prospect in its scope. I strike down the hill and now I'm in the highway and meet two well-dressed Spaniards, mounted on fat mules, their heavy spurs rattle and jingling as they pass at a slow trot. These I know from certain indefinable appearances and signs to be gamblers. Here on the hill-side, I meet a covered wagon, two large bay mules are driven by one who looks like a Western farmer, and his courteous "good morrow" is confirming evidence. And yonder's an ox wagon, three yokes, and the manners of the driver betoken a Down Easter. "Whoa hare, Buck, likewise, Bright, *consequently* the whole team." He never swears save in one strain, "go long, darn ye!"

Around the hill on the right hand side of the road is a tall canvas house, a tavern kept by one *"Smith,"* who seems impressed with his dignity as Landlord of the "Chimney Rock House." Behind the house is a tall black rock of chimney shape, by the side of a rippling brook; from this the "stand" received its name. "Mine host" has "prospected" the ravine hard by, but found little of the Oro. Smith is a young man, short in stature, with a head of red, wiry hair, an ungainly sandy colored phiz, and his "better half," a female old enough to be his mother, is tied to him, *not* in the bands of wedlock. Curious taste his…I'll stop a moment and buy a pie. Good morning, madam. "Good morning, sir, and I wish you a Happy New Year. Won't you have a nice warm punch?" The draught was far more intoxicating than her appearance, but alas for vanity, her looking glass had told her what *any eyes* could not approve. I bought a slice of ginger bread heavy as its size in lead, and wandered on the road to Greenwood, munching and ruminating. Dr. Franklin did so, why not I?[7]

The road here winds around hills, through valleys, up hill and down, and at the entrance of a level is the comfortable, neat looking, double, hewed-log house of my acquaintance, "Harry," whose sign board advertises "accommodations for man and beast." I drink a glass of Champagne Cider, light my pipe, and start off with a whiff of satisfaction. This pipe of mine (all Californians have pipes) is a fanciful one and quite aristocratic for these neighborhoods. A Chinese bowl (with a forest scene on its front, a stag chasing past the decayed trunk of a dead old standing tree) long bone stem, and it's pleasant to draw, and it's nice to see the white smoke curling upwards. I often fashion my ways after those good old Dutchmen who think hardest when they puff fastest. Yonder's an urchin in a *"corral"* hard by the road side; descries my assistance to catch a fractious mula. He swings the *"lass,"* and *"mula"* is noosed, and I am away again and soon cross the pine log bridge thrown across the sluice-way of a saw-mill, two miles from *the "Valley."* Just on the verge of the hill which looks down into the town of Greenwood Valley,—or as it is now denominated, Louisville,[8]—is one of those two-horse, covered vehicles known in the West as Dearborns, filled with man and women, dressed in holliday attire, doubtless on their way to a New Year Ball a few miles down the road. One woman has in her arms a rosy, chubby little infant. I warrant me it is the happiest of the flock. Just behind them on horseback ride three well-dressed young men, neat as a maid. All are Mormons.

I will now look into the town of "Greenwood Valley," or as it has lately been called, Louisville. This town is built up in the midst of a beautiful green valley, some four or five miles long, running in rather a circular form from the S. E. to N. West, and much deeper than is usual with valleys on the ridge. Numerous oval and conical shaped hills rise on either

---

[7]In his autobiography, Benjamin Franklin describes himself as a youth, newly arrived in Philadelphia, walking up Market Street, munching on a large roll while carrying two others in his arms. Franklin, *Autobiography,* 24.

[8]The town of Louisville (also spelled "Lewisville") was named for the son of storekeeper and former mountain man Lewis B. Myers. When the post office was established in 1852, the name of the town was changed to "Greenwood," as there was another Louisville in the vicinity. Sioli, *El Dorado County,* 185–86.

side, and between them are countless ravines, which convey the water from the hills during the winter season into a small stream winding through the Valley. This stream is quite auriferous at the present time; one year ago it was much richer. Gold was first discovered by one "Greenwood"[9] and a Mormon by the name of "Gates."[10] The former builded the first house, and from him the Valley has taken its name. At the present time it is a considerable village, being the main depot for provisions and stores supplying the different placers generally within a circuit of ten miles. There are more than 100 houses of all descriptions usual in California trading towns from frames to rag houses. Some of the frames are really excellent buildings, though very plain. There are perhaps a dozen stores besides as many drinking Houses, gambling and Bowling Saloons, one apothecary shop, one book store, several express offices, a dozen physician's offices, and one Post office. The Magistrates' offices, of which there are two, are in the store room of one officer, and the other in a drinking house. The lawyers are always to be found in Gambling and drinking houses.

Louisville is situated midway between the extremes of the valley and is built up similar to almost every other trading town in the mines of California, being what is called a long "string town" with but one street running through the entire length, or more properly the houses are erected, without pretension to exact regularity, on both sides of the highway. The good frame houses of one story and attics, which latter are generally fitted up for sleeping apartments, are first in order; secondly, the rougher frames with floors of rough unplaned boards laid loosely on sills; then the frames with no floors save the hard ground. Next are the houses composed of pine clap-boards nailed to posts set into the earth; then are the rough or hewn log cabins, some with, some without floors, and these are decidedly the most comfortable in winter; finally are the tents or cabins of the miners. The best houses are generally lined and ceiled with calico or canvas, and generally are covered with clapboards,

---

[9]Apparently the mountain man Caleb Greenwood (c. 1763-1850) who, sometime in 1849, settled with his family in what came to be known as Greenwood Valley, where his half-Indian son, John, kept a public house. Hafen, *Mountain Men and the Fur Trade,* 9: 187-92.

[10]Probably Hiram Gates, a Mormon immigrant to Utah who fled to California in 1849 to avoid arrest for kidnapping the daughter of Mormon leader Orrin Porter Rockwell. Davies, *Mormon Gold,* 113, 361-62; see below 122n.

though some are roofed with canvas which is equally water proof. The brook which is now flowing through the valley is totally dry during the dry season, and water is supplied the inhabitants by wells. The village is now at the acme of prosperity; two or three years will find it deserted, and pity for it so to be, for the situation is beautiful. "Our" old friend, Henderson, has been stationed here during the last seven months, building houses and making "gold Rockers" and "long Toms." Yonder he is now, measuring a pile of lumber which he has just bought. Now he spies me and wishes me a "Happy New Year!" He is an eccentric old Bachelor, and quite an humorous companion. He hails from old Scotia, and is impregnated with many Scottish peculiarities. His hobby is to get rich![11] How many more individuals in this same community have a like desire? and all for different objects when taken in detail, and very similar at first appearance. At all hours of the day Miners may be seen busily engaged digging among the roots and rocks, rocking their cradles and working "long Toms," though to-day they are generally idle. But it is time for me to move onward.

Taking a Northern direction, leaving Louisville behind, I strike into the hills and annihilate the space 'twixt the Valley and Spanish Bar. The valleys and ravines now become deeper, and rivulets supplied from mountain springs, more numerous. Log cabins are scattered about by the side of the brooks and on the breasts of the hills, pick axes, shovels, and rockers lie about the doors, and occasionally a deer-skin is stretched out between two trees, while the antlers are placed over the door. Evidence of Anglo-American enterprise strike the eye on every side. The mule trail on which I now travel, winds beautifully through pleasant vall[eys] and around conical shaped hills in an ascending direction, or occasionally plump down into a deep Cañon. In this deepest one, three miles from the "Valley," is the "Hoboken *House*," a rag tent, where is "accommodation for man or beast," and the sign post says, *"Barley, Cakes, Pies, Hay, Whiskey, and Beer."* A tall flag pole shoots up into the sky, and on its summit is flying a banner of red flannel with yellow flannel spots for stars... How one pants and puffs and blows ascending the

---

[11]John Henderson, a Scottish-born carpenter and a former Ohio resident, is listed in the 1850 census as living in Louisville in January 1851. 1850 Census, El Dorado County, California, 451; 1852 California Census, El Dorado County, 66.

acclivity at this place; yonder grey stone beneath that green spruce tree I hail with grateful feelings. It is a nice resting place.

Here are the Spanish Dry Diggings, on top of the mountains which o'erhang the Middle Fork at Spanish *Bar*. These "diggings" were discovered by some Mexican Spaniards last winter,[12] and large quantities of gold were digged. The yield is not half so great this year and double the number of Miners were engaged. Here are some 3 or 4 stores and boarding houses, and in the first one I hear a confusion of voices, and stopping for a glass of water discover a party of Miners enjoying a New Year Dinner. One of the hombres drinks a toast, "here's hoping that this fair land of California may soon be thronged with the fair sex." A patriot, thinks I. Farther on is a party of Germans a little "how came you so"[13] engaged in knocking down bottles with a broom, their eyes being blindfolded. At last I arrive at the apex of the mountain overlooking Spanish Bar Bridge and a portion of the Bar a mile below. On my right the mountain pitches down almost perpendicularly even to the flashing stream, its base bathed in the cool, clear waters. Far, far below I see the tops of the waving trees, looking like shrubs in the distance. To the left it is equally precipitous and far more rugged, though two thirds of the distance down the declivity changes into a kind of plain or bench, and a second bench desends to the river. The mule trail strikes straight down the ridge or "backbone" (it is far too rugged and steep for a wagon road) and this is my course, but for a moment I must admire the glorious prospect from the summit.

This place commands a most extensive view of the surrounding country, and any one who takes a delight in the [b]eauties of mountain scenery, cannot fail to take at least one view from the grey granite rock on which I stand. To my right in a north easterly course the deep cavity between the mountains discovers the tortuous course of the river, some of the mountains rugged, rocky, and almost completely barren, often intercepted in the deeper declivities by precipices, frowning perpendicularly hundreds of feet above the waters of the Fork. Others present a regular surface, sometimes steep and sometimes sloping gently, and covered with White Pines, Cedars, Spruce Pines, and oaks, and with a red

---

[12]Spanish Dry Diggings were discovered in 1848 by Don Andrés Pico, brother of Governor Pío Pico and the hero of the battle of San Pasqual. Gudde, *California Gold Camps*, 329.

[13]Drunk.

barked and beautiful foliaged tree, known to me as the "Smimmelah." The river winds down, rushing and foaming o'er a rocky bed, between the cliffs on either side until near the bridge, where the channel deepens and a smooth and glassy surface is presented. The bridge is a narrow wooden structure with strong natural abutments, and with the white tents and cabins on the banks in the distance, reminds one much of the travelers' description of ..[illegible]..scenes among the mountains of Switzerland. The trail is now winding along the breast of the opposite mountain for several miles until lost in the forests. Below the bridge, the stream suddenly becomes shallow and rushes over rocks and stones, and making a sudden turn around a small mountain which starts up suddenly as a kind of a first bench to this one,—and for a short distance is hidden from view, but below this mountain it again appears tumbling over rocks, rushing and foaming and sparkling like gold in the sunlight, then becoming smooth and alternately keeping in a tolerably straight course for several miles, it finally fades from the view among the mountains below. On this straight line may be seen the Oregon and Union Bars, and on the banks are scattered numbers of white tents and humble log cabins, while men appearing no larger than little boys are moving about, chopping wood, or operating among the rocks. Some five or six miles below, the course of the river is discovered by the old "Blue Rock" at Murderer's Bar, darkly and dismally ornamenting the breast and summit of the Mountain.

After noting these nearer scenes, the eye wanders to the distance, and the tall and rugged snow capped summits of the Sierra Nevadas are discerned describing a line of white in the blue sky of Heaven. No forests are seen on these cold, bleak, rugged peaks to relieve the eye, nothing but a garment of purest snow. One can scarce refrain from shuddering at this chill looking prospect, notwithstanding the spring like atmosphere around him in this beautiful season. This line of white describes a complete half of a circle as it is viewed from this place, or as I should more appropriately term it, the intervening space is one vast amphitheatre. From the extreme east, verging close upon the south, I follow this long line of white in the field of blue, extending to the Northeast, and North, and West to North West, almost fading as it approaches the latter point.

Then, directly between this ridge and the point on which I stand, though separated by many miles of mountains and valleys from the Middle Fork, is the beautiful plain or Valley of the Feather river, level as the surface of the ocean in a calm, spreading out and along that stream for miles upon miles. At this point the view is indescribably beautiful. Seen in a bright sunshiny day the Feather River Valley at first appears like the Ocean in the distance. At the base of the mountains on this side, the soil is barren of verdure and presents a yellow sand appearance, reminding one (and at first deceiving) of the sea beach; as I look farther onward, the green foliage of scrubby oaks and thickets of bushes scattered about, and waving in the wind, it first strikes upon the fancy that old ocean is heaving up before him. The illusion of the yellow soil and waving green tree tops at first glance is perfect, but a second glance shows the white summits of the Nevadas, and nearer still the tall mountains on the Feather and Yuba streams, and the truth is revealed. To-day the sun is arrayed in all his glory, "shining alike on the just or the unjust," imparting his generous warmth to the earth, tinging the Mountain tops with golden hues, and giving additional splendor and beauty to every scene.

Leaving these fair scenes behind, once more I am on my way, now plunging sheer down the side of the mountain, and now winding round the rough and rocky trail, stopping for an instant at a tall grey rock, placed as if to watch from this lofty post, performing watchman's duty in night as in day, through wintry storms and spring day smiles. Now in zig-zag course and now bring up at what Scott's Muleteer calls the "half way house," being a level spot about ten feet square, caused by the washing of earth and stone and lodging against the roots of mancinito bushes. Here to my right is a cliff of dark rocks impregnated with white and reddish quartz; and straight down is the bridge, the trail to which turns off at acute angles on the right, a few steps before me, whilst the trail to Spanish Bar turns abruptly to the left at right angles. I now descend, winding through a ravine and around the "bench Mountain," and at last I greet my friend, Scott, with "a Happy New Year." I am somewhat fatigued, but I am better able to grapple with these mountains than in times past.

My friend has a neat canvass house on the bank of the river, and has on hand a fine stock of goods suited to his market, neatly arranged on shelves and in boxes. Like most of Mining traders he has a boarding house connected with his store and his customers are satisfied with his cuisine. Certes, he had a fine supper and I enjoyed it with a zest and enjoyed the pleasures of smoking a fragrant Habana, by a good warm stove and until bed time listened to some fine singing by a small party who had assembled.

Thus have I passed New Years Day. How different from the last! I look back to those sunny hours of the past with a melancholy pleasure and a sigh of regret. Yet again I do not regret, for duty hath called me hither and ambition and hope which springs from my breast repays me for absence from my Home…

[Marginalia: "A party of Cribbage players in Cromwell's store on Murderer's Bar while I transcribe from my memoranda are a source of annoyance."]

CHAPTER FOUR

Return to Murderer's Bar

Spanish Bar—Middle Fork of the American.
Thursday, Jan. 2nd, 1851.

What a magnificent winter season we've had thus far. Instead of the wet, stormy, inclement and muddy weather I had been led to expect in California, it has been, with the exception of a few rains, clear and pleasant, bright sun shiny days, warm and genial as Spring, with cool, clear and frosty nights. But man is thankless in whatever situation he may be placed...This one wants a bright, clear sky and it rains; that one rain, and it shines. Alas, poor short-sighted mortals cannot think that all is ordered for the best.

The dry weather has operated against the present interests of those engaged in Dry Diggings. Much dirt has been thrown up, and water has been too scarce for washing. Miners are disappointed, traders sell but little produce, and business is dull in the cities. Many in the Dry Diggings are becoming discouraged with California, selling out and going home... Many who despair of rain are returning to the Bars of the rivers, where the diggings have been paying very fair wages. For myself, I have concluded to cease rambling and settle down at Murderer's Bar. I have spent much time in "prospecting," and am weary. I have rambled over a considerable portion of the country, digging holes in divers places, and in the end have found them the graves of the hopes with which I began their excavation. My "luck" thus far has been hard, but I despair not. Robert Bruce after being defeated in twelve battles was successful in the thirteenth essay. I shall try a thousand times if necessary.

Friday, January 3d, 1851.

At sun rise this morning I left my couch & soon after seated myself at Breakfast and made my last compliments for a season to my friend's good cheer. After Breakfast I collected my blankets, books &c. together, mounted Scott's—"Little Billy"—mule and with the two Packers with mule train, rode up the mountain. This to me was hardly so tiresome as walking would be, but the mule panted as though *he* felt the exercise. Reaching the Spanish Dry Diggings, I dismounted and walked to Greenwood over the same trail I passed on New Years Day. The atmosphere during this walk was so warm as to be troublesome, indeed it was like a day in May. Spring seems to be budding thus early in the year; from the earth, flowers and grass are sprouting and the pine buds are bursting from their confinement. Birds sing blithely and flit about gaily among the bushes; and *I* have an attack of the Spring Fever.

Dinner in Louisville is not so poor as it *might* be, neither so good. Tough beef, heavy dark bread, molasses, and water. One sits down at table in this country with some queer specimens of humanity; some are polite and gentlemanly, some assist their neighbors without a word, and others gruff and seem sadly troubled at the request of one next to him to pass a dish. Such a set of whiskerados doubtless were never seen congregated together in any other country; beards and mustaches of all shapes and colors, often three or four inches long, decorate their phiz's. A smooth shaven face is a rarity, but I must say they appear much the neatest. I do hate to sit opposite a man with a long fierce moustache when he is eating; it makes me uneasy, and looks so filthy, that I scarce can eat at all.

I passed the afternoon and evening in perusing "The Count of Monte Christo," in which I became greatly interested in the fate of Edmond Dantes, though his great fortune, so suddenly come upon him, is *rather* too marvelous for the general interest of the work.

Saturday - Jany. 4th, 1850 [sic]

In company with Henderson and Jemmy MacWilliams[1] I started for

---

[1] James McWilliams is listed in the 1850 census as an Ohio-born miner living in Grass Valley in October of that year. He was probably the James McWilliams who was later employed as a policeman, porter, and watchman in Cincinnati. 1850 Census, Yuba County, California, 274; 1860 Census, Cincinnati, 16th ward, 134; Cincinnati city directories 1861-75.

Murderer's Bar, my pack on McWilliams' mule. Trouble enough had we with our baggage, having no pack saddle, and on the highway we met several parties of prospectors. More unfortunates, thought I, and my sympathies were enlisted. I, too, have had my experience on that road to fortune, and a hard one was it to body and mind. How wearisome it is to travel over the mountains from day light in the morning until the stars peep forth at night. Sometimes the "prospector" abides for a day in a spot, digging a hole here, another there, carrying a sack or pan of earth often several miles before finding water. And then the blasted hopes of the unsuccessful essay! But if the yield is *good,* with what a light and fleet step and sparkling eye does one return to try again. In the neighborhood of Nevada City and Grass Valley there are many holes sunken in the earth by my aid, and they exist as monuments of disappointment...

Taking a different trail on my return, from that which I had followed several days previous, I meet with fewer striking scenes, though there are some of rare beauty... Two miles from the bar on the road leading thence to the city, I leave my companions who are all bound for "Junction Bar," and strike downward, passing soon a log house where are several busy urchins playing in the door yard. Just below the house is a curious shaped hill which is composed of a mass of blue shelly granite rocks, lying about in all manner of shapes and forms. Within this hill is a large cave or grotto which I have not yet visited. At this place the ravine widens into a valley several hundred yards in width. On the left is a small frame house, tenanted by a small family, on the right is a second one, also containing a family. Farther on to the left and at the foot of a hill is the snug log cabin of my friend Dr. Piggott of Mississippi.[2] I called to see him and passed an hour in conversation and partaking supper.

After leaving the Dr.'s cabin, I strike through the hills and in a short time stand on the summit of the Mountain, overlooking the Middle Fork at "Murderer's Bar," formerly "Livingston Valley." The view from this point is most enchanting, not so grand as that from the mountain at Spanish Bar, but far more beautiful. The eye is first directed to the Northwest, where the course of the river is detected by a deep chasm

---

[2] Probably the "A. R. Piggott" listed in the 1852 California Census as a 28-year-old physician, born in South Carolina, living in El Dorado County. 1852 California Census, El Dorado County, 148.

between mountains frowning above. One in particular is remarkable for its sugar loaf shape and for being destitute of trees, though it is green with waving bushes. The river is suddenly discerned rolling abruptly from behind a hill on the eastern side, while on the west is a high flat of earth and gravel which has been thrown together by the floods of winter. The waters soon find a deep channel and flow smoothly and bright as a mirror; and *now* may be seen a little flat bottomed ferry boat, the road crossing at this point.

Soon, however, the smooth and quiet waters move in swifter current, and several hundred yards from where first they are seen, suddenly leap wildly down a perpendicular fall, fall 25 feet, soaring like the sea lashed into fury by the storm, scattering the spray in a thousand rocks starting up on the shore, and sparkling in the sunlight like pearls. The abyss of waters beneath is boiling and foaming as though a thousand furnaces were burning under it. On both sides of the stream tall cliffs and large masses of green hued rocks rise abruptly, many feet into the air, and imparting an air of terror and grandeur to the scene. The bed of the river below, for several hundred yards distant, is choked up with rocks, and the waters whirl round them with mad impetuosity, and not until they take a second fall less abrupt, of four or five feet, and flow over a rough bed on an inclined plane do they again become smooth.

Midway between the two Falls on the West side of the river is a small level flat of semicircular form covered with a beautiful carpeting of green grass, shaded with scattering pines, oaks, and Mancinito bushes. The mountain above rises gradually from this plain for perhaps a half mile, and suddenly ascends precipitously, with dark masses of rocks jutting out from its side seeming to form a roofing for the earth beneath. On this plain I encamped with my brother last summer whilst engaged in Mining. I can even now see the clump of bushes which Harry Hubbell and I fashioned into circular shape, hollowing out the center for a sleeping apartment, and increasing the already pleasant shade into one impervious to the rays of the sun.

Beneath the summit of the mountain on which I stand, I see the tops of pines waving in the breeze, and now immediately at its base is the small town, or trading post of the bar. A few roughboard houses and canvas tents, with Col. Jos. Potter's[3] log cabin, comprise the improvements. On the opposite side of the river is Buckner's Bar, now rough and broken, miners having disturbed its evenness. The mountains of the color of burnt clay rise above at acute angles and are barren save in thickets of chaparral. From the town huge grizzly bears are often seen stalking along the sides of these, picking berries from the Bearberry shrub. The summit of the "Blue Rock" looms up commandingly in the N. West course, the river is lost in the distance, but the opening between the everlasting hills denotes its winding. This view of Murderer's Bar is one of the loveliest I have ever beheld. The mountains, pitching down so suddenly on either side of the river, and now sloping gently, or starting up from the very river side; the road cut in the side of the mountains winding round and round, now in a straight line; the plains and bars; the sudden appearance of the river seeming to start from the earth, its momentary quietness, its quick change to rapid descent, and finally the magnificent leap over the falls, rushing, roaring and foaming, presents indeed a picture of rare beauty. And this too is enhanced by the thoughts of the Miner who here lays claim to a portion of the river bed. The idea of gleaning most precious metal from the bosom of the stream is brightness itself. The scene by moonlight is indescribably lovely.

About half way down the hill is a beautiful spring of cool, clear water, bursting from the crevices of a grey granite rock, and often when warm and fatigued, burning with thirst, I have seated myself on its mossy banks and cooled my parched tongue with its grateful waters. It is an "oasis" of the hill side, and many a wearied "prospector" hath found relief therein. Just above are numerous deep furrows made by logs drawn from the summit to the river for Fluming purposes. A portion of the raceway constructed in the river below the falls by a Vermont company is now visible, a monument of disappointed hopes!

Today the hazy and half clouded sky indicates a change in the weather; the air is damp and the wind howls mournfully through the forests.

---

[3]Joseph C. Potter was one of the earliest inhabitants of Murderer's Bar. In the summer of 1850 he fought the first duel in what is now Placer County with George Melville, an English sailor with whom he had a dispute over a mining claim. Neither was injured. Potter later served as clerk of the California assembly. Sioli, *El Dorado County*, 184; Angel, *History of Placer County*, 89; Bancroft, *California*, 6: 657.

E. Cromwell's Store, Murderer's Bar. Sunday, January 5th, 1851.

As I yesterday surmised, there has been a change of weather during the past twelve hours. It rained during the night, and this morning the clouds look lowering & stormy. "Murderer's Bar" in dark weather is a gloomy place, dull and lifeless as a church-yard. Miners are seen going back and forth with heavy, long-legged boots on their feet, and cumbrous, long India rubber cloaks thrown over their shoulders; some going to their "leads," some cutting firewood, while others, and the great majority, wend their course to the trading houses; which all have their "Liquor Bars"—and there pass the time in playing cards for a "drink." A limited number remain by their own firesides engaged in various occupations, some wash or mend their clothes, some sleep, and some few read.

The character of this community has undergone a complete change since the last summer, attributable to the desertion of the Bar for home or dry diggings of the old settlers, and the arrival of new-comers who have settled upon the leads still legally held by those who were last year proprietors.

During the last summer the community, though composed of persons of all ranks of life, was far more intelligent than any of the same size with which I am acquainted in California. Many young and middle aged men from the first ranks of society, all in good circumstances, some wealthy, well educated, and of polished manners; students, Lawyers, and Physicians from every state in the Union. True, there were many of the ordinary stamp of mankind, but in lesser proportion than is usual in such situations, and some, chiefly sailors, of the most depraved and dissolute character. Taken as a body the community was remarkable for its intelligence in the abstract, though separate interests, often conflicting, frequently made those who composed it appear strangely inconsistent and devoid of the intelligence of which I speak. They were liberal, free hearted, generous, and fearless; Kentuckians, Western and Southern men, with many from New England. Shrewd and enterprising business man and industrious miners. All were jealous of their rights, extremely watchful and quick to frown upon any infringement; as the majority were too honorable to take advantage of their neighbors' short-sightedness. Men are not angels, and to say that they quarreled not would argue that this were the Valley of Alhama[4] in peacefulness. They quarreled much, although in extenuation it can be said that this was the effect of a few evil minded and designing men. How true it is that one intriguer or grumbler will poison the enjoyment of many. A little spark often kindles a great flame. This community, so intelligent and industrious, however, frequently relaxed and entered into dissipation, and at night "glasses jingled merrily." I became acquainted with many persons of sterling worth, and I was warmly attached to a few. Indeed there were some associations to which I shall ever turn with pleasure; ties were then and there cemented to which I shall often revert with sweet remembrance.

At this time, with the exception of a number of the old settlers who have remained, the community is composed of a number of wild, uneducated Missourians—whom the "old on's" designate as "Yellow bellies" or "Greybacks"—who lately arrived, "jumped" the old claims, and made a new set of Laws, arbitrary and partial to their own interests, inviting all who will to take up leads not *actually* and personally occupied by the owners. This is for the purpose of gaining greater numbers for their defense against the legal proprietors who return in the spring. They will meet with most serious and, I fear, bloody opposition. Their course has rendered them obnoxious, and thus the epithets "Grey Backs," &c. are bestowed upon them. They are not generally challenged by that intelligence and urbanity of disposition which belonged to the old inhabitants, although they are industrious and fearless men. They seem to feel the cold looks of the old residents and naturally keep by themselves. The chasm will be widened by future occurrences. Several meetings have lately been held by both parties, many of the old claimants having got wind of their proceedings. The plot thickens!

I am at the present time stopping with Cromwell, and shall continue with him until such time as will enable me to finish my cabin shall elapse. At Cromwell's I have anything but felicitous opportunities for "posting up" my Journal, his store or boarding house being the Head Quarters of the old residents, who assemble at nightfall in his establishment and pass the evening at cards. At the present time "Cribbidge" is the favorite game, and there is nothing to be heard but laughing and

---

[4]Alhama was a Moorish city in southern Spain, conquered by Castille in 1482. Bickham's references to the "Valley of Alhama" are obscure.

talking, calling out the count, and the various terms used. However all parties afford me every facility possible under the circumstances.

Cromwell's is a curious place, and he is a queer individual.[5] His house consists of a frame of timber covered with canvass, in one end of which is the "bar," and the other end, not partitioned, is cook house, bed room, reading room, drawing room and gen'l amusement room. Crom' is a New Yorker and taking him all in all is a "pretty good fellow," although I cannot sometimes perfectly understand him. He is a decided wag and often affords his customers considerable amusement. His countenance is perpetually playing in a kind of suspicious smile, which frequently puzzles those with whom he associates to say whether he is jesting or in earnest. The "Butt" of the company's jokes is the "old Captain," who is pestered almost out of his life by all hands, but Crom's tongue and ever smiling visage is more trouble to him than that of any other. The Captain's limited acquaintance with the manners and customs of the United States opens him to the attack of all hands, who stuff him with any "cock and bull story" which they are able to muster, and he is often compelled to believe against his own convictions. His good nature renders it safe for all to pester him, where they would stand aloof from others.

Cromwell has a queer party with him each night; indeed they are almost *fixtures*. Some laborers at home, others farmers, and all singular representatives of each vocation. Morris, the constable of the District, is a large, wellformed, and decidedly good looking man, and *in his way* is a very good fellow.[6] He holds much the same station here as he would in Boston, his home. He is, though not a professional gambler, one of the best card players ever on the bar, equally acquainted with every known card game. The only gambling now done here is for "something

---

[5] Elias C. Cromwell, (d. 1861) a native of New York, sailed to California in 1849. He was one of the original inhabitants of Murderer's Bar, where he opened one of the first two stores. In 1852 he was appointed an aide to Governor Bigler with the rank of colonel of cavalry in the state militia. Haskins, *Argonauts of California*, 441; 1850 Census, El Dorado County, California, 467; 1852 California Census, El Dorado County, 140; Sioli, *El Dorado County*, 184; *Alta*, May 26, 1852; *Bulletin*, December 3, 1861.

[6] Hezekiah Morris was elected constable of Murderer's Bar in May 1850. He is listed in the 1850 census as a 31-year-old miner, born in New Jersey, living on the Middle Fork of the American River in January 1851. Morris is listed in the 1870 census as a "common laborer" living in Bakersfield, California. BL: CB 383.2: Records of the El Dorado County Clerk; 1850 Census, El Dorado County, 467; 1870 Census, Kern County, California, 366.

to drink" and eat, and he is nearly always engaged, and *seldom* is the beaten party. Pete Horton is a youth of about 19 years, hails from New South Wales, and is a decided bore, being the noisiest and most profane youth I ever saw. He is always at night at the card table, which indeed is the heighth of his ambition. Uneducated of course. Col. Joseph Potter of N. Y. is a well informed and tolerably well educated gentleman, about 35 years of age, and one of the Bar Aristocracy. He has his little faults, but take him all in all is a very gentlemanly personage. Mr. Tracy of Florida, about 30 years old, is a Southern gentleman, is of medium stature, rather slender and well formed, dark hair (what there is of it), piercing dark eyes, Roman nose, and finely chiselled lips. His tolerably good looking countenance is ornamented with glossy black whiskers and moustache. His manners are courteous though they are tinctured with considerable haughtiness. His profession is that of lawyer and civil engineer. Dr. Piggott of Mississippi is an occasional visitor and may be termed one of the "coterie" of queer and choice spirits which assemble at "The Den." This party is one of the queerest of those companies which are contained within the boundaries of California, and I have above briefly signalized them that I may in future times when thinking of these evenings be enabled to call forth the names of the *dramatis personae* with the never to be forgotten picture which they presented when sitting at the card table or around the stove passing jests, relating anecdotes, and sipping hot punches or Brandy Stews, and smoking their pipes, those invaluable articles to the Californian in the placers, and without which they would be almost miserable. Oh the many, many hours of soothing comfort my favorite pipe has afforded me. It has served to invite thought, or to drive away sorrow and perplexing cares. The company of the Den with their curious shapen pipes, all smoking together, look a party of Germans, smoking together in a favorite Beer House.

To-day being stormy, there is a full attendance of the "Company" and "Cribbage" with the accompanying toddies, is in high repute. Peter is out doing himself in making noise, and Cromwell is unceasing in his attention to the old "Captain," boring the old fellow to desperation. Some three or four are sitting around the stove discussing the future prospects of Miners in California, and in Murderer's Bar particularly.

Cromwell's or "The Den," Monday Evening—Jany 6th, 1851.

It rained pretty much all day, and to night it is storming fiercely. After breakfast I repaired to the opposite side of the river to lay the foundations of my new cabin, and by nightfall accomplished considerable, though the rain impeded my operations thoroughly, soaking my garments. This is my first attempt at building, and I find it a job not so easily accomplished as I thought for. The site of my house is upon my last summer's camping ground, entirely separated from any other habitation. My acquaintances wonder at my selecting such an isolated position, but I tell them my desire is to be where I will suffer no molestation. I prefer to be alone where I may read and write at my pleasure, particularly as there is now no person on the bar without a partner with whom I wish to associate so closely as under the same roof and at the same table.

Tuesday Evening, Jany 7th, 1851.

To-day it was nothing but rain, rain, but I continued my operations on the cabin until nightfall. I met upon returning to Cromwell's Sam'l Ayers[7] and Wm. Huntington[8] of my own city, and my old friend Jas. Stuart, a canny Scotsman. The former are new comers on the bar, but Stuart was here last year. All intend locating here, and propose assisting me in my cabin. This pleases me as they are agreeable associates and will make the time pass pleasantly. These three add to the company of "The Den" and make the evenings pass more agreeably.

Wednesday Evening, Jany 8th, 1851.

I worked part of the day at my cabin, but was not troubled with rain, the sky having once more become cleared. At two PM I was called across the river to attend a meeting of the last season's Members of the Bar, and

---

[7]Samuel Ayers had been a bricklayer in Cincinnati and later resumed this trade in California. He had come overland to California in 1849 with the Cincinnati and California Joint Stock Company, which included several other acquaintances of Bickham. Cincinnati city directory, 1849; *Republican*, April 23, 1849.

[8]William Huntington had come to California with the Cincinnati and California Joint Stock Company, together with Samuel Ayers and other acquaintances of Bickham. He may be the William C. Huntington who was later an importer and dealer in China, glassware, and fancy goods in Cincinnati. Haskins, *Argonauts of California*, 406; Cincinnati city directories 1865-95.

was honored with the appointment of Secretary for the Company during the ensuing season. Col. J. C. Potter was Chairman. This is the first meeting of a series which will be held, and I shall witness some curious struggles between the old Members and the "Jumpers." The old claimants assume the direct position as being Legal owners; the "Jumpers" assert that the ground is public domain and being *personally unoccupied,* assume that it belongs of right to any who *will* occupy. The principal object of the meeting was to take measures with regard to Damming and Racing. The question as to who are the owners of "Bank Leads"— river claims are not jumped because they could not be worked by anyone—was not settled. I cannot conceive how a race can be constructed until the difficulty is adjusted, for if the "Jumpers" retain the Banks they may, if disposed, prevent a race from crossing their leads. Law suits and, I fear, worse things will result.

The Den is the scene of considerable amusement to-night, and Captain Barker is in a tight place. To-morrow Ayers and Huntington intend beginning with me to work on the Cabin. It is just 12 Midnight and I must to bed.

Thursday, Jany 9th, 1851.

Cabin not finished but in a state of forwardness. Ayers and Huntington, having builded cabins previous to this, are adepts, and Saturday might well witness a consummation of our desires. The weather is very clear and beautiful.

Friday, Jany 10th, 1851.

I have labored hard to-day with my associates and this evening I am much fatigued. "The Den" has an unusual number of visitants to-night, and at the small table is a party making considerable noise at a game of Poker, substituting beans for money. Sam Ayers is busy in the game. Crom. and Peter are at my table playing chess. Huntington is reading, and Tracy is walking back and forth in meditative mood. Frank, the cook and bar keeper by turns, is preparing some "Stews."

Sunday, January 12th, 1851.

This morning the inhabitants of the "Den" laid in bed until a late hour, having that night been kept out of their beds by a party of card players, who made too much noise for even sleepy ones to rest. The weather still continues clear, but I fancy rain will fall within three days. Ayers, Huntington, and myself to-day continued operations upon the cabin and before the going down of the sun we were gratified at seeing our house completed. This is another incident in a California life. Each man who makes the "placers" his home is compelled to erect his own cabin on the coming of winter, and sometimes he finds it a comparatively easy job; at other times, as in our case, it is superlatively troublesome. Cabins erected in the forests where timber is plentiful, can be tossed up in a trice, and "chinking and daubing" is merely nothing; when timbers are scarce, as with us, and have to be rolled and carried from a distance, and roofing has to be hunted up from every corner, both time and toil are requisite. Our house is neither of the ancient orders of architecture, the *Comic* being substituted for the Ionic, Doric, and Gothic. The north side consists of a fallen tree, chinked between the two main limbs with a log laid above; the east end is of large logs, while the south and western side and end are built of stones with logs on top. Roofing consists of blue canvas. The Chimney and fireplace are made of stones and logs. Sam. Ayers acted as Mason and Plasterer, Huntington as Carpenter, and I was "Jack of all work." The interior arrangements are not yet complete, but our room wears a most pleasant appearance. We intend moving to-morrow and then I look for more agreeable evenings...

The "hombres" of this community to day seemed to turn out almost generally upon a spree, guzzling Rum and swaggering about in fine style. This has been the besetting sin of the Bar, the great majority being practitioners *at* the *Bar.* To-night, there are present in the Den some half a dozen men, English, French, and Americans, in a "darkly, deeply, beautifully blue" state, some of them vaunting of their bravery and deeds of prowess. By the bye, I have noticed that *nothing* so much delights a great many present at this place as talking of Shooting and fighting. Every night, I hear some story of a hard fight, somebody shot, or that certain persons "were going to fight, shoot, stab, assassinate or annihilate somebody, only *something* prevented the catastrophe." Oh what a country! it ought "to be fenc'd in."

I write with all these "drunken sojers" around me, or in the room, and I feel as though I were in a regular pandemonium. Pete's dealing "vingt et une," and about every two words spoken, I hear an awful stagger at swearing. I might as well say that the talk (it's not conversation) is not seasoned by oaths, but that oaths are besprinkled with a very little talk. I wish I were an artist, I would draw a comical picture.

CHAPTER FIVE

The Blue Cabin

This morning Stuart, Huntington, Ayers and I removed from our Lodgings at the "Den" to our cabin, which last evening was sufficiently complete for its constructors. Blankets, Cooking utensils, a few books and our provisions constituted our movables, and one trip across the river sufficed. All hands seemed highly satisfied with the interior arrangements as well as the situation of "our home."

The place where we are living is one of the most pleasant imaginable for a California Miner, and is really a most beautiful situation for a village, decidedly romantic and picturesque. About fifty yards distant, the Middle Fork rushes along its rocky bed, the mountain rising up from its brink on the opposite side gradually to within a few hundred feet of its summit where it starts up abruptly into tall broken cliffs. Several brooks lead down and contribute to the constant stream, and in their descent form numerous pretty little cascades. The upper limit of the semi-circular flat is shaded by large and tall masses of a greenish granite stone, full of fissures and little grottoes; behind us the mountains rise gradually as on the opposite side of the river, and terminate at the summit in the same manner as the facing mountain; below, a sugar loaf hill juts out to the edge of Buckner's Bar, and in the sunshine looks like a huge pile of clay burned red, as one will see in brick yards. At night the dull, heavy rolling of the waters over the falls sounds most mournfully, and the rushing over the ripples is like the sound of the wind among the trees. A few steps from our door in the side of the mountain is our spring, and on every hand we gather our fuel. No other cabin is near us and our seclusion is perfect.

Jim and Wm. H. have commenced sinking a prospect hole on the flat, and "Samuel" with myself made additions to the interior of the house and finished the chimney. To night I am engaged with Macaulay's Essays.

[Marginalia: "Plague the talk, it bothers me."]

Blue Cabin, Jany 14th, 1851.

The weather continues clear and pleasant, days sunshiny and warm; nights beautifully moon-lit and very cool. This morning a heavy white frost covers the earth and air very Keen. "Samuel" and I work at the cabin to-day, and "Jeemes" and William dig. I perceive the village on the opposite side of the river is receiving daily accessions. New tents and new cabins spring up as if by magic, and the lately dull neighborhood is lively as a swarm of bees. All the vacant lots of the village are staked off and claimed and in a few days three ten pin alleys will be opened to the public. Already there are three business houses in operation, and five or six more are soon to be established. Murderer's Bar is becoming quite celebrated and I believe the population during the coming summer will be double that of last year.

"Samuel" and I have just returned from the "Den" where we have been passing the evening playing Eukre, eating Oysters, &c. We were a moment ago congratulating ourselves on having a quite pleasant home where we could enjoy ourselves without interruption. "There's no place like Home, be it ever so humble." *Our home* is a pleasant one, and our "mess" is most agreeable. "Sam" is amusing, rather noisy, and makes "fun" for us all. Twelve O'clock. I must to bed.

Blue Cabin, Jany 15th, 1851.

Wm. H. and James S. went to work in the "Coyote Hole" now twenty feet deep, and "Sam" went with me to my old claim to make some money. We were so much impeded in our operations by the water that we gave up and were returning to camp when we met Wm. who said they had given up at the Hole until a future time, and that he had picked a place on the other side of the river in which to work. All hands worked until 3 o'clock when "James" left to attend a meeting of the Livingston

Co. We were not very successful in getting dust, but made enough for one day's board. Passed this evening at the "Den," and not very agreeably.

Thursday, Jany 16th, 1851.

Frosty morning. Rose at sunrise and ate breakfast which Sam. prepared, and all hands after taking a smoke went to work. Received dates up to the 1st of December from the East, containing accounts of State's elections, Unionist meetings, and the speech of Henry Clay before the Legislature of Kentucky.[1] Also received late dates from San Francisco, containing accounts of the "Gold Bluffs" at Trinity.[2] This is the great excitement of the Winter in California. I expect it to turn out much like the El Dorado Cañon excitement of last winter, and the last summer's "Gold Lake" humbug.[3] Over 100 vessels in the port of San F. are "up for Gold Bluffs," and grand inducements offered to adventurers.

I heard today of a man being killed in the neighborhood of Todd's Ranche by a grizzly bear. He went out hunting and had not returned by next morning. Two of his friends went in search and found him horribly mangled and near him lay two huge grizzlys which he had doubtless slain. Two weeks since, three or four miles from here, another man lost his life in the same manner. He went out hunting with a friend and became separated from him. His friend heard the report of a rifle and supposed his companion had shot a deer. He saw him no more and returned home. His companion not returning next morning, a party of men went in search and soon found the hunter horribly mangled and [he] had evidently been dragged some distance down the mountain. The

---

[1] In his speech of November 19, 1850, to the Kentucky legislature, Henry Clay (1777-1852), the noted statesman and Whig party leader, defended the Compromise of 1850, of which he was the principal architect, and declared that his loyalty to the Union was stronger than his party affiliation to the Whigs. *New York Daily Tribune,* November 20, 1850.

[2] In April 1850, gold was discovered mixed with black sand at the foot of a series of cliffs north of Humboldt Bay. At least eight shiploads of prospectors departed from San Francisco for the "Gold Bluffs" during the early part of 1851, but the gold particles proved to be too fine to be easily separated from the sand, and the excitement soon died down. Jackson, *Gold Dust,* 325; Gudde, *California Gold Camps,* 132.

[3] During the summer of 1850, hundreds of prospectors in the Northern Mines searched the headwaters of the Feather River for a rumored lake whose shores were reportedly lined with huge gold nuggets. No such lake was found, although rich deposits were discovered in the upper Feather River valley. Jackson, *Gold Dust,* 262-64; Gudde, *California Gold Camps,* 135.

party went in search of the grizzlys and succeeded in killing two after shooting one 30 times, the other 11.

During the latter part of December, in the neighborhood of the "Pilot Hill Diggings," a young Englishman named Avery started out on a short hunting expedition, stating "when he left camp at day-light" that he would return to breakfast. Several days elapsed and he did not return. His friends began to fear lest he should have fallen in with Indians. A party started in search and on the same day found a party of Indians having Avery's rifle and hunting equipment in their possession. Several of them were taken prisoners and conveyed to Pilot Hill, where one of them confessed they had murdered A., and only for the sake of his equipments and boots. Three of them were hanged by the populace and a fourth one shot. The whole neighborhood was highly excited, and large parties scoured the forests and mountains in search of more of the murderers, but were unable to find any. The Indians were driven entirely out of the neighborhood and have not since made their appearance. Young Avery's body was found six days after his disappearance buried under leaves and dirt, and not more than fifty yards from the City Road. The body was horribly mutilated, his face and arms being terribly cut to pieces, and his throat cut from ear to ear. A young Indian boy who was taken prisoner at the same time with those who were hanged, was suffered to escape death upon guiding a party to the place where A. was buried, and after giving a complete account of the transaction. He stated that A. was attacked about sun rise by a party of 13 or 14 Indians, that he was brought down by a pistol shot fired by the Chief, Pico. A. shot one Indian through the body with his rifle, but was so fiercely beset by numbers that he was unable to club his gun to resist longer.[4]

The first week of this year was signalized at Salmon Falls, on the South Fork of the American, by the hanging of a man by "Judge Lynch" for stealing stock. At Auburn, Sutter Co., in the same manner was hung

---

[4]According to the *Sacramento Transcript*, Avery was the son of a widow who kept the Pilot Springs House, and was "generally esteemed." The conflict in which he lost his life was begun by a party of whites who burned an Indian village in retaliation for thefts which the Indians had reportedly committed against them. According to the son of the chief, three other whites were killed the same day as Avery. *Sacramento Transcript*, January 4, 9, 1851.

another man for shooting down a fellow being for a very slight provocation. Judge Lynch is most powerful in this country and his decisions are listened to with fear. As singular as it may appear he is nearly always correct in judgment and the mass of the community feel more secure under his Jurisdiction than they do under that of Uncle Sam.

Friday—January 17th, 1851...

The Express man arrived to-day from the city with dates from the Atlantic to Dec.1st, also late dates from San F. giving astonishing accounts of the newly discovered region at "Gold Bluffs." An agent of a vessel at Sacramento accompanied him and endeavored to obtain passengers for said vessel to the "Bluffs." Most of the "Bar" Men looked upon the affair as being a grand "humbug." However he obtained six passengers, who start to-morrow.

The papers are filled with most extravagant accounts throwing into the shade all other stories with regard to California ever before published. Men publish affidavits of a most extraordinary nature inviting all to go and partake, assuring the adventurer of a princely fortune in an incredible short space of time, saying that any man may be sure of $100,000. One company, it is said, *"design loading a vessel with the precious metal and then sail[ing] to some port where it is not so plentiful!"* One man had accumulated (?) 30,000 pounds; others have claims from which they obtain 100 pounds per day, and this all on the sea shore... It is my opinion that these stories are inventions for the purpose of attracting a large emigration from the States during the ensuing season. Fears are entertained by those who are interested in the immigration that it will be small in comparison with that of last season, and it is therefore necessary that something should be done to excite the people of the old States into the California Fever. It may be that ship owners are at the head of the movement, as there are many hundred vessels lying idle in the port of San Francisco, and this excitement is raised for their benefit. However I think the ulterior object is to seduce an immigration from the East...

Passed this evening at the "Den," but I was so discontented that I intend to stay at home hereafter. A Monte Bank was opened, and during the evening was broken. The excitement was great.

Saturday, Jany 18th, 1851...

After breakfasting—and at not a very early hour—I passed an hour reading the last papers received from the States and went over to the "Den" to attend a meeting of the Murderer's Bar racing and Damming Company. I was much surprised to see so large an[sic] general attendance, as I had thought the Members so widely dispersed nothing like a full meeting would be held. However I was gratified at seeing several warm friends of mine from whom I parted in October last with the thought that we perhaps should not meet again, at least in California.

Col. Jos. C. Potter again acted as Chairman and I as Secretary. Mr. E. H. Phetteplace, a young lawyer formerly of Kalamazoo, Michigan, as Ch'n of the "Business Committee," presented the report on the several subjects for which the Committee was selected and also a "Plan and Specifications" of a Raceway, all of which were received and adopted with great unanimity. A Committee prepared a string of resolutions with regard to the race and Contract and they were also passed in their order... The Secretary had a very nice *little* job of writing allotted as his portion of the work, in addition to what fell to his share in a regular manner. [Marginalia: "I penned all these resolutions, drew up the memorials, &c."]. I was pleased to notice the great unanimity of those present in the several propositions offered. All seemed imbued with a spirit of enterprise and speculation. A determination to succeed in their object was manifested by all parties and I trust they may not be disappointed in their hopes. The race is to be planked and lined inside with canvas, to be firmly made and secured; dimensions three feet in depth and fifteen feet wide inside, the whole to be ready for the admission of the water on first day of July, 1851.

This morning, whilst lying in bed, I heard loud shouts proceeding from the village and when I repaired thither I learned that they proceeded from a party of eleven men who had given the cheers as a parting salute to Murderer's Bar, they having started for the "Gold Bluffs." I hope they may not have cause to repent of their adventurous spirit, but reason bids me fear. Nevertheless, if it were not for my having an interest here, I too should go.

I remained at my cabin during the evening of this day and I busied myself preparing several copies of the minutes of the proceedings of the meeting. Sam and James Stuart went to the Den to pass the time. Appearances denote rain at this time. 11 P.M.

Sunday—January 19th, 1851

I was again caught napping this morning by old Sol, who, contrary to my expectations, rose in an unclouded sky. I have lost so much sleep of late that it appears necessary for me to sleep in the mornings, although I much reprehend such a course of action. My messmates seemed equally disposed to court the attentions of the sleepy God, but "Jeemes" says that Monday morning must mark a change as he then begins work upon the Livingston Co.'s race-way.

After breakfasting we repaired to the village which we found in a state of lively commotion quite unusual for this season. The Murderer's Bar Co. Committee had just letted the Contract for racing their portion of the river to S. C. Tyler[5] and E. H. Phetteplace at the rate of $8.00 per running foot, and were now in session with committees of several other companies endeavoring to make an agreement for constructing a dam, and connecting races. W. H. Dulany[6] and myself acted (after my arrival) as Committee from the Dulany Co. Four copies of an agreement to assess the Livingston Company in building a Dam at the head of their Leads, and further to allow the 4 race-ways to be connected were signed by the respective Committees. Thus is the ball put in motion and with the most pleasing equanimity. How different from last summer; then all was jarring and discord, now all are united in one harmonious whole. After attending to all necessary business, Tracy and I started off afoot for Greenwood Valley, he on business, I for letters. We arrived before sunset and, contrary to expectation, were compelled to remain all night. I was sadly disappointed at not receiving any letters, and felt gloomy during the entire evening...

---

[5]Probably Stephen Tyler, a former inhabitant of Vermont, who had been one of the contractors entrusted with the construction of the Middle Fork flume in the summer of 1850. The following year, Tyler became a partner in a sawmill near Greenwood Valley. Sioli, *El Dorado County*, 83-84, 186.

[6]William Henry Dulany (1818-1914) a successful Missouri tobacco planter, came overland to California in 1850, and was mining in Murderer's Bar in the summer of that year. By the following January, he was shipping goods by wagon from Sacramento to the mines. According to one account, he had accumulated $11,800 by the time of his departure from California in early 1851. After the Civil War, Dulany entered the lumber business in which he remained active for the rest of this life. Shoemaker, *Missouri and Missourians*, 4: 121-22; MHS: W. H. Dulany papers.

Monday Evening, Jany 20th.

I trudged from Greenwood to-day with 20 pounds of Sugar and Coffee on my back, and am this evening somewhat fatigued. I have just finished browning coffee and cooking a kettle of Beans. My loaf of bread also smiles in the pan on the hearth stove. I don't like to be master of the culinary department but "Sich is life" in California.

Operations on the Race-way were commenced this morning by the Livingston and Murderer's Bar Cos. I perceived this evening a round tent for a Coffee room standing on a lot which yesterday was vacant...

James, Wm. H. and Sam are all at the Den, and I sit here all alone listening to the mournful and sullen roar of the waters of the river as like the course of time the[y] flow ever onward, and like time too they leave no perceptible trace of their passage. Sometimes, aye often, I gaze half abstractedly into the blazing fire and muse on the future; think of the past, of home and friends so far away. Then again I seize my pipe and take desperate whiffs, sending the white smoke curling to the roof and —don't think at all. This is when I'm desperate. I've been desperate several times to-night and all caused by a bad cold, the burning of my beans, and upsetting of a kettle of water two or three times on the fire; the latter two occurrences would disturb the equanimity of a good natured "woman" and I don't believe I can be blamed for hurling one or two anathamas at the offending articles...

Tuesday, Jany 21st, 1851.

I have been quite unwell all this day and consequently have remained within my cabin. Samuel remained with me busying himself patching his striped unwhisperables with a striped calico shirt, being unable to procure a different material. Sam tore his breeches by sitting on a log covered with pitch; said pitch, having great adhesive power, retained two delicate pieces when he rose. I entertained both him and myself with the potent sermons of Dow, Jr.,[7] a copy of which has lately been added to the

---

[7]Elbert Gerry Paige, founder of the *New York Sunday Mercury*, wrote weekly sermons under the name of "Dow Jr.," taking the name of Lorenzo Dow, a revivalist preacher. Dow Jr.'s sermons, unlike those of his namesake, were, according to historian Franklin Walker, humorous with some "homely wisdom." Walker, *San Francisco's Literary Frontier*, 118-19.

Library. This evening I have been engaged in writing a letter to Mr. S. S. L'Hommedieu[8] of Storrs Township, O.

Wednesday, Jany 22d, 1851.

Today my health has resembled that of yesterday, but I essayed to dig a little. I perceive more new tenements and new inhabitants in the village across the river.

I went to Dulany and Hill's[9] store to attend a meeting of the Dulany Race-way Company after supper, but finding but few members present I returned and passed the evening until within a few moments, finishing my letter to Mr. L'H. At sun-down the sky was o'ercast with clouds and the atmosphere gave indications of rain, but now all is clear and cool. What a remarkable winter!

Thursday, January 23d, 1851.

The earth is this morning clad in a mantle of pure white frost and the atmosphere is keen and piercing. It is just sun-rise and I must to work.

Sam Ayers worked with another party to-day and Will H. and I kept our rocker going. Poor success. The water of trouble among the mining companies is beginning to heat. The Livingston Co. has been in session all day, discussing the right of claimants to a portion of its ground. The members seem not in a very good humor. This, I think, is the forerunner of other quarrels. Jas. Stuart went over after ten to confer with his partners about their interests. Sam and Wm. H. went along to find amusement, and I remain alone to pass the time reading and writing.

Friday, Jany 24th.

My mess-mates did not return home until near the break of Day this morning, and they were much disposed to sleep when I called them up

---

[8]Stephen S. L'Hommedieu (1806-75) was one of the proprietors of the *Cincinnati Gazette* from 1829 to 1848, and served as president of the Cincinnati, Hamilton, and Dayton Railroad Company from 1849 to 1871. After the death of Bickham's father, much of the Bickham family property was apparently entrusted to L'Hommedieu's management. *Biographical Cyclopædia. . . of Ohio*, 3: 797-98; DMCL Bickham Collection, WDB-Sketch, 2.

[9]Wesley Hill, listed in the 1850 census as a 44-year-old Kentucky-born merchant, was William Dulany's business partner and resided in Murderer's Bar in January 1851. 1850 Census, El Dorado County, 467; MHS: W. H. Dulany papers: letter from Dulany to his wife, January 7, 1851.

at sun-rise to breakfast on Slap-Jacks and beef. Slap-jacks are usually substituted for bread by the Miner when in haste, and this morning James, being hurried, fed on this delectable (?) article. It consists of flour, saleratus, and water. The experienced cook often shows surprising dexterity in turning them in his pan, giving them a scientific toss several feet into the air and catching them the cooked side upward in his pan. Remarkable stories, for the truth of which I am not prepared to vouch, are related of b'hoys who would toss them out of the cabin chimney and, running out by the door, would catch them in prime order on the other side of the cabin!! What armies of accomplished Knights of the Kitchen will be sent home from the wilds of California! The province of women will be sadly invaded! What scores of washer*women* (men) too will be entitled (?) to diplomas!... A murrain on cooking and washing say I. Chiefly washing! O how my poor knuckles have suffered from the rubbing I have given my unlucky shirts for being dirty! Oh, woman, what are thy troubles even though this should be the greatest... But alas,— yes *a lass*—for the Miner say I, he must do his own cooking and washing. Lord a mercy, what cooking I have seen in this land, such mussing, such loaves of bread, heavy as lead, tough as gutta-percha... Will H. is a first rate cook, I only tolerable. I am the lark, however, who keeps the dishes clean.

Jany 25th.[10]

Three of us felt unwell to-day, and consequently were idle. The "Express Man" brought papers up to 11th Dec. from New York, and from N. O. to the 14th, containing the President's—Fillmore—message[11] and congressional reports. All in this country are delighted to hear

---

[10]Bickham's dating is confusing. The succeeding day, which he lists as "Saturday, Jany 26th," should be the "25th," as it follows Friday, January 24th. This January 25th heading was apparently inserted by mistake, and the succeeding paragraphs still pertain to January 24th. Bickham gave the wrong date for the succeeding day as well, but corrected his dating for Monday, January 27th.

[11]Millard Fillmore (1800-74), a native of western New York State, was elected as Zachary Taylor's vice president in 1848. He succeeded to the presidency upon Taylor's death in July 1850, and served out the remainder of Taylor's term. In his message, Fillmore supported the Compromise of 1850 and expressed the opinion that California's mineral lands, which he had previously been in favor of leasing, should be divided into "small particles" and sold under such restrictions as to insure the best price and "guard most effectively against combinations of capitalists to obtain monopolies." *New York Daily Tribune,* December 3, 1850.

of the dissemination of Unionist sentiment at home; they never did believe that a dismemberment of the confederacy could be effected. We say for our country "est perpetua." ...

We all passed the evening at the Cabin, reading and writing before a bright blazing fire. This is decidedly a more pleasant manner of passing time than by repairing to "the Den" where there is nothing done, save card-playing, tippling, and talking; and nothing sensible is said (save occasionally). The last evening I spent at "the Den," I was amused with a conversation relating to "gentlemen miners." It appears that the Missourians or "Jumpers" who have lately arrived at the Bar have conceived a violent animosity toward us of "the Den," deeming that we decide in favor of the old claimants and that our influence being cast against them is detrimental to their interests. We happening to be old acquaintances, and aligning to-gether as is natural for old friends and acquaintances, and the majority of our party being residents of cities, are by the "Jumpers" denominated "Gentlemen Miners." What a hidea! But "Sich is Life."

Heretofore the great body of Miners and adventurers have mingled to-gether in one great body, forming but one society, one community and strictly Democratic, but now party lines are beginning to be drawn, and those totally devoid of education withdraw themselves and look upon men who have education either of the ordinary or an excellent character as "aristocrats," "gentlemen miners," and "speculators." The populace are ever jealous of those in better circumstances than themselves.

Saturday, Jany 26th [25th].

Rose at sunrise this morning and went to work quite early, and at night was gratified to discover better results to our labor than we have had for some days...

I passed the evening with Sam. at the Cabin, reading to him the Message of Fillmore, &c. The others of the Mess went to "The Den" and did not get home until 4 O'clock.

Sunday, January 27th [26th].

In consequence of retiring at a late hour last night, we all felt disposed to sleep this morning and therefore did not rise until the sun was far advanced in his daily course. The morning is delightfully pleasant, balmy as spring. At home I should say that in few days rain would follow, here I know not what to say. After a short visit to "the Den" I have returned home to write a letter to the Gazette, and I am no[w] enjoying the solitude of my cabin undisturbed by any one. Periods of this description rarely occur, and when they do I seize upon them with alacrity. Thought and fancy then ramble or concentrate as it may happen, and I feel more contented than at other times...

As I fancied this morning, so it has proven. The rain is pattering on the roof.

Monday—January 27th...

I have just returned from my daily labour, which offered discouraging results, three of us making but *one dollar,* (O California!) have eaten my supper, cleaned off the table and am again at my writing. But everything is so dull that I can write nothing. No one in my hearing has said anything for a week worthy of note save an Irishman in the Dry Diggings on the hill who has had a large pile of dirt laying dry for months, and he waiting for rain. He was swearing hard at the weather, and said "Be C'asus and it's the *Driest wet saisin* ever I did see!" This is all I have heard save a continual clatter about "claims," "diggings," "monte and Poker" or "Seven up." These topics are discussed morning, noon, evening and midnight; and since July last my ears have been continuously ringing with the sounds.

Tuesday, Jany 28th. ...

About eight o'clock Wm. Huntington started for "Bird's Town" and "Eldorado Cañon" upon a prospecting expedition. We have become tired with our poor prospects here and wish to better ourselves. Sam and I went across the River to work, but, I being called upon to attend a meeting of the Dulany Raceway Company, he returned to camp. At the meeting appropriate resolutions were passed and a Committee appointed to obtain the names of owners of Leads in the Co. and the Nos., and to advertise a plan and specifications for Contract, &c.

The village increases daily. A Baker has started a bake house, and a new "Round Tent" is occupying a piece of ground which yesterday was vacant...

Wednesday, January 29th.

Being out of provisions in the meat bin, we this morning breakfasted on bread and Coffee. Bread's the staff of life, but it's a walking stick which taken by itself is rather shaky. Sam and I went to work at sun-rise, but George Boone,[12] a friend of his, arriving from Weberville, we desisted until the middle of the afternoon. Mr. B. dined with us. He gave information of an Indian fight on the Cosum[n]e river in which a friend of our Mess from the Queen City, Jas. Foulds,[13] participated. Nine of the red skins gave up their hold on life; the leader of the white men, Dr. Slaughter,[14] received a slight wound in the shoulder, and had his cap and clothes perforated by several balls. This is fight No. 2 for Jas. Foulds…

Thursday, January 30th, 1851.

We were up this morning and had eaten our breakfast before sun-rise. A heavy dew fell during the night. This is about the third time I have noticed it among the mountains. It never falls in the summer. Samuel and I went to work on our claim quite early, hoping to make more than $3.40, the amt. of yesterday's work. We placed our rocker under a spout and conveyed water from a brook running from the mountains, thus laboring more rapidly and easily.

Well-a-day, only $4.50 for our day's labor. This *is* hard luck, but who the d-l cares, better do this than be idle. If it were not for the wear and tear of the poor body,—which really is awful,—it wouldn't make any difference…

Sam Ayers told me yesterday that Truman Conclin said to him, the

---

[12]Probably the George W. Boone listed in the 1850 Census as a 30-year-old miner, born in Illinois, living in Greenwood Valley in January 1851. He may have been the George W. Boone listed as a hotel keeper in El Dorado County in the 1852 census, and was very likely the George W. Boone listed as an Alameda County cattle dealer in the census of 1860. 1850 census, El Dorado County, 449; 1852 California Census, El Dorado County, 99; 1860 Census, Alameda County, California, 111.

[13]James C. Foulds, an Ohio resident born in Louisiana, came overland to California in 1849, and was a tavern keeper in Weaverville, El Dorado County, in September 1850. He was still living in El Dorado County at the time of the 1852 census, but by 1859 had returned to Cincinnati and become a grocer. *Republican,* April 23, 1849; 1850 Census, El Dorado County, 253; 1852 California census, El Dorado County, 3; Cincinnati city directory, 1859.

[14]Dr. Samuel M. Slaughter, a native of Virginia, was one of the first members of the El Dorado Medical Society, and served as justice of the peace in that county from 1853 to '54. In 1860 he was practicing medicine in Sacramento. Sioli, *El Dorado County,* 140; BL: CB 383.2, Records of the El Dorado County clerk; 1850 Census, El Dorado County, 253; 1860 Census, Sacramento County, 223.

day T. C. started home for the States, that I would become one of the wildest of gamblers before I left California, as I was "one of the wildest, quickest fellows he ever saw!" God forbid that I should become so. No, I am *too proud* for this, and esteem my name and fame too much. Beside, have I not a mother and sisters! If his "clack" should create any uneasiness on my account at home, he shall hear from me in such manner as will make *him* look "wild."

Friday, Jany 31st, 1851.

The last day of January and my fortunes not improved, and in truth appear in any other light than flattering. The weather continues very beautiful. No work to-day, the discouraging results of several weeks labor having an evil influence. Not very well.

Saturday—February 1st, 1851.

I did not rise at a very early hour this morning, but when I did, I employed some time mending my clothes. About 11 A.M., Samuel and myself went to town, and had not long been there before Dave Scott arrived from Spanish Bar in pursuit of two absconding debtors. Hearing no tidings of them at this place, he gave up the search and after buying a can of oysters which he and I demolished, he started homeward. During the afternoon Sam, James and I started for Greenwood Valley and Spanish Bar, but turned back after having half ascended the hill, upon meeting Tom. Smith. Sam and I went up to the Falls to take a view, and there we laid ourselves down on the brink of the cliff o'erlooking the cascade, and in the genial warmth of the sun admired the beauty of the picturesque view presented at this point—and indulged in the meantime in various ruminations. An hour before sunset we returned to the village where we met Wm. Crawford and turned in with several others on a regular frolic. After supper Morris and I went to the ferry where we passed the evening eating oysters for which I finally had to pay, making a hole in my funds the size of a half ounce of gold dust. After returning to the village, we found the boys of the place wide awake on a Saturday night frolck, and as we were unable to cross the river to our cabin we were compelled to remain out of bed nearly all night.

Sunday, Febry 2d, 1851.

At an early hour I arrived here at my cabin, prepared breakfast and went to bed. I passed the day in sleep. A pretty piece of business for a young man. During the evening I heard that the "Gold Bluffs" stories had already proven to be a grand humbug. Just as I anticipated. Hundreds of poor fellows are now in that section of country unable to get away.

To-day two old Members of this community started for home, one with over $3,000 in dust, the other with rising of $2,000…

Monday, February 3d, 1851.

I arose this morning shortly after day-light and prepared breakfast;— after this started for the opposite side of the river intending to work. I had scarce set one foot on shore upon leaving the boat when a sudden feeling of indolence passed through me, making me totally disinclined to labor. The lazy atmosphere had much to do with this feeling, and I was prompted during the day to believe that I was under the influence of Spring Fever. Certainly this splendid winter weather among the wild scenes has a singular tendency to produce indolence. Sam and I are both lazy today and without any license so to be for we are too poor to buy beef. We were laughing to-day at the queer figure we make standing up at our table, masticating a dinner consisting of nothing under the broad heavens other than fried Mess Pork, Bread and Coffee. Quoth Sam, at the same moment bursting out into a hearty laugh, and the which I echoed, "How they would pity us at home if they could only see us in our present situation! Poor Fellows, I don't see how they can stand it!" "Yet, Sam." said I, "we are more happy than many who would pity us, & more contented than we would be at home, for a life of excitement and adventure are as necessary to us as a tongue is to a woman." But jesting aside, *it is* rather hard work to dig and roll big rocks all day, carrying dirt some distance to the rocker and only making two or three dollars, especially when one thinks of days when two or three ounces could be obtained without half the labor…

Well, we did not work to-day but busied ourselves in the morning first by going to the Ferry to see if our partner, Will H., had sent a letter to us from Birds. This took one hour; the remaining portion of time I passed in reading; how Sam killed time heaven only knows. I saw him endeavoring to smoke it away. To-morrow I work whether he will or no.

To-night I am alone in the cabin, reading, writing, castle-building, and reflecting. I have enough of the latter to do and my reflections are not altogether of a consolatory nature. I find that action is preferable to reflection sometimes.

Tuesday—February 4th, 1851.

Having read until a late hour last night, I felt drowsy this morning and therefore did not rise very early. I have been troubled for the past two weeks with severe pains in my breast for which I cannot account unless it is caused by eating so much pork grease or smoking. I feel the effects of working in the water last summer, my joints being stiff. Persons may and do boast of the excellent health they enjoy in this climate, and with justice, but they are deceived by the very thing in which they feel such security. Working in water from noon till night and sleeping upon the hard ground, though it seems not to affect the system at the time, it will eventually be attended with evil effects. During the summer men feel hale and hearty, and quite lithe and active, but when winter comes they become stiffened and the bones ache *somewhat*.

At noon I returned and read a short time, when Sam went with me to the Empire Bar a short distance above the cabin. This bar is of very great extent and width and the distance to the bedrock is, I suppose, at least 30 feet. The labor necessary to expose the gold which must lie on the bed rock appears so great that as yet no one has prospected. Last summer two dams and races were constructed, but so imperfectly that they proved useless. There was no fair prospect, the bed rock not being approached. This year, I think, will see the whole worked out, and with eminent success. The Bar is sandy and full of boulders, and with all presents a very pretty appearance. The river must certainly here at someday have run through it, although there are oak trees growing in its midst several hundred years old.

On our return towards the Cabin we became excited from some cause, and indulged in all manner of pranks, rolling big rocks down the mountain side, climbing cliffs over-looking the falls, whooping and yelling like Indians, *and* various other antics were played. The last we engaged in was climbing to the top of a tall rock overlooking the falls. The summit was more than one hundred feet above the bed of the river. We tossed off rocks and listened to the distant crashes. Just before departing, I carved the initials L. C. H. & W. D. B. on the trunk of a small oak tree growing from the side of the rock.

Wednesday—February 5th, 1851...

Cards, cards, nothing but cards, are talked of by Sam and Jim. Will Crawford is with us again to-night and cards again the topic. Jim and Will have just been making sport of Sam, telling him that he knows nothing of Cards. Sam has a great conceit of his abilities, and this raillery "riles" him. I know little concerning cards, but have sufficient acquaintance with them to detect cheating. Sam thinks he can "put up" cards quite skillfully, but he can only deceive "green ones." I, in perfect good nature, made a remark to this effect, when he turned upon me and used most insulting language. This of course disturbed my equanimity and I read Samuel a lecture on gentlemanly principle. I was tempted to strike, but reflected and soon recovered my usual good nature. Sam is still sulky, but he will recover before to-morrow.

Just at this moment the conversation is touching upon emigration, &c. Will Crawford says he is pleased to learn that the immigration of this year will be comparatively small, as "he is tired of seeing so much poverty."[15] Quoth I, poverty knocks pretty starkly at our door...

It is now twelve o'clock and I must lay aside my book, Macaulay's Miscellanies, and go to bed, perhaps to lie awake an hour or two and reflect upon the past or indulge in fancies for the future. This is my nightly custom and always banishes repose.

Thursday, February 6th, 1851.

Old Sol has opened his peepers and so have I. His light is just tipping the top of yonder mountain, and the reflection is glancing hitherward.

---

[15]Crawford was correct. The number of emigrants to California declined drastically in 1851. Although over 15,000 still took the Panama route, only slightly more than 1,000 took the overland trail as opposed to 47,000 in 1850, and hardly any came by the Cape Horn, Mexican, or Southwestern routes. Jackson, *Gold Dust*, 315.

What a glorious sight is a California sun rise! how the first rays bathe the hills and valleys in a flood of brilliant beauty! And what a magnificent thing is a California sun *set!* How lovely are the valleys as the long lines of brilliant light defile. How magnificent the mountaintops are, tipped and pointed with shining gold. But it's morning, and speculations on Sun set are mal-a-propos…

Sam says it's my turn to get breakfast and I suppose I must. So here goes for the woodpile.

Sam played and I worked, and it's hard to tell who was most fatigued at supper time this evening. I know, however, that I was most contented.

What a queer picture we present in our cabin at night when we are all at home. Jim lies on the bed with a short stemmed chalk pipe between his teeth, and Sam sits on the end of a pine log at the foot of the beds before a bright blazing fire, reading Lalla Rookh by my light, while I sit upon a camp kettle covered with a griddle, at our table covered with my blue blankets, and before me lies my Journal in which I jot down *what* happens to come uppermost. Sometimes the scene becomes changed; all hands light pipes, and then engage in conversation. We laugh at our "situation," speculate upon former times, and wonder what our friends would say if they could only see us now. Only think; what *would* our "auld acquaintance" say if they *could* see us? To-night Will Crawford is with us, and we are making time fly merrily. He and Sam are taking turns reading Moore's Melodies,[16] and occasionally have a good-natured contest about the volume. Says Will, "Let me have the book to find one particular Psalm." Quoth his friend, "here is *one Sam!*" Will says, "Jim, lying on the bed, looks like the fellow whom the Irishman said 'laid in Salvation seven weeks.'" …

Friday—February 7th, 1851.

Last night, after retiring to bed, the rain began to patter on our house top, and the music of the falling drops lulled me to sleep. This morning all is bright and clear, and only the freshness of the air indicates the past shower. It's quite early, and breakfast is ready, and I shall eat, then to

---

[16]These were a series of 130 poems written and set to music between 1807 and 1837 by the Irish poet and composer Thomas Moore. They included such well-known works as "The Last Rose of Summer," and provided a sympathetic if highly sentimental view of Ireland.

work, though not until I put some beef on the fire to make soup for dinner. This shall not be "hasty soup.".…

It's 10 o'clock, and Will Crawford and Sam Ayers are "making night hideous" in their attempt to sing "Oft in the stilly night." I am tired as I have been working all day, and I shall cease writing and help the boys make noise.

Saturday—February 8th, 1851…

I washed 31 buckets of dirt to-day and received for my labor only $1.25. That's poor pay, and very discouraging. Samuel has been flying round doing *nothing*. Harder work than mine, for there's nothing here to help a man pass time. Jas. Stuart started for Greenwood early this morning to buy lumber for the Livingston Company.

To-night we are passing in the same manner as the past two nights. It's impossible for me either to read or to write, consequently I assist in creating uproar. Dow Jr.'s Sermons assist us greatly in our enjoyments.

Sunday—February 9th, 1851.

I awakened this morning with a severe head ache, and felt altogether quite unwell. However, I bathed myself as is my custom on every Sunday morn, and put on a clean shirt. I went to the village to learn whether the mail had yet arrived, and was disappointed. After cruising around the village an hour or two, passing compliments with the "gentlemen miners," I returned to the Blue Cabin down under the hill, and read until late in the afternoon when Sam, Will Crawford and I again went to the village. I went for the purpose of going to the top of the mountain with Morris to see his sweetheart, Sarah. I was, however, left in the lurch as I was so late in crossing the river that M. despaired of seeing me and went alone. He has been after me for a long time to go to see Sally, and I will some day accompany him to see what enjoyment I can have. He says she is pretty. Next Friday night there's to be a ball at Pilot Hill where the "gals" will appear in their finest feather…

Monday—February 10, 1851.

Wonder if my head will ache forever! I feel as though I were *standing* upon my caput. No work to-day I see very plainly.

It's night again and the loveliest night which ever shone. I have just seated myself after a walk in our amphitheatre, musing upon the past and endeavoring to peer beyond the mountains. Fancy's a jewel, but to-night I have not a jewel of a fancy. I'm somewhat in the field of blue, troubled with the indigo fiends...

William and Sam are enjoying themselves with pipes and Dow Jr. Wm. and his partners have a quartz rock lead which will make them rich men. He is down here endeavoring to dispose of his interest in the bar that he may give his whole time to working the Quartz ledge...

Tuesday, February 11th, 1851...

James Stuart returned to-day and I was surprised, nay worse, was shocked, to hear that he had made up a match for a prize fight; wager $1,500.00. A singular mess mate for me, but I shall soon be relieved of him. He is a clever and whole souled fellow, but his tastes and mine do not harmonize. At his request I wrote a note to a friend of his in the city, requesting him to make preparations.

Sam received a note from Will H. this evening which contained such very unflattering intelligence that he would not tell me the contents. Poor Sam seems sadly discouraged at his ill fortune. He is minus the ducats and he is consequently troubled with the blue devils...

Wednesday, February 12th, 1851.

To-day I worked hard and only made $1.60; awful! About the time I got through my labors, Judge Lauck and Col. Davis arrived on the bar on their way to the city from the quartz ledge in which they are interested, along with Wm. Crawford and his company. They brought with them a wagon load of gold-bearing quartz which they intend having assayed in San Francisco. Col. D. pressed me to accompany them, and it was my intention to have so done had it not been for an unlucky accident which befell me whilst running a foot race with two hombres. I got thrown when under full weigh, and my face and nose struck the ground first, swelling the former and badly bruising and scratching the latter. I had been jumping a few moments before and came off victorious, and in the latter contest I fared not so well though the race was not decided.

I remained with my partners in the village until a late hour, and had almost reached the cabin when we heard a noise on the opposite mountain side as if proceeding from someone struggling and calling for "help, help, help;" it seemed like the voice of one being choked. We listened awhile and heard it again, though not so distinctly, and we immediately crossed the river, procured arms, and searched the cliffs and mountainside, but without discovering anything. We all thought the voice proceeded from a woman and consequently were eager in our chase. Will Crawford had a double barreled shot gun, Jim Stuart no arms, Sam a revolver, Jacoby[17] a pistol, and I my butcher knife. It looked queer to see us five scattered about over the mountain at 12 o'clock at night, all hunting eagerly for something. If any poor fellow had happened to have been met it would have fared ill with him. After returning to camp, we built a nice fire and before we went to bed many strange stories were told about "strange noises, cries for help, night walkers, somnambulists, Ghosts and hobgoblins."... [Marginalia: "I have since discovered the source of the noise. Ours was literally a 'wild goose chase.' This is the season for the flight of geese, and from a flock of these came the strange sound which startled us."]

We now go to bed, it being only two o'clock.

Thursday—Feb. 13th, 1851.

Morning cold and frosty. My nose looks like a drunken man's nose the day after a fight and feels as though some one had struck me on that prominent feature "Ker-diff." We went to the village for breakfast, and soon after Sam and Will Crawford started for Crawford's Cabin twenty miles distant. I went to work and stuck to it hard all day, making but two dollars and a half, whiles I paid $3.75 for board and cigars.

At an early hour after dark I came over to the cabin and wrote two or three paragraphs in this diary.

Now tis ten o'clock, the moon is in the fullness of her glory, shedding silvery rays on the cliffs of the mountains. My eyes are dim and I shall retire.

Friday—February 14th, 1851: St. Valentine's Day.

The only damsel to whom I to-day can send a Valentine is that fickle

---

[17]Henry Jacoby is listed in the 1850 census as a 28-year-old German-born merchant, living on the Middle Fork of the American River in January 1851. He later became a prominent businessman in Spanish Flat, El Dorado County. 1850 Census, El Dorado County, 467; Sioli, *El Dorado County*, 192.

beauty, Fortune, and I almost fear to trouble her, because she has for some time past been cross towards me... One year since I was busy in writing and receiving billet doux amours, this day I suppose I must keep my rocker busy. I would go to the ball at Pilot Hill House, but my nose is too much scarified. Cromwell, Col. Potter, Mas. Moss,[18] Morris, "Oregon," and Hopkins[19] are all going and wish me to go with them, but the Gods have forbidden and I must remain at home.

It is evening and the Bar delegation to the Ball, dressed in their best toggery, have started and are determined to uphold the reputation of the Village. Stuart and I have to stay in the village on account of the boat being on the opposite [side] of the river.

Saturday—Feby 15, 1851...

About 3 o'clock this afternoon the "hombres" who were at the ball returned and were pretty well "how came you so." This would sound badly at home, but it is a necessary consequence in California. They seemed in raptures with the affair, saying that it was one of the most pleasant affairs imaginable. California girls to the number of 57 were there, looking as beautiful as Sultanas, beside there were present several married ladies. Widow Gates[20] of Greenwood and Miss Leffingwell[21]

---

[18]Mason F. Moss, a native of Kentucky, was a Murderer's Bar saloon keeper in January 1851. Local historian Paoli Sioli lists Moss as one of the first two storekeepers in Murderer's Bar, together with E. C. Cromwell. Sioli, *El Dorado County*, 184; 1850 Census, El Dorado County, 467.

[19]William R. Hopkins, a native of New York, is listed in the 1850 census as operating a ferry on the Middle Fork of the American River (presumably the one at Murderer's Bar). He was elected to the state assembly in 1851, and later prospered as a Sacramento merchant. After his property was destroyed by fire in 1853, Hopkins returned to New York, where he became a member of Roscoe Conkling's political machine. 1850 Census, El Dorado County, 468; Bancroft, *California*, 6: 657; *San Jose Pioneer*, February, 1901: 23.

[20]Emily Gates, the daughter of Mormon leader Orrin Porter Rockwell, was reportedly abducted by Hiram Gates (see above 81n) who brought her to California and married her in 1849. The Gates settled in Greenwood Valley where Emily was the first white woman. Hiram was killed in the fall of 1850, apparently by Indians, but possibly by his father-in-law. The eighteen-year-old Emily is listed in the census as living in Greenwood Valley in January 1851. Davies, *Mormon Gold*, 113, 129, 267, Appendix 15c; Schindler, *Orrin Porter Rockwell*, 35; Sioli, *El Dorado County*, 186; 1850 Census, El Dorado County, 450.

[21]Probably Cynthia, the 18-year-old daughter of William Leffingwell, who had been a captain and high priest during the 1847 Mormon migration to Utah. In January 1851, Leffingwell and his wife were operating a hotel in the vicinity of Pilot Hill. Davies, *Mormon Gold*, 217-18; 1850 Census, El Dorado County, 474.

were married according to the Mormon Ritual. New idea this, of having weddings at Balls. Mrs. G. appeared in the ball room during the evening with three different dresses; Miss L. with two changes was content. Huzza for California. On the evening of the first of March another Ball is to take place at Harrison's on the mountain overlooking our village. I shall attend this one. By the way, tickets to the Pilot's Hill ball were a half ounce, and the six who went from here spent $6.00. Huzza a fudge.

Sunday, February 16th, 1851...

I rose with the sun and enjoyed his first beams, and after breakfasting took a bath and dressed for Sunday.

There is less working in the mines on Sunday than last year, but enjoyments are entered into with the same feeling as of yore. However, there is more conversation upon interesting subjects than at the time of my arrival in the State. Politics, Religion, Science and *so forth* are each discussed, and Preachers are more sought for, and books have more attention.

As beautiful as is this day, its charms are to a certain degree lost on me. I feel dull, stupid, insipid, can't read, can't write, can't play, can't— well what *can* I do? I never felt thus at home. Thank heaven I'm not homesick. The longer I remain here, the more I like the land; almost one year gone of the four I intend to remain.

In my remarks of Jany 5th I mentioned the change which had taken place since last season in the character of the community. I now have the pleasure of noting the return of many old residents of the correct stamp, as well as new ones who are a great addition to the Society of the Bar. This community will now rank with the highest mining community in California.

The Jumpers have been permitted to retain the bank leads, they being thought the legal owners as the banks had been deserted, but *now* they *claim* the *bed* of the river. This will cause much trouble as they say they will resort to force before they will yield. They have a troublesome body of men to contend with, brave and fearless to a fault, men who will rather die than be imposed upon. As it appears to my mind the question of ownership is most easily decided, yet the Jumpers of course advance reasons contrary to the opinions I hold.

Last fall, after the failure of the Racing enterprise, many persons who held leads on the banks conjointly with the bed of the river were so poor in purse that they were forced to desert their claims to search for winter-quarters, with good reasons deeming that they would not be able to work the river during the rainy season; yet, previous to their departure they took every precaution within their power which they deemed necessary to enable them to hold their claims until the next season for racing should open. They supposed that the fact of their having expended labor and money on their claims, and the general knowledge of their failure and intention to return at the proper time would cause their title to be respected, and as additional security posted notices to that effect on the very ground, the sum and substance of the notices being a declaration that the "claimant or claimants" intended to return at the proper time, &c. ["]to work the bed of the river."

During the latter part of December, a company of Missourians arrived on the bar and forthwith went to work on the above mentioned bank claims. To this there was little objection as the ground was public domain and unoccupied; but in addition to this they laid claim to the bed of the river which neither they nor any other person *could* work, and proceeded to let the job of racing for the summer to contractors. They laid claims to the river bed on the ground that it could not be a separate interest from the bank, that the bank and river were one and indivisible. Now, the very notices which they tore down were sufficient to show men who would listen to reason that the interests were separate and distinct, for they stated that "the undersigned intend returning at the proper season to work the bed of the river to construct a Dam and Race-way, etc." Every miner knows that one individual may hold a *bank* claim and another the *bed* of the stream. Those who take up original claims, often take *only* the *bed,* and allow any who choose to work the bank. Legal advice has been taken on the question, and decision given in favor of the old claimants. The matter may be decided by legal tribunal and may not. As I have said, the Jumpers declare their intention to hold possession vis et armis, and if they adhere to this determination, the affair will terminate in bloodshed and in their discomfiture.

Monday, February 17th.

Work was the order of this day, and I had some of the severest description such as moving boulders from a deep hole, &c. I was able only to wash 56 buckets of earth and my remuneration was $6.00. My next neighbor from 60 buckets recovered $14.00, and one next to him $12.00. This thing of working in a hole, digging dirt, rolling and lifting huge stones, carrying two heavy buckets of earth to the cradle some distance and there washing it, may be amusing and pleasant to some, but for me the practice is one I would willingly forgo if I could find other employment...

CHAPTER SIX

The Blue Cabin; Alone

Tuesday—February 18th. [1851].

This morning I awakened soon after day-break—cooked breakfast and prepared to set out for work, but the sky became clouded and rain set in. I therefore settled down and read awhile in Macaulay. About ten o'clock I went to work and had washed 3 buckets of earth when the rain again drove me away. I worked no more but busied myself reading papers which had just arrived from the States of date 26th Dec., '50 and Jany 1st, 1851... In my reading I am much like both matron and maid, looking first at "Marriage" and "death" lists. I presume all Californians from the States do likewise. In all the period since my landing in this country I have not seen more than a half dozen "Cincinnati Gazettes." This vexes me, as my old connection with that paper, and the long time it was our family journal, has made it more acceptable to me than all the other Citz papers together. I also have a private interest in wishing to obtain it as some of my humble epistles are therein honored with insertion.

In the New York Tribune of 11th December appeared the President's Message and accompanying Reports of the Heads of the different departments. In the first document and in several of the reports are made allusions to California, recommendations for the disposition of Mineral Lands, &c. There are several distinct propositions mentioned, such as 1st "dividing the lands into small lots and Leasing them," thus creating the distinction of Landlord and Tenant between the Government and miners, 2dly "dividing into lots and after advertisement selling to the highest bidder;" and thirdly, "that a certain per centage of the amount taken from the mines shall be paid to the Government." Some slight allusions are made with regard to allowing said Lands to remain as they are, "open in common to all." The first and third are objected to in all the reports, but the second seems to find favor, and only because no better plan has yet been devised.

Whether this proposition would be suitable to the purpose, should it be adopted as recommended, is to my mind a matter of question. Some of its features are very good, while on the other hand, some are decidedly objectionable. The recommendation is "that the lands be surveyed and divided into small lots, subject at first to an increased minimum, and after due public notice, shall be sold at Auction to the highest bidder. If at this time they should be unsold, they will be subjected to an increased minimum and sold in the usual way." The principal objection to this recommendation is the selling at Public auction. In the first place it will subject the mining district to the monopoly of Capital and will thus prevent the masses from enjoying the wealth of the country as freely and uninterruptedly as they might under other circumstances. Again it will interfere with the operations of the hundreds of thousands who are here seeking for competence and who have left pleasant homes in the hope of accumulating that which will increase their sum of happiness, or at least will enable them the more easily to meet the rough breakers on the ocean of life. Selling at auction will deprive the adventurous miner of much of his ambition, as it is necessary that he should have somewhat to stimulate him in his exertions. If he is aware that so soon as he shall have discovered a good "placer" after spending his money, and undergoing the severest hardships and hurculian toil, that government will step in and sell the very ground for which he has sacrificed so much to one who may possess more money than himself, his incentives will be gone. Thus the country itself will suffer, for, there being less inducement for the miner to search for "diggings," the resources of the country will remain undeveloped, this therefore will be so much loss to the State and to the whole country, as they are affected by individual success; but should these lands be divided into small lots and subjected to an increased minimum—not too great—and then sold to the finder or present possessor, there would be inducements for the emigrant, and I think there would be few to find fault with Government. The Government would then receive revenue for the lands, individual prosperity would be increased, and the state in a corresponding ratio be benefited. I prefer that the mineral lands should be held in common for the use of all.

I am now Solitary and alone in my cabin, Will Huntington having sent word that he intends remaining at Stony Bar. Sam Ayers has gone to him and Jim Stuart has taken up his abode in the Village, he preferring the *life* of such a place to the solitude of this. I have every day a chance to learn how deceiving are first impressions of persons, though the contrary is held. Jim Stuart I have and have not been deceived in. He, I know—and at first thought—to be a generous hearted fellow, but yet I was not aware as now that his disposition is not so lofty as I could wish. He is a *very* good companion for sportsmen, none whatever for me, though I would trust much to his honor. Will Huntington has a very limited education, but he is every inch a gentleman and one who has very few enemies. Sam Ayers is a mixed character, some of his qualities I like, and some I much dislike. I may say I have contempt for them. Much is owing to education, but nature shows itself in strong light. I never felt secure with him because I knew not what moment I would be compelled to strike him. I never could trust him. He is liberal according to the common acceptation of the term, but there are little things in him which occasionally show themselves that are not pleasing. Sam is a pretty good fellow to meet in a general crowd of men, but as a mess-mate and partner I do not like him. Very probably he thinks the same of me. He never could discriminate between a *suggestion* and a *fault-finding*; he always supposed the former to be the latter and frequently made considerable noise about "fault-finding," &c. and acted very much like a spoiled child on those occasions. I used to laugh at him when he would speak cross, though my fiery disposition tempted me to speak rather scornfully, and more particularly too as I had frequently controlled my temper in peculiar occasions, which made him think I was *afraid* of him. Ha! ha! I don't believe Sam is an *exceedingly* brave man, nor do I believe him a coward. Certain am I that I am glad we never had open rupture, for California quarrels generally end seriously; I always felt that it would be thus if I should have to meet him hand to hand. Thank fortune we parted friendly. Will Crawford was only a visitor and he is now absent.

To-night the sky is o'ercast and the rain drizzles on my canvas canopy, while the blaze of my pitch pine fire roars and crackles and sparkles cheerfully. My two tallow candles at the present moment have long knotted wicks which the dames of ancient times would say betokened letters for me. Pray heaven it may be so, for I have not received any of later date than Oct. 18th, 1850, "now four months wasted."

Wednesday, Feby 19th, 1851.

To-day the weather is wet, and therefore I shall not trouble mother earth about her gold, but shall content myself with Macauly *[sic]* until dinner time, and then will go to the village. By the way, I have been so exceedingly unfortunate as to lose my valuable and trusty companion, my gold pen; what *shall I do* without it? I have examined every pocket of my clothes, and have searched back and forth over the ground which I passed yesterday, but the pen, as the lawyers would say, is non est inventus. I'd almost as soon scrape with a stick as to try to write with this abominable iron stylus, but as there's no other resort I presume I must make the best of circumstances...

Thursday—Feby 20th.

Beautiful day. I worked from morn till dewy eve, and made $6.00.

To-night I have been reading the Secretary of Treasury's report (Thos. Corwin).[1] I was deeply interested, and consider it one of the ablest documents of its nature which I have ever perused.

Friday—Feby 21st, 1851.

Raining again this morning. This California weather is as fickle and capricious as some women I have met in my time. At night when one retires the sky is clear and the stars sparkle with brilliancy; morning comes and is dark and drear as a wintry morn in the far north; or it is the converse, night dark and gloomy, and morning clear and bright as a morning in September at home. Of all places in all this wide world, in rainy weather save me from a situation in the mines of California. Everything is wet, drizzling, and muddy; everything has a sombre, downcast look; ground in cabins and tents wet and sloppy; water drip-

---

[1]A former congressman, Ohio governor, and senator, Thomas Corwin (1794-1865) served as Fillmore's secretary of the treasury, and was U.S. minister to Mexico during the Civil War. *DAB.*

ping from the eves; wind blowing in disagreeably from every crack and corner; every living animal one sees: horse, mule, or ox, drizzles and steams, and steams and shivers, hold down tails, hold down head, looking stupid and senseless; every *man* is either covered with mud up to his hips and soaked with water to the skin, (there's generally too much whisky within the skin to allow water to permeate), or he is encased in long legged boots and a suit of nasty, sticky gutta percha or oil cloth from which the water runs off in streams, forming behind him as he travels a perfect little brook; in the bar-rooms and stores the stench of wet garments by the fire, whisky and old pipes is similar to a hospital not well kept;—a German Beer house would be Paradise to such a place—cards are turned up and liquor down; money turned out of a wet purse on the gambling table and not turned in again, and, to bring up the whole affair, perhaps two or three coves may be seen lying about in different corners dead drunk. Save me from such things as I have witnessed, and from those miserable feelings I have experienced *several* times this winter. I am really happy when I return from the village to my lonely habitation, for here I can do as I please, meeting with none of those disagreeable scenes, and can pass the time agreeably by reading or thinking! without being disturbed.

Saturday, Febry 22nd, 1851…

Saturday evening again, and I am very much fatigued, having labored incessantly since early dawn, and have made only $6.00. Better this than nothing. I must retire and rest.

Sunday, February 23d, 1851.

I did not rise very early this morning, but after I did I got breakfast, mended my "unmentionables," took a nice bath, dressed myself, pulled on my long legged boots, tramped over to the village, shaved myself, bought a new shirt, and then took a bird's eye view of affairs to discover what was in the wind. The first discovery I made was that there was an unusual number of persons in the village; the next that their business was to attend a meeting of the Murderer's Bar Company; and next that there was a female (I can't call her a woman) dressed in a man's costume on the bar. Some of the green 'uns who had not seen anything like a woman for a long time stood around with eyes open and mouth agape, staring at her as though she were one of the seven wonders. She came in company with a gambler, astride of a horse a la homme and as they started her fellow said of her, "if *she* were placed on a wild mustang horse, *she* would be at home." ...

The meeting held on the Bar to-day was one of the most interesting and exciting which has been there held for a long time. The avowed object of the meeting was for the purpose of settling the controversy between the old claimants and the Jumpers. I soon discovered by the series of resolutions proposed to the meeting that there was a scheme laid for the purpose of depriving the old members of the Bar of their rights; that the articles were most speciously glossed; but the tail of the devil stuck out of the not perfectly closed door. Mr. Phetteplace attacked the resolutions with such a hearty good will, that the new party soon began to shy off. The whole affair was finally settled by the adoption of some resolutions and the appointment of a judicial tribunal to whom those cases of disputed claims on the Bar are to be referred. Thus is one grand difficulty removed, and I hope the meeting next Saturday will bring to a close this series of disturbances.

After the meeting, Morris and I walked up the Hill and called on Miss Sally Mayfield, at Shelton's.[2] This is the first young lady whom I have visited in California, and I am constrained to say that I did not reap much satisfaction therefrom. The house, being used as an "Inn," was crowded with strangers, and all the chat I could hold with her was by snatches. I soon discovered that she was not afraid to look at a man, but she was evidently afraid to talk with a stranger. She is quite a nice look- ing country girl, with all their hoydenish actions, and don't know how to talk about anything of sense, unless it be about the cows and farm affairs, and I am inclined to think she'd consider a fellow green who would talk about such things... Sally Mayfield is a "purty" nice gal, however, and cooks well. But didn't I put the milk down; and the fresh butter too, the first I have had since I left Mrs. Jones' *hospitable* mansion, among the Santa Cruz Mountains. One thing kind o' stuck me here, I called on the lady, took tea with her, praised the old lady's butter, the young lady's bread, said all manner of nice things about the kitchen fixens, &c., and

---

[2]Sebert C. Shelton, a veteran of the Mormon Battalion, and his wife, Elizabeth, kept a hotel in the Pilot Hill vicinity in January 1851. With them lived the four Mayfields, Elizabeth's chil- dren by a previous marriage, the youngest of whom was 16-year-old Sarah (Sally), together with Elizabeth's four younger children by Sebert. 1850 Census, El Dorado County, 474; Davies, *Mor- mon Gold*, 140-42.

then had to pay for my supper in the bargain. Oh the ways of this wicked world! But the practice of going to see the girls is a good one and I shall keep it up. I shall dance with Sally at the Ball next Saturday night if nothing occurs to prevent.

I had a severe time returning as the night was very dark and the path quite rough. Lost once or twice, but finally succeeded in reaching the village, where I had to remain all night, the boat being this side the river. I slept with Jim Stuart and Jo. C. who was drunk, and a sweet time I had of it... I had the night-mare, and looked to have frozen and sundry other evils too numerous to mention.

Monday, 24th Febry.

Rain all day. I staid in the village until almost night, smoking cigars, playing eukre and domino, amounting to nothing at all.

Jemmy McWilliams came up from the Junction to see me, and told me how tired he was of the country, and how he intended to leave the d—d place so soon as he could get enough money. Poor Jemmy, he is not a philosopher. I believe I am. At all events I have been so unlucky that I am determined to have revenge.

Tuesday—February 25th.

Sky all clear again this morning and a heavy frost whitens the earth.

I worked very hard during the morning and made only $1.40. I did not say much but thought a great deal upon my ill success, and was musing upon it after returning to my cabin, and soon after there arriving I had the good fortune to find my pen. Glory enough for one day, thought I, though I worked in the afternoon and made sufficient to amount for the day to $4.00.

Wednesday—Febry 26th, 1851...

I imagined upon rising that it was quite early, but what was my surprise when I looked forth to find the sun far above the mountain top which answers me in lieu of a time-piece. My cabin, not having a window, is very dark and thus my deception. I could not accomplish much, thought I, in the way of digging, and therefore concluded to pass the time until noon chopping wood.

After dinner I went to work and made $2.35.

Thursday—Febry 27th.

This morning I made sure of rising early enough, and at sunrise was digging away as though my fortune depended on the day's labor. Soon after, a friend of mine, Perry Simpson, a young Georgian,[3] came down and asked if I wanted assistance, and, [I] not objecting, he began, and at night-fall we had washed 90 buckets of dirt and made $10.00. One of our neighbors made over an ounce. *Sich is luck,* for he did not labor as much as we.

The village continues to increase in size, and though it has not so great a population, yet there are many more houses and tents than during last summer. To-day was quite an era in the history of the place, on account of the immigration of an old man with four daughters who came to keep a boarding house. As they entered the village all hands set up a yell of welcome. First one, then another, and so on ad infinitum. Wonder the poor *"gals"* weren't scared, but this is the way things are done in this country. It does good to the male part of creation in this wild region to see any of the fair sisterhood... The "b'hoys" have now something about which to talk, and to-night will there be much conversation relating to the grand addition to our population. If a real genuine lady should happen to drop among us and pay us a visit, I believe she would receive more genuine homage and see the exhibition of more real politeness than she ever even imagined could exist...

The town's agog with regard to the Ball at Harrison's next Saturday night. The boys are beginning seriously to think of throwing off their old mining clothes and putting on new toggery for the occasion. Fine shoes and boots, white shirts, etc., etc., are in great demand.

There was quite an excitement day before yesterday, 25th, which I forgot to note, about town lots. A German Jew named Jacoby, who keeps a store in the village, has been taking up all the vacant ground upon which he could step his foot for speculative purposes. This property, belonging to Uncle Sam, is open to any one when not possessed by another. An old man had gotten on to a lot which the Jew claimed, and he wished to eject the occupant, the public said no, and the matter ended.

---

[3]Probably James P. Simpson, a 24-year-old native of Georgia, listed in the 1850 census as a miner living on the Middle Fork of the American River in January 1851. 1850 Census, El Dorado County, 467.

Saturday, March 1st, 1851.

At a very early hour this morning I was digging and rocking for the purpose of making sufficient money to defray my expenses at the Ball on the hill to-night. Perry S. came down at half past eight and we worked with a will until dinner hour, at which time we "knocked off" for refreshments; and upon weighing our dust found that we had $14.00.

At this time I found the young hombres of our community in a state of excitement making preparations for the dance, purchasing new shoes, new boots, white or "chawed shirts," pants, coats, etc., &c. and generally shaving. It was quite amusing to see those who were tolerably dressed for the first time in California, strutting about the town "large as life and twice as natural." Some did not know how to walk and others would not sit, and one fellow threw off his coat, swearing he would wait until night before he put on his miseries.

After dinner we washed 40 buckets of earth, and made $10.00, and then I prepared myself for "*Le Bal*," all about which I must reserve for

Sunday, March 2d, 1851

Well! about the Ball. At dusk last eve a goodly number of the population of Murderer's Bar, "rigged in holiday attire," set out upon their toilsome march up the mountain side, full of enthusiasm and joyous anticipation for the pleasures of the evening; my friend, Phetteplace and I in the rear rank of the column but in the vanguard of the hopeful. The shades of evening gathered thickly around us before we accomplished the ascent, and the consequence was that we had no little difficulty in clambering the steeps, tumbling over logs, brush heaps and stones, but Fortune befriended us, and we escaped without bruises, our clothes without rents, and our boots without tarnish, and arrived at Harrison's in good time to discover all that was passing in a thickly crowded assemblage of Miners, Farmers, Gentlemen Gamblers, and Traders.

Upon first entering the room where the bottles containing the substance with the invisible spirit of wine shone from shelves circling in a corner, I discovered the majority of the male part of the company toasting each other in bumpers of Milk Punch, Brandy Cocktails, dry Whiskey and Brandy Straight; putting the Spirit down to keep the spirits up. In the corner to the left as I entered the door I discovered the "Old Man" and Ans. Sawyer dealing forth monte and catching the "boys" in the door; opposite to them, on the right, sat another individual bolstered up on two tobacco boxes, turning for the cards a la "Vingt et un" to a solitary individual; the game being only for "suckers," and very few of them being there, it went off rather slowly; opposite this table in the back part of the Whisky apartment, occupying a sly corner, sat a little cunning looking, black eyed customer, with his tricks spread out numbering 1.2.3.4.5.6., and in his hand, his dice box, playing at the celebrated game, Chuck-a-luck. This was also for suckers, but all present seemed to know that the more money they put down, just so much less would they take up. Here was my first introduction to the ball: cards, whiskey, and dice; laughing, talking, and swearing.

From this place I sauntered into the sanctuary or Ball room, which was tolerably well suited for the occasion, being large enough for two cotillions at once, though I must say I have seen many barns in the Buckey[e] State which surpassed it in appearance immeasurably. I met my friend, Dr. Piggott, one of the managers, on first entering, and was informed that the band for the occasion had failed to appear according to appointment, and that the d-l was to pay because of the want of music. The whole establishment was soon in a perfect uproar, and messengers were dispatched to the "Bar" to get a fiddle and a fiddler, and all hands dispatched themselves to the *Bar-Room* to "fire up." I entered the dining room and discovered some of the party making up for lost time over a tolerable supper; here Mons. Harrison[4] was sweating and swearing and half crying over his disappointment, and laying all the fault to the managers. Well, this was the first blight to my hopes.

About 9 o'clock the *fiddle* came from the Bar but no *fiddler;* fortunately for all assembled, one of the guests volunteered and "all our stern alarums changed to merry greetings." Each ticket to the ball was numbered and consisted of pieces of Eukre cards, entitling each gent to his supper and a dance when his number was called.

At last the curtains before the ladies' dressing room raised, and the fairy procession glided gracefully into the room, and to the benches

---

[4]Isaac Harrison, an Ohio native, had come to California in 1847 as a member of the Mormon Battalion. In January 1851, he and his Scottish-born wife, Catherine, were listed in the census as managing a "hotel" in the vicinity of Pilot Hill. Bancroft, *California,* 3: 777; 1850 Census, El Dorado County, 475; Davies, *Mormon Gold,* 74.

along the wall, there awaited the attention of the beaux. First there was Mrs. Brizee, lately the widow of the Mormon Elder Gates, and now a new made bride. She headed the procession of ladies as if by right due to experience and some degree of beauty. Her figure was tall, well-formed, and rather muscular; her hair, brown, teeth white, eyes indescribable, the principal features being boldness, impudence, scornfulness and lasciviousness; complexion fair, cheeks rosy, and lips looking as though they would be nice to the taste. Her voice was rather masculine; her hands and feet neither very large or very small; in short they were what might be termed sizable. Mrs. B. was attired in a figured purple silk dress which fitted her well formed person with exactness, her neck was bare, but not too much so for delicacy; her hair "done up" very simply and plainly; her fingers ornamented with several brilliant rings, and her feet encased in an elegant pair of ladies' cloth and patent leather booties. Her "tout ensemble" was very good. Unfortunately for her general praise, the expression of her features were too closely scanned by most of those present. This is more the case with Californians than with any other people with whom I have met; they always judge of women by the expression of the countenance in connection with the slightest action. All countenance readers do this, but the Californian is *always* studying the countenance.

Mrs. Burns came next and, though not possessing the same striking appearance of the leader, she won much more upon the regard of the gallants of the party by her pleasant, smiling countenance and womanly demeanor. Mrs. B. the 2d was dressed in striped lawn with frills and ruffles, and her hair arranged with more skill than that of her leader. She was my favorite among the married ladies.

Mrs. Tubbs or, as I termed her in one of my moods, Mrs. O'Tubbs, was a strapping big country g-i-r-l, who looked as though she could chop wood, shoulder a barrel of Beer, or thrash her husband at will. She was about as tall as myself, 5 ft 9 in, though rather stooping, had a face as large as a full moon and almost as round, a nose like the plate of a sundial, eyes the color of whey and *feet and hands*, my eyes but how does she manage to turn over in bed! Mrs. T. was dressed in striped calico with flounces and ribbands to a degree before unchronicled; three flaming red ribbands hung gracefully down from her hair, which was fastened into a knot something like a chanticleer's comb on the top of her head; from her ears were suspended two massive specimens of gold, and her fingers glistened with a large gold ring with a glass setting.

Another lady whose name I did not learn came *fourth* and *forth*, and with her appearance I was much pleased. She wore a mouselin Le Laine with flounces, tight sleeves, and low in the neck, but over her shoulders was thrown a black silk mantilla which set her off to advantage; after her appeared another of the fairer part of creation of the Mrs. O'Tubb school, though *not quite so much so,* the main difference I conceive consisting in this, that one was married and the other single; bless me how she did squeeze my hand when I swung her in the dance, and her hand was harder than mine own; but that was not in anywise to her discredit for she doubtless has made her hands hard in striving for fortune. Behind this one was a lass of 14 or 15 summers, dressed in white linen, with light yellow hair tied up with red ribbons. Her feet were her distinguishing features, they being so large that the bottom circle of her dress was not capable of covering them, but she couldn't help that.

Finally came the star of attraction, the last, and the least in size but the first in consideration, Sallie Mayfield, upon whom I called last Sunday evening, [who] appeared in a dress "a la Grisette," white skirt with green bodice, which became her petite figure very much. Her hair was arranged simply without ornament, and no jewelry marred the beauty of her face or pretty little hands; and her feet, small and delicately formed for one in her station of life, were encased in stockings of matchless white and little black slippers.

Mrs. Harrison, the hostess, was mostly confined to the kitchen but danced when called upon. Eight ladies only were present, a grievous disappointment to all, as there were present perhaps one hundred gents. All the ladies but one or two were of the Mormon Faith. Of the gents I cannot speak in such particular manner as of the ladies, as it would fill my Journal were I to do so. There were Mormons with long hair tied up with ribbands like a woman's, generally fantastically dressed, having numerous stars, crescents, &c. stuck in their coats, hats, &c., and one of them, the Lord of Mrs. *Brass-ee* (Brizee) appeared in black velvet pantaloons (I forget the Spanish name for them) open to the knees and garnished with silver buttons placed about 1/4 of an inch apart.

Of the attire of the gentlemen I cannot speak at length, but will notice the most conspicuous personages of the company. My friend, Dr. Piggott, one of the Managers, was plainly but well attired, and would not have been considered as outré in any company. A few others were also dressed in the same manner, viz. cloth coats and pants, white (or "chawed shirts") and nice boots or shoes; such were Dr. Whitely, Jno. Palmer, and myself. Dr. Flewellen[5] of Georgia, in lieu of a dress coat wore his white blanket, and on his head a white wool cap with black brim turned up all around a la Polka. The Dr.'s tall figure stood a head and shoulders above the crowd. Will. Crawford appeared in a dark cloth overcoat, cassimere Pants and calico shirt. Jim. Stuart swore he was the best dressed man in the crowd being attired in the tallest kind of a pair of boots into which his unwhisperables were thrust en militaire, a calico shirt, (no cravat) and a white wool "roundabout." McDermot appeared with red top boots, his pants being shoved into the tops, a la B'hoy. O Moses, how McD'd shake those feet! Some of the hombres had no coats and some short rounnabouts[*sic*]; some were in their mining clothes, and many in the only suit which they possessed; but all wore clean shirts. Some of the *tallest* specimens of boots I ever have seen showed their fair proportions "in the mazy windings of the dance["], and chick shirts, calico, flannel, and "chawed" shirts, met and parted, and circled round about the room like the sails of a schooner in a gale.

About nine o'clock the music struck up a lively tune, numbers 1.2.3.4.5.6.7. and 8 were called, and gents representing these advanced and chose their partners. Two cotillions were formed and soon "all went merry as a marriage bell." It was rare fun to see the large feet of the elegant Mistress Tubbs "flitting in the dance," and what tickled me most was that my friend the honest but gruff Jim. Stuart had her in tow, and he, not exactly understanding the steps and cotillions according to her notions, received sundry scowls and frowns with now and then a jerk

---

[5]Dr. Robert Turner Flewellen (1821-99) a native of Georgia, graduated from the medical department of the University of New York in 1845. The following year he began practicing medicine in his home town of Culloden, Georgia, specializing in orthopedic surgery. In 1851 Flewellen departed for California, partly, according to Bickham, because of having killed a man in a fight, and he arrived in San Francisco by steamer in June of that year. In 1853 he moved to Texas where he served in the state legislature and as president of the Texas Medical Association. Daniell, *Types of Successful Men of Texas*, 237-8; Webb, *Handbook of Texas*, 1: 611; Rasmussen, *Passenger Lists*, 1: 35; below 158-59.

from the fair one for his awkwardness. I saw him wince and grin several times and once heard him grunt. I went into the Bar-room to laugh then, and did not see him again until after that dance when he told me that he "was struck after that woman." "Oh," said Jim, "she's a 'fit woman' and knows how to dance as well as to look dark." The next cotillions were called and I enjoyed myself exquisitely looking at the participants. Mr. Bisee [*sic*] shook his buttons with a vengeance, and I thought several times would have kicked the delicate shins of the ladies. If he had been so unfortunate as to have touched Mrs. T. there would have been a row. I now procured my ticket which chanced to be number 16, and forthwith engaged Sallie Mayfield whom I observed danced elegantly and demeaned herself with lady-like propriety. I told her my number was "sweet sixteen" and she accepted; not the numbers but the representative, with charming naiveté.

Soon my number was called to fill the place of an hombre not ready for the dance and I was sorry to find Sallie engaged in the other cotillion. Dr. Piggott advanced with me to Mrs. Tubbs. (horror, thought I, though submitting to the last alternative with grace). The acquaintance does me honor, said I, but Mrs. O'Tubbs, will you do me the honor of accepting me as a partner for this cotillion? *"Yes I will,"* quoth the amiable, "but my name ain't O'Tubbs, it's Mrs. Tubbs, T-u-b-b-s." I apologized but was very near making a worse mistake by calling her Mrs. Wash-Tubbs… However I escorted the lady to the floor and was soon being whirled about in the giddy trance. I danced about her, up to her and around her, but she danced harder than I. Once I was chatting with Sallie in the other cotillion when it was my turn to swing, but did not here [*sic*] the call. The pleasant Mrs. T. caught me by the arm and gave me a whirl which made my head swim and said, "Young man, please tend to your business." My dear Mrs. O'Tubbs, quoth I, squeezing her hand tenderly, I won't offend you again. My appeal was touching and the lady afterwards said I danced very well. She gave Will Crawford a lecture after the same fashion, but he looked so thunderingly at her that she didn't try it again. I poured soft nonsense into the lady's ear until she thought I was a "proper young man."

The next amusing circumstance which I witnessed was the tall, spare, though graceful figure of Dr. Flewellen bending and bowing over the short little miss with the white dress, red ribbands, and big feet. The Dr. looked as grave as a sexton, though occasionally I could see something like laughter in his eye. However, his gentlemanly Southern breeding prevented an ebullition. Good Lord, but how the little witch did dance! Her feet would glance out by the side of her dress like the oar blades of a skiff handled by strong rowers. I saw the bottom of the right foot *every* time, but the left foot "nary" time. I did think for a while that she didn't move the left one at all.

During this time the ball did not progress so harmoniously as all wished. The Mormons took too much upon themselves and crowded out all they could who were not of their own party, and several times I looked for a general row, but fortunately none occurred, though the humbug ball gave very decided and general dissatisfaction. The bar was far better patronized than the dance, for there was heard a constant jingling of glasses, and rattling of bottles. Whilst the ladies were resting, the gentlemen got up "Buck Reuben" or "Stag Cotillions" and had quite a merry time, and, by way of changing the performance, we had one or two hoe-down trial dances and several hornpipes. At two o'clock the ladies departed, and with them the glory of the evening. I went with Mrs. Tubbs to the door to say good night and wish her happy dreams, and rec'd an invitation "to call." Yes I will, thought I, *in a horn!* A number of the Bar delegation started at the same time, but I thought it too dark to venture down the mountain and with a half dozen others sat before the fire until daylight. Oh "sich" a Ball, and it was only a *little* expensive. However, I had plenty of fun and made the valuable acquaintance of Mrs. O'Tubbs.

Sunday, March 2d, 1851...

At sun-rise I came down the hill and took a few hours repose, and then went back to the Sheltons on the hill to see Sallie Mayfield and drink buttermilk. Col. Potter, Mason Moss and Jim. Stuart went up also to bid farewell to Col. Suffron, an old resident of the Bar. The Col. left last fall but came up yesterday from the city on a visit. At Harrison's we gave him welcome and he responded in a speech to which I was delegated by the assembled company to make response. After this the Col., who is a fine singer, sang several fine songs; among the rest, "Woman,

Dear Woman." Such songs as this are great favorites with Californians. They love to talk, sing, and think of that part of creation with whose presence they are not blessed so much as they wish. I warrant me Californians are the most gallant men to ladies in the known world. In due time we adjourned to Shelton's where the Colonel sang several more songs, and then he and Jim Stuart drank buttermilk whilst I talked to Sallie. At just about the same hour one year ago I was smothering a good bye to _____, my sweetheart! I wonder if she's married yet. I hope not, for I want her myself, and *will* have her if she doesn't get tired of waiting. But—the rest of the party seeing me so well engaged and wishing to grant me indulgence, proposed waiting for supper, consequently, I luxuriated on milk and fresh butter at tea and did not get down the break-neck Mountain until the deep shades of night had darkened the land. I crossed the river, fell over the stones in my path sundry times on my way to the Blue Cabin, and after arriving bade the world good-night, and left it for a few hours to make a journey to the dream land, which is now my dear old home on the Banks of the Ohio.

Monday—March 3d,

I was up at an early hour and at work, was driven to shelter by rain. At ten o'clock the sky was clear, went to work with Perry S. and we made $4.00 each, a falling off from Saturday.

Sunday—March 9th, 1851.

During the past week I have not kept up my Journal daily as previously on account of other engagements such as writing letters and reading late Papers from the Atlantic, moreover there has nothing of interest transpired within the circle of my observations. I worked during the week a portion of the time assisted by Perry S. and part of the time alone. Perry injured himself lifting large rocks and was compelled to retire from labor. The weather after Monday morning was very warm, though exceedingly pleasant.

This morning, after taking a bath in the river and mending my clothes, I "dressed up" and went to the village where I passed off a portion of the time chatting with the two girls, Fanny and Jenny. I enjoyed myself passing well, although I felt melancholy to a degree, thoughts of home forcing themselves on my unwilling spirit; and in addition thoughts of discouragements numerous had a saddening effect. The day was warm and pleasant, and the sky filled with light hazy clouds. About 10 P.M. I returned home and went to sleep.

Monday, March 10th.

To-day I have been very unwell and consequently have not worked. This evening I feel somewhat better, but am low spirited and feel lonely, and there is no company in the whole of California of which I can think which to-night could dissipate the clouds which enshroud my spirit.

Sunday, March 16th.

The past week rolled away much like the preceding one, nothing worthy of note having occurred saving the departure of two Monte Dealers, old residents of the Bar, for their homes, having about $2500.00 between them. Cromwell also opened his new house. His bar is decidedly pretty and is the most tastefully arranged of any that I have seen in the Mines. Tracy, his partner, our newly elected Justice of the Peace, stands behind the counter to pour out the liquid. Torrence with his wife have a "Vingt et un" table, and the two young hombres deal Monte on the south side of the establishment. The ten pin alley is not finished.

This morning after a bath, "dressing up," taking a fragrant Habana, &c., I seated myself by the fire and read Mrs. Ellet's criticism of Schiller's writings.[6] At ten o'clock I repaired to Reid and Byrd's, there to attend a meeting of the Dulany Company. I was elected Secretary and also a committee man, very much against my desires; and made several speeches on matters of vital importance to the interest of myself and several members. I opposed an odious resolution, and was fortunate enough to defeat it, but thereby got the ill will of two or three of the Missouri "Jumpers." After the meeting I repaired to the Bar and took dinner at Hamilton's.[7]

At 3 o'clock Dr. Piggott, Moss, Col. Potter and myself beside two or three others went to Phillips and proceeded to the female department

---

[6]Elizabeth Fries Ellet (1818-77) was a literary critic, translator of German, French, and Italian literature, and the author of works on the achievements of American women. The book to which Bickham refers is apparently *The Characters of Schiller* (1839).

[7]Probably David Hamilton, a 28-year-old hotel keeper, born in Massachusetts, living near Pilot Hill in January 1851. 1850 Census, El Dorado County, 473.

and had quite a lively little tea-party with Mrs. Lannus and her daughters, Fanny and Jenny, and Mrs. P. Several bottles of wine were destroyed, and Mrs. P. was *very* near being tipsy. After laughing, chatting, &c. until near Sunset, Dr. P., Col. P., Charley Parsons[8] and myself all went to Shelton's on the top of the mountain to get some milk and see Sallie. I went particularly to see the latter. We destroyed numerous quarts of buttermilk until it was used up and then went to work on the sweet milk. At supper the company enjoyed a hearty laugh at the expense of Charley Parsons and myself. Some sweet potatoes meshed into a sort of a hash were placed before us in a bowl, and we, thinking them to be sugar, sweetened our coffee with them. I was making signs to Sallie at the time, but still thought something was out of order in Mrs. Shelton's housewifery, as never before had I noticed such stringy, sticky sugar placed on the table, nor in truth anything else out of order. The sweet potato jest had its rounds, and I enjoyed it as well as any, laying all the fault on Sallie. We arrived on the Bar at 9 o'clock.

---

[8]Charles Parsons, a 29-year-old New Yorker, is listed in the 1852 census as living in El Dorado County, and was Whig candidate for county coroner in 1853. 1852 California Census, El Dorado County, 148; *Union,* August 8, 1853.

CHAPTER SEVEN

Last Months in Murderer's Bar

Monday, March 17th, 1851.

This morning I took a partner in my claim and we worked until 3 PM when I went to Col. Potter's and Lewis's hotel to a public dinner given to the Bar on the occasion of opening the establishment.

Tuesday I commenced boarding at the new Hotel at $12.00 per week, being heartily tired of keeping Bachelor's Hall. Bruce[1] and I made a half ounce each to-day.

The town is quite full of strangers; Monte dealers and others.

A grand jumping match came off after supper in front of Moss's round tent between all who wished to engage. Col. Potter pitted me against the field for an ounce. Cromwell selected one of his partners, Torrence, and I beat him nearly two feet...

Saturday 22d.

Was clear and pleasant, but I worked only during the morning. During the afternoon I attended to business pertaining to the Delany [*sic*] Company

This evening I notice a considerable increase in our population. Among the new comers were Wm. Fay, a tall young Irishman, the antagonist of Jim Stuart in the prize fight which is to take place during the summer, also his trainer, Tom. Gayner, a tremendously built man, a very giant in frame; in addition, a short, thick-set shoulder-striker traveling in company. They issued bills this evening of an exhibition to be given

---

[1]Possibly George Bruce, a 36-year-old Scottish-born miner living on the Middle Fork of the American River in January 1851. He was probably the George Bruce listed in the 1870 census as a 55-year-old laborer living at Placerville. 1850 Census, El Dorado County, 468; 1870 Census, El Dorado County, 120.

to-morrow afternoon at Tammany Hall, viz. Cromwell's. Just before they came into town there occurred 5 grand fisticuff engagements in dead earnest between several belligerent individuals of this place. Damages, several black eyes and bloody noses. After dark the fancy "shoulder strikers" had a grand spree, singing songs and "making night hideous."

Sunday, March 23d, 1851.

After taking a bath this morning I went forth to see what was going on in the *city*, and passed the time until the dinner gong rattled with the girls at the Illinois house. After eating an excellent dinner I went to Tammany Hall and witnessed the first sparring match in my life. I had considerable amusement in seeing others knocked about, and finally put on the gloves myself, having for my antagonist a large, heavy framed German. I knocked him down twice, receiving one scratch on the nose in return, when we agreed to quit. During the evening I enjoyed myself in the same manner, knocking down one antagonist and getting some sound raps myself.[2] Singular employment for me on Sunday. Shame!

Rain again to-night and disagreeably cold.

Monday. Rained after dinner. I have felt so lonely and half miserable for several weeks past that my Journal has been sadly neglected.

Tuesday. Clear. Made $8.00 to-day.

Wednesday. Rain. Weather miserably unpleasant. The only warm place in town is in bed. I never have suffered so much with cold as during the last 10 days; not sharp, piercing cold which bites, but cold which chills the blood and causes that most unpleasant of all sensations, a chilly shivering.

Thursday. Rain and snow with a perfect hurricane of wind.

Towards sunset, the sky is clear and the hombres of the town, like chickens, are out sunning themselves and "sky-larking." ...

Saturday, April 5th, 1851

During the past week much rain has fallen, and I have been unable to work but three days. Yesterday the river rose 8 or 10 feet and came booming down its channel in wild fury. I never saw such a terrible rain storm

---

[2]Bickham continued to enjoy boxing after his return to Ohio. In the later 1850s, while working for the *Cincinnati Commercial,* he and his editor, Murat Halstead, regularly repaired to Murphy's Gym to "put on gloves." According to Bickham's son, Daniel, "none in the county could beat them." DMCL Bickham Collection, "High Spots."

as that which occurred about 2 o'clock of that day. My boarding house was flooded, a small mountain torrent having bursted its way through the canvass sides. Not a comfortable place was to be found save in bed.

I have had much sport upon the clear days, skylarking with my companions of this neighborhood, running races, jumping, &c. I have proven to be the best Jumper on the Bar and am believed to be as good at running as the best. To-morrow I try my speed with *one* of the best. Rivalry.

About ten o'clock to-night whilst sitting in Tammany Hall, some four or five men came running in, all breathless and pale, stating that they had been running for their lives from the Indians, who had come upon them suddenly in their camp at Brown's Bar, 27 miles above this place, and that some of their companions were slain. They stated that they were encamped at the lower end of the Bar, and that from the one camp above one of their friends had come running down, naked all to his shirt with face all pale and covered with dirt, shouting to them to "save themselves, for God's Sake, that the Indians were upon them." Thereupon, they started off in a fright; being unarmed they thought running away to be the best plan. It was agreed immediately after the story was heard that a party of men should start for their Bar from here, early to-morrow morning, to hunt the murderers whoever they might be. All hands then retired preparatory to an early adventure.

Sunday, Apl. 6th, 1851.

This morning, according to the resolution last night, we began to prepare ourselves for an Indian Hunt. We assembled at the Eldorado Saloon and, just about the time the party were ready to start, a man came down from Brown's Bar and informed us that the whole affair was nothing but a hoax.

Tuesday, April 8th, 1851.

Sunday was a clear and beautiful day, and with exception of the Indian Volunteer excitement in the morning, passed off as it usual[ly] passes in our Village. In the afternoon I heard two temperance addresses and after supper witnessed and shared the glory of several foot races. I was picked up for a "Sardine" in running and beat the best of the runners.

Monday afternoon was stormy and in consequence there was no labor.

This morning it rained some little, but about 10 o'clock the sky became clear and I worked all day. John came over from Bear River to take up his residence at this place.

Wednesday is clear and warm. A good day's work was done by Bruce, John, and myself. Quite an exciting case came up this morning before Esquire Tracy. The Plaintiff sued for damages and prayed the ejectment against sundry individuals who had jumped his "claims." Defendant denied the charge and urged that the said "claims" had been deserted last Fall and had not since been taken up by Plaintiff, that they were open to all comers. The jury looked very much like a packed jury to me, and, as I suspected, returned verdict in favor of Plaintiff. A new feature in judicial proceedings was presented in this trial. The jury had agreed, and the Foreman, upon announcing the verdict, stated that "We the Jury give our verdict (*which I consider a most unjust* one) in favor of the Plaintiff." ...

Wednesday, Apl. 23d, 1851.

Nothing worthy of a place in my Journal having occurred for many days, I have passed over the time in silence. The weather has been varied, though for the greater part of the time it has been wet, cold, and extremely disagreeable. I have suffered much with a severe pain in my right side. I attribute it to the constant use of the shovel at my mining operations. I have made only sufficient money to pay current expenses, and see but little to encourage me in the hope of making more.

To-day I have been unable to work, and John informs me that our claim is exhausted. I think I shall on Monday next bid farewell to the Bar and proceed to Sacramento, there to try my fortune.

I this evening received a letter from home of date Nov. 21st, 1850, containing an account of the serious accident which befell my sister Eliza[3] and her alarming illness following it. This is the only letter I have received during five months, and the tidings which it has brought have made me feel sad, very sad. I think I am on the path pointed out by duty, yet when I hear evil tidings from home, I fear that I may be wrong in being away...

---

[3]Bickham's third sister, Eliza, sometimes called "Lida," was eleven at the time of the 1850 census. During the later 1850s she taught school in Cincinnati. She later married a Mr. "Lair," and was still alive at the time of her brother's death. 1850 Census, Springfield, Hamilton Co., Ohio: 130; Cincinnati City directories: 1859, 1860; DMCL Bickham Collection, "Biographical Notes;" *Dayton Daily Journal*, March 28, 1894.

Thursday, April 24th, 1851...

I judge this morning from appearances of the horizon that the Dry Season has commenced. The air is very clear, and the weather is very warm and beautiful. The last rain we have had was on Monday afternoon, Apl. 21st.

This evening the Whigs held a meeting at Stuart & Gaynor's Round Tent, and the Loco-Focos[4] met at "Tammany Hall." The object of the meetings was the organization of the parties of this district and the selection of delegates to represent them in Conventions to be holden at Coloma on the 29th inst. I called the meeting, the first ever holden in this Co. A goodly number of Whigs assembled and organized by the appointment of Dr. M. G. Sherman[5] of N. Y. to the Chair, and Wm. D. B. as Secy. Five delegates were chosen, myself among the number. Several short speeches were delivered, and one of an hour's length delivered by K. Anderson Esq.[6] of Mo., who was listened to with earnest attention. We as Whigs were delighted to find our party so large on the Bar, and were very much pleased at the speech delivered by Mr. A. The Locos were much chagrined to find that they were in the minority, and of course found fault with the addresses. The delegates were instructed to vote for no candidate who is unwilling to pledge himself to support the Compromise acts,[7] and who would not favor the existence of the present law relating to Mineral Lands.

---

[4]The term "Locofoco" was originally applied to a radical faction of the New York Democrats who, in 1835, during a meeting in Tammany Hall, lit candles with loco-foco matches when their opponents tried to end the meeting by turning off the gas. The Whigs used the term to designate all Democrats, and Bickham employs it in this sense.

[5]Mason G. Sherman is listed in the 1850 census as a 45-year-old physician, born in Vermont, living in Louisville, El Dorado County, in January 1851. During the Civil War Sherman served with distinction as an army surgeon in the Stones River, Chicamauga, and Chattanooga campaigns. 1850 Census, El Dorado County, 454; *War of Rebellion*, Series I, 16: 1,139; 20: 532; 30, part 1: 716, 765; 31, part 2: 151, 154, 184.

[6]Kemp P. Anderson, a native of Kentucky, is listed in the 1850 census as a 40-year-old blacksmith living at Coloma in November of that year, and was among the earliest inhabitants of Murderer's Bar. He died at Auburn, California, in 1859. 1850 Census, El Dorado County, 396; Sioli, *El Dorado County*, 184; *Herald*, April 4, 1859.

[7]The series of statutes passed in September 1850, which helped to postpone the Civil War for a full decade. They included the admission of California as a free state, the organization of New Mexico and Utah as territories with no restrictions regarding slavery, a stronger fugitive slave law, and the abolition of the slave trade in the District of Columbia.

Sunday, April 27th, 1850 [sic].

Weather warm and beautiful. Busy to-day reading papers from the Atlantic States of the 11th March.

Went to sleep after dinner and rested until 4 o'clock, at which time went to the Illinois House to see Sallie Mayfield who was paying a visit to the girls. Had some amusement.

Monday, April 21st [28th] 1851.

This morning I rose at an early hour and after breakfast resumed the late papers, which kept me busied the greater portion of the day. About 3 P.M., Wm. Stewart,[8] formerly of Madison Ia., now Treasurer of this county, visited the Bar and brought the Whigs notice of a meeting of the party at Coloma on Saturday next at 1 P.M. Stewart being a Whig, the Whigs of the Bar of course had a "talk" with him and among themselves generally. He informed me that the Democrats intend taking Major Jno. Love[9] of Belmont Co., Ohio, or M. S. Latham Esq.[10] of Columbus O. as their candidate for Congress. Several Whigs are spoken of as candidates. We intend to endeavor to have our friend, Dr. A. S. Piggott of Miss., nominated for the office of sheriff of this county.

---

[8]A soldier, journalist, author, poet, and self-taught scientist, William Frank Stewart took part in the war with Mexico before coming to California in 1849. He served under filibuster William Walker in Nicaragua and published a book about his experiences. He edited several short-lived Placerville newspapers during the late 1850s, and published a book of short poems in 1869. During the Comstock rush, Stewart moved to Nevada where he served as state geologist and state senator. He died in Boston, aged 59, while examining mining conditions in Maine. *Call,* June 21, 1882; *Union,* June 6, 1882; Goodwin, *As I Remember Them,* 192-96; Kennedy, "Newspapers of the California Mines," 348, 525-26; Stewart, *Pleasant Hours in an Eventful Life.*

[9]Apparently the Major John Love who led a 59-man party overland to California in 1849. He may have beeen the John S. Love who served as assistant secretary of the California state senate, California land commissioner, and warden of San Quentin prison. Harker, "Morgan Street to Old Dry Diggings," 51; CSL Biographical Information File; Bancroft, *California,* 6: 675.

[10]A native of Ohio, Milton Slocum Latham (1827-82) practiced law in Alabama before migrating to California in the winter of 1849-50. He served as clerk of the San Francisco Recorder's Court for six weeks, then moved to Sacramento where, in 1851, he was elected district attorney of Sacramento and El Dorado counties. After serving as congressman (1852-55) and as collector of the port of San Francisco (1855-57) Latham was elected governor of California in 1859. After five days in office he was appointed to the U.S. Senate to fill out the remainder of the late David C. Broderick's unexpired term. He failed to win reelection in 1863, became a San Francisco banker and railroad magnate, and later served as president of the Mining and Stock Exchange in New York. Phelps, *Representative Men,* 156-60; Melendy and Gilbert, *Governors of California,* 92-98.

About Sunset-hour, the Loco-Foco delegation left the Bar for Coloma, their Convention being appointed for to-morrow. W. Crawford of Cinti. was among their number.

Tuesday, April 29th, 1851...

At 10 o'clock I went to the top of the mountain to pay Sallie Mayfield a visit. I found her at home and unengaged and immediately entered into the merits of my case, enjoying myself exceedingly in her conversation. I remained until near sun-set; Mrs. Shelton's milk pans suffered considerably from my attacks in the interim.

I arrived at the Bar about dusk and was informed that there were at Cromwell's ("Tammany Hall") *Six* letters for me. I hastened thither and lo, 'twas even so. They had for some time past been accumulating at Spanish Bar with Dave Scott, and he had sent them. I was over-joyed upon receiving them and somewhat disappointed upon opening each to discover that but *one* hailed from my home... The letter from home was dated Jany. 11th, '51, and contained paragraphs from Mother, Sisters Emma,[11] Angie,[12] and Eliza, the latter having recovered from her severe illness. The letter contained much that was most pleasant and agreeable, and after reading it, I immediately commenced answers...

Wednesday, May 1st, 1851.

This is May-day, and is one of the most delightful days imaginable. Not a single cloud mars the sereneness of heaven, and a cool pleasant breeze blowing through the valley wafts delicious fragrance from the flower clad hills. I passed the greater portion of the day writing letters to Emma, Angie, and Lida.

---

[11]Bickham's eldest sister, Emily C. Bickham, continued to live with their mother in Riverside into the 1870s. In 1875 she married Austin Glazebrook, a prominent wholesale grocer in Louisville, Kentucky. She died in 1887, one year before her husband. Cincinnati city directory, 1872; 1870 Census, Cincinnati, 21st ward, 702; DMCL Bickham Collection, WDB-Personal, 3; Bodley, *History of Kentucky*, 3: 1,007-08.

[12]Bickham's second oldest sister, Angelina, was fourteen years old at the time of the 1850 census. She later married J. W. Chapin of Columbus, Ohio, who was successively an insurance agent, clerk in the state adjutant general's office, pension attorney, and deputy city auditor. 1850 Census, Springfield, Hamilton County, Ohio, 130; DMCL Bickham Collection, Biographical Notes; Columbus city directories, 1866-1911.

Thursday, May 2d.

This has also been another beautiful day, but I have felt rather unwell.

Upon visiting the Illinois House to-day, I was informed of an infamous slander which had been uttered against me by a contemptible scoundrel of this village. I immediately called upon him and confronted him with the old lady of the house, and being satisfied with his guilt, proceeded to give him the sound castigation he so richly deserved. A portion of the crowd assembled were warmly in favor of sending the scoundrel an invitation to leave the neighborhood, but finally concluded that he had received sufficient punishment at my hands.

Business is exceedingly dull here at this time owing to the high stage of the river caused by the melting of snow on the mountains, the miners from this cause being unable to operate. My claim failed some 12 days since, and I now have to search for other "diggings." Good Lord, but I am tired of mining; however I must grin and "bear it." Must "Wait and Hope."

Friday, May 3d.

The atmosphere is really chilly this morning. I feel quite unwell, being rather bilious.

Sunday, May 4th, 1851.

Friday evening I went to the top of the mountain for the purpose of procuring a horse to take me to the Whig Convention at Coloma. Rested that night at Shelton's, passing the hours before bed-time chatting with Sallie, &c.

Saturday morning procured a mule of Mayfield at an early hour and started alone—the remainder of the delegation being unable to procure animals—for Coloma. My ride among the mountains was an exceedingly pleasant one, my course following the windings of numerous valleys embellished with thousands of beautiful wild flowers, and my senses delighted with the murmurings of rivulets and gay warblings of birds. This is the season when nature is arrayed in her most beautiful dress, and it is more lovely here than in any other land in which I have yet sojourned...

I journeyed with mingled feelings of pleasure and anticipation, thus ruminating until the flashing waters of the south-fork burst upon my view. Here the scene changed. My solitary path changed for one of more stirring nature. Occasionally I would meet a fellow man, or pass a number busily engaged on the banks of the stream with Pick, shovel, and cradle, industriously separating the dross from the pure, the child from the parent, the precious gold from the earth. My pleasant course among flowers and through valleys had changed for one more abrupt and broken, though not less worthy of admiration. By 11 o'clock I arrived at Coloma and called to see my friends, Jo. Gordon[13] and Frank Stewart, by whom I was warmly received. I also had the pleasure of meeting my friend M. S. Latham Esq. of Sacramento City. I discovered soon that quite a goodly number of representative delegates from various precincts of the county had assembled to attend the Whig Convention, thus evidencing the interest taken in the affairs of our common County and good Whig cause.

After dinner I repaired to the District Court-room where I found assembled quite a large number of Whigs, and the most intelligent looking body of men I have seen in the Country. The venerable Mr. Thompson[14] of Coloma was called to the chair, and A. W. Bee[15] of Weaver, selected Secy. The object of the meeting was stated by E. L. Sanderson Esq.[16] of Salmon Falls Town and who submitted some eloquent remarks

---

[13]Josiah Gordon, a native of Florida, was appointed El Dorado county clerk in 1850 and served in that office until 1853. He was a delegate to the Whig state convention of 1852, and served as president pro tempore of that body. According to Coloma pioneer E. S. Hall, Gordon's leading role in the attempted lynching of a gambler in the autumn of 1851 cost him considerable popularity. In 1853 Gordon lost the election for county recorder, and in November of that year he left California as an express agent for Adams and Co. BL: CB 383.2: Records of the El Dorado County Clerk; *Union*, August 8, November 21, 1853; August 20, 29, 1885; *Alta*, June 8-9, 1852; 1850 Census, El Dorado County, 397; 1852 California Census, El Dorado County, 179.

[14]This was the Reverend Thomas Thompson, possibly the Thomas Thompson who was the first Disciples of Christ preacher in California. *Union*, May 6, 1851; Garrison, *Religion Follows the Frontier*, 217.

[15]Albert W. Bee, a native of New York State, arrived in California in June 1849, and settled in Placerville where, by December 1850, he was established as a trader. He and his brother, F. A. Bee, later constructed the first telegraph line across the Sierra Nevada, and he played a major part in the construction of the first transcontinental telegraph. 1850 Census, El Dorado County, 321; "In Memorium, Everett Newton Bee," *CHSQ*, 15: 95.

[16]E. L. Sanderson, a native of Vermont, kept a hotel in Salmon Falls, El Dorado County, in October 1850. After running unsuccessfully for district judge in 1851, Sanderson returned to the east, where he practiced law in Brooklyn, New York, and was active in local politics. His brother, S. W. Sanderson, served as chief justice of California during the 1860s. *New York Times*, October 23, 1876; 1850 Census, El Dorado County, 385; Steele et al. *Directory of the County of Placer for the Year 1861; Union*, August 29, 1885.

in addition. We then entered into business, several warm discussions arose upon questions of order but were speedily settled, and Committees appointed, one to draft resolutions expressive of the opinions of the Whigs of El Dorado County, and the other to select candidates for the State Convention.

After a half-hour's absence the Committees returned, and each in turn presented their reports which were excepted. Twelve delegates were elected to attend the State Convention, and among the number Dr. M. G. Sherman (at his request myself alternate) of Murderer's Bar, and my old friend Geo. W. Kinney[17] of Portsmouth, O., from Cold Springs. One of the resolutions presented, viz. to the effect that our candidates for Congress should pledge themselves to support the Compromise acts. The resolutions were 13 in number and all passed without alteration and unanimously, save the 11th resolution, which read, "Resolved, That in the mines of California we recognise the chief aim of support to the State Government and the people that our representatives in congress be *requested* to oppose the agitation in any manner whatever of the question relating to the laws governing the Mineral lands of California."

Upon hearing this resolution, I immediately proposed the substitution of the word *instructed*, not deeming the word "requested" as sufficiently forcible or expressive of our meaning. With my motion, which was speedily and earnestly seconded, I advanced my reasons for altering. I was answered by Dr. Howe[18] of Hangtown, who seemed to have long entertained a favorite idea, that "Congress must of necessity legislate upon the question as government had expended both blood and treasure in the acquirement of California, and therefore must have remuneration." The gentleman was opposed to leasing or selling the lands, and he considered that there was but one other method by which the Government could be remunerated and that was by inflicting a tax of some

---

[17]George W. Kinney is listed in the 1850 census as a 28-year-old miner born in Ohio and living in the Placerville vicinity. He later moved to San Francisco where he worked at various times as an accountant, mining agent and hotel clerk. 1850 Census, El Dorado County, 269; 1852 California Census, El Dorado County, 103; *Placerville Mountain Democrat*, March 4, 1854; San Francisco city directories, 1867-86,

[18]Probably John W. M. Howe, a native of Ohio, living at Placerville at the time of the 1850 census, who was elected justice of the peace of El Dorado County in 1854. At the time of the 1870 census, Howe was practicing medicine in Susanville, California. 1850 Census, El Dorado County, 328; BL: CB 383.2, Records of the El Dorado County Clerk; 1870 Census, Lassen County, California, 441.

description. He repelled the insinuation that he was in favor of the principle of direct taxation, but it seemed to me that his arguments or explanations conduced only to that belief. He did not seem to remember that the Government was the People, and the People the Government, and that the People remunerating the government was but taking money from one pocket and placing it in the other, or that the prosperity of the government increased with the increased prosperity and industry of her citizens. Would anything be more unjust than to tax the Miners here and then again tax them after they had entered into other walks of life. Frank Stewart followed him in support of my motion and delivered a forcible and eloquent speech. The vote was taken and passed unanimously, save the voice of Dr. Howe, and thus we said to Congress and to the Government, "Let us alone."

I was the only delegate present from Murderer's Bar, and consequently had a larger share in the deliberations of the assembly than I desired, yet I was much flattered with the attention I received. Adjd. at 6 P.M.

After supper the Whigs met in Mass Meeting and listened to a number of capital speeches. We were overjoyed at the enthusiasm manifested and felt assured that with diligence and activity the day will be our own when the contest shall take place. I met many old acquaintances and formed numerous new ones. Among the former, Geo. Kinney of Portsmouth, O., Milt. Elstner[19] of Cinti., and Capt. Hall,[20] who knew my father and myself when I was but a lad. I always am gratified when I meet with old acquaintances and friends of my father; the pleasant remembrances of the past are brought before me so vividly; I seem

---

[19]Milton Rains Elstner, an Ohio native, journeyed overland to California in 1849, settling in Placerville, where he built and operated the first hotel and served as alderman. In later life he superintended mines in Aurora, Nevada, and Bodie, California, and was active in the Nevada Democratic Party. *Call,* June 28, 1896; Colcord, "Reminiscences of Life in Territorial Nevada," *CHSQ,* 7: 118; Harker, "Morgan Street to Old Dry Diggings," 35, 43, 49, 51, 52, 68; Sioli, *El Dorado County,* 178, 208, 209, 218, 220.

[20]Elnathan S. Hall, a native of Connecticut and former Ohio resident, managed the Rogers Hotel in Coloma together with his wife, Catherine, in the autumn of 1850. He is listed as a lumberman in the 1852 census, and was deputy recorder of El Dorado County during that year. In the 1860 census he is listed as a Marysville hay dealer, and in the census of 1870 as a "laborer" living in Amador County. In 1885 Hall contributed a series of articles on Gold Rush Coloma to the *Sacramento Union.* 1850 Census, El Dorado County, 398; 1852 California Census, El Dorado County, 125; *Journal of the Third Session of the Legislature of the State of California, Proceedings of the Senate,* 458; 1860 Census, Yuba County, California, 947; 1870 Census, Amador County California, 339; *Union,* August 15, 20, 29, 1885.

almost to return to the happy days of boyhood. Capt. Hall introduced me to his wife, and upon departing, pressed me to renew my visit.

This morning previous to departing I met Mas. Moss and took the rounds of Coloma with him and at ten o'clock set out for Murderer's Bar much pleased with my trip. I arrived at home about 4 o'clock, quite fatigued and not very well, and was busied for some time giving an account of the convention to the Whigs present.

Perry Simpson starts for the Atlantic States in the morning, and Tom. Smith follows him in a few days. Both old friends of mine, and I regret their departure.

Wednesday, May 7th, 1851.

Weather pleasant, though rather cool this morning. This is now the third week since my claim has been worked out, and since then I have been too unwell to labor. During this time I have felt totally indisposed to labor, read, or write. Have been ill. To-day opened a correspondence with "The Sacramento Daily Union."

Thursday, May 8th, 1851.

Slight shower of rain this morning and air heavy and damp. Still feeble and unwell.

May 9th, 1851.

Fair weather and warm.

This morning one of our old residents, Thos. Smith, bade farewell to his friends on his departure for Independence, Mo. Tom, the only son but one of perhaps the wealthiest man in Missouri, by his generous and gentlemanly demeanor has made many friends among us, and this morning we parted with him, as became us. We regret his loss and again rejoice at his departure, well knowing that it is to his advantage and happiness. Quite a number met together, and as he rode up the hill accompanied by several of our citizens, we gave him the farewell cheers. He took charge of several letters from me to Mother and sisters and my friends, Wm. D. Ludlow[21] and H. Morris Johnston.[22]...

---

[21]William D. Ludlow is listed as a clerk in the Cincinnati city directories of 1849-51. He was later involved in the manufacture of scales, iron railings and grates, and in patent rights. Cincinnati city directories, 1849-57.

Sunday, May 11th.

A warm and beautiful morning. I am troubled with a severe cold and sore throat. John's old comrade, John Charbonneau,[23] the "half breed" Indian, came to see us and perhaps to take up his abode with us.

Times at this place are exceedingly dull owing to the scarcity of dust, the river being so high as to prevent Mining operations. Provisions in consequence of the "great fire at San Francisco"[24] have risen in price but I think will soon fall.

Well, well, it seems to me that I have lost my ambition of late. I am too unwell to work, have no desire to read, and find it utterly impossible to write satisfactory letters. I should write to the "Gazette," but to save me I cannot.

After dinner with Dr. Flewellen and Mr. Weeks, I went to Shelton's and passed the evening in the delightful valley in which they are situated. We imbibed sundry glasses of milk and talked with Sallie.

Saturday, May 17th.

Rosy-footed May is waning but is changing its beauties for the

[22]Henry Morris Johnston was a book keeper in Cincinnati during the 1850s. He became a commission merchant and meat packer during the following decades, and in 1869 served as vice president of the Cincinnati Chamber of Commerce. During the 1880s Johnston was vice president of a white lead manufacturing firm in Chicago, where he lived until his death at the turn of the century. Cincinnati city directories, 1856-79; Stevens, *City of Cincinnati*, 194; Chicago city directories, 1879-1901.

[23]Jean Baptiste Charbonneau (1805-66) the son of French fur-trader Toussaint Charbonneau and his Shoshoni wife, Sacajawea, spent his infancy with his parents on the Lewis and Clark expedition. In 1810 his parents took him to St. Louis where he received an education and was placed under the guardianship of William Clark. In 1823 he was befriended by German traveler, Prince Paul of Württemberg, and spent the following six years in Europe with the prince. Returning to America in 1829, Charbonneau spent the succeeding fifteen years as a fur trapper and trader in the Rockies and Southwest. In 1846 he served as guide and hunter for the Mormon battalion on its march to California. He was appointed *alcalde* of Mission San Luis Rey in December 1847, but was pressured to resign the following year because he was believed, as a half-Indian, to be excessively partial to his charges. He was prospecting for gold in Murderer's Bar as early as 1849 and remained in California for the following sixteen years. In 1866 he departed for Montana, the scene of his youth, where new gold fields had been discovered, but he died of pneumonia before reaching his destination. He was, according to the *Auburn Placer Herald*, "of pleasant manners, intelligent, well read in the topics of the day, and was generally esteemed in the community in which he lived as a good meaning and inoffensive man." Hafen, *Mountain Men and the Fur Trade*, 1: 205-24.

[24]The fire of May 4, 1851, was the fifth and greatest of San Francisco's early conflagrations. The fact that it took place on the anniversary of a previous fire aroused suspicions of arson and contributed to the formation of the first Vigilance Committee.

delights of the most lovely of the summer months. The last three or four days have been cold and disagreeable, but this morning the sky is clear and the air warm and pleasant. The river continues to fall, and in a few days we may expect to see the owners of river claims busy at work on their races and flumes. Our village is unconscionably dull owing to the scarcity of dust. The *hombres* sleep a good portion of the day and after tea assemble in the street to enact sundry impromptu farces, &c. Jas. Humphries, a little bodied, great souled fellow from Georgia, is one of the principal actors, generally playing upon others, "I'll tickle you, and you tickle me," *if you can.* Jo. Colgan,[25] a jovial Irishman hailing from Baltimore, is generally the principal object of our pranks, and always makes great sport for us. He is good natured and a queer chap. Our sports would in the East appear to be of a rather ridiculous nature, being exceedingly rough, but here we are not particular. Last night Joe. struck Jim H. with an old coffee sack; Jim returned the salutation, and by degrees all hands were drawn into the scrape. Joe was compelled to run the gauntlet with about a dozen striking at him with old bags and rags. His bald head is the subject of many a jocose remark which he takes with excellent grace.

In the early part of my journal I made mention of the good fellows and principal persons of our village; since then we have had many additions, the chief of which are several Georgians. Dr. Flewellen is one of the noblest fellows I ever knew; a general favorite with all who know him; courteous, affable, and kind, a true type of the generous and high-minded Southerner. A man of commanding intellect. His personal appearance is noble. He is not what would be called a handsome man, but his tall and graceful person, with his strikingly intellectual countenance and magnificent forehead, would distinguish him in any company. He is quite wealthy at home, and is only a citizen of California because of a difficulty in which he was engaged at home, and in which he killed his opponent. He had been attacked in the street by his adver-

---

[25]Joseph Colgan, a native of Ireland, is listed in the 1850 census as a miner living on the Middle Fork of the American River in January 1851. He was later a merchant in Iowa Hill, Placer County, where he died in 1861. 1850 Census, El Dorado County, 467; 1852 California Census, Placer County, 178; Steele et al., *Directory of the County of Placer for the Year 1861; Bulletin,* April 13, 1861.

sary who was enraged because of the Dr.'s successful rivalry in a love affair, and the result was as I have stated. Dr. F. left his home in order that the affair might blow over. Next autumn he returns. He is very anxious to see his wife and little boy, whose daguerreotype he received a few days ago. His son he has never seen, he having left home before his birth. Since the reception of the miniature the Dr. has been one of the happiest men imaginable. He doats *[sic]* on his "Carrie and the boy," and takes delight in showing daguerreotype to all his friends. The last thing he does at night, the first thing in the morning, and a dozen times through the day is to look at the picture. We often jest with him upon the matter, but who can wonder at him![26]

Judge Hammond, Jas. Humphries, and Jas. Lothe all hail from Ga. The judge is the senior of the quartette. He is an old gentleman whom I much respect, though I differ with him with regard to politics and matters of local concern, North and South. We have many arguments, but he is rather irritable, and I as a young man cannot take liberties with him as with others. He and Jim Humphries in this country deal "Monte"; in Georgia they are Planters. All these I regard as warm friends. Mr. M. G. Sherman of N. Y. and G. W. Torrence of Texas, two very worthy gents, are of our number, but not intimate associates.

Old Charbonneau is now with us on the bar and is as full of life and fun as any boy of 18. He can be heard laughing and making merry at any hour between breakfast time and midnight.

"Rounce" for "tods" or cigars is now the favorite game of this village, and a party of 6 or 8 seated round a table, talking and playing back and forth, present quite a lively scene. All hands went fishing yesterday. Result: plenty of fun, much noise, and few Fish.

Yesterday I rec'd a "Daily Union" with a portion of my letter in one of its columns—signed *"Pick."* Editorial notice desired me to continue my correspondences. *"Storrs"* was my signature, but was changed by the Editor.[27]

---

[26]See above, Chapter 6, note 12. Dr. Flewellan's first wife, Caroline Elizabeth, the daughter of James Bivens of Culloden, Georgia, died at their residence near Chapel Hill, Texas, aged 23, in 1854. Rocker, *Marriage and Obituaries from the Macon Messenger,* 167.

[27]In his letter to the *Union,* printed in the May 14 edition, Bickham praises Murderer's Bar and its inhabitants, regrets their neglect by the Sacramento press, and describes the local Whig meeting of April 24 and the subsequent county convention at Coloma.

Sunday, May 18th, 1851.

Strange to relate, rain is falling upon us this morning. It has been the general supposition that the "dry season" had set in. Miserecordie. What an unpleasant, disagreeable day. I've the Blues.

Finished the perusal of Colton's "Three Years in California." Some portions of it not very interesting, and take it all and all, it is not a work of very great merit.[28]

Read late city papers. The citizens of San Francisco since the great fire of May 3d have builded nearly 400 new houses. In consequence of this conflagration, produce, provisions, lumber, Clothing, building material, &c. have enhanced in price from 25 to 100 per cent.

Heard to-day of an outbreak among the Indians in the neighborhood of Hangtown. Gov. McDougal[29] has issued his proclamation authorizing Col. Rogers[30] to raise 1000 volunteers for the purpose of suppressing the insurrection.[31]

The conduct of the Executive of this state in regard to the Indian wars seems rather reprehensible, and to say the least, his *present* conduct appears very suspicious. Congress during last session appropriated the sum of $300,000 as a partial reimbursement to our state for the customs

---

[28]A native of Vermont and graduate of Yale, Walter Colton (1797-1851) arrived in California in 1846 as naval chaplain of the USS *Congress*. He served as *alcalde* of Monterey during the American military occupation and co-founded and edited the *Californian*, California's first newspaper. His memoir, *Three Years in California*, gives a lively picture of California between the conquest and the Gold Rush.

[29]A native of Ohio, John McDougal fought in the Black Hawk War and the war with Mexico, and served as superintendent of Indiana State Prison before coming to California in the winter of 1848-9. After an unsuccessful attempt at mining, he became a Sacramento merchant and represented that district in the 1849 constitutional convention. According to historian Theodore Hittell, McDougal owed his election as lieutenant governor in November of that year to his "mercurial temperament, easy disposition, and readiness to catch and side with the popular humor of the hour." McDougal became governor in January 1851, upon Governor Burnett's retirement, and he served out the remaining year of Burnett's term. He never again ran for public office and died of apoplexy in 1866. A genial, if pompous man, and a notoriously heavy drinker, McDougal was noted for stating that he feared "no one except God Almighty and Mrs. McDougal." Hittell, *California*, 4: 62-88; Melendy and Franklin, *Governors of California*, 38-47.

[30]William ("Uncle Billy") Rogers (1793-1877) a native of Kentucky, came overland to California in 1849. He was elected sheriff of El Dorado County in 1850 and served as major of militia during the El Dorado Indian Wars of 1850-51. In 1859 Rogers was appointed Indian agent for the Shoshonis in Nevada, and he spent the remainder of his life in Ruby Valley near present day Elko. *San Jose Pioneer*, September 15, 1877; *Alta*, December 16, 1875.

paid into the U. S. Treasury prior to Dec. 1, 1849, and also for monies expended in Indian wars. This $300,000 is to be used in defraying the expenses of war, and the Gov. has appointed Col. Rogers paymaster general of the volunteers. Col. R. pockets 10 per cent, or $30,000 of this for his services, in addition to the profits accruing to him upon the purchase of many war claims. It looks very suspicious. Are not Gov. McDougal and Col. Rogers partners in this affair and as such are interested in this war. Col. R., I remember, received from the Legislature last winter, as remuneration for past warlike services, only 22 town lots in San Jose.

Monday, May 19th, 1851...

I feel lively and animated; quite different from myself one week since. After writing some notices of a Whig Meeting to be held to-morow evening, I went to Shelton's with Dr. Flewellen and had a chat with Sallie.

Our village is awfully dull, and my Journal suffers from the want of incident. This evening the dreary monotony was changed a little by the introduction of a game of foot-ball.

Tuesday, May 20th.

Cloudy and cold to-day, with a drizzling rain.

This evening more pleasant. The dreary monotony of our village relieved to night by the appearance of a "magician," master of the art cabalistic, phrenologist,[32] &c. A large crowd assembled early in the evening at the Illinois House and were greatly amused during two hours by the novelty of the performance. The greater portion of the audience were green 'uns from the backwoods of Illinois and Missouri, who never

---

[31]On Friday, May 10, 1851, seven miners prospecting on the South Fork of the American River near Hangtown (Placerville) were attacked by a party of some twenty-five Indians who killed one miner and wounded two others. When, on the following Sunday, a party of twenty-four whites returned to the site, looking for the dead miner's body, they were, in their turn, attacked by a much larger Indian force. One white was wounded, and at least four Indians were believed to have been slain. Sheriff William Rogers was ordered to lead the militia against the local Indians. He had conducted a similar campaign the previous fall with little result, but considerable expense to the state. His 1851 campaign was equally uneventful, despite a spurious report of a battle with the Indians, and peace was eventually negotiated. Sioli, *El Dorado County*, 157-59; *Sacramento Transcript*, May 13, 1851.

[32]A pseudo science, popular during the nineteenth century, phrenology was based on the belief that a person's characteristics could be discerned from the contours of his or her skull.

before witnessed a performance of such description. After sundry feats of "slight of hand," the performer called upon the audience to designate an individual whose phrenological organs should be examined. Morris, Mas. Moss, and myself took the stool in turn and were made acquainted with ourselves; at least we as well as the audience were informed of our merits and short-comings. The most amusing incident of the evening occurred upon my taking the stool. The landlady of the House stated in presence of all that she wished "Mr. Magician to tell her all about me, as I wanted one of her gals." Roars of laughter greeted this remark; the poor girls simpered and blushed, and though I was hit awfully hard I laughed too. After the examination was concluded the old lady again exclaimed, "Well, Will, I believe I shall yet say Yes." This was worse and worse, fuel upon fire. It almost non-plussed me, but I had to support myself under the difficulty. "O, these wimmin!"

After the performance was concluded, one of our "men about town," in order to have some sport, entered a complaint before the Justice of the Peace against the Performer for exhibiting without license. A writ was served upon the hombre, and everything gotten ready for the trial, when we came to the conclusion that it was too base to deprive the fellow of an ounce or two, and thereupon quashed the affair. We generally go all lengths for sport, but do not like to injure the persons or property of our victims, and we have gotten the name Abroad of being "awful fellurs."

During the afternoon I was seated in the jury box. A case of trover occupied the attention of the court. My friend, Dr. Flewellen, appeared for defedts. and K. Anderson for Pltfs. The testimony was conclusive against defdts., but during the trial we were greatly amused at the questions of counsel and answers of witnesses. Dr. F. made an eloquent speech, but the subject of the trial being a Beef, the Dr.'s eloquence partook of the sublime and ridiculous. Anderson in his answer to the Dr's allusion of the head of "Yorick's" being recognized but not a precedent in this case, committed a most laughable error, confounding the names of Warwick the Kingmaker, Garrick the actor, and Yorick the fool. Kemp has lately read "The Last of the Barons."[33]

---

[33]Anderson was confusing Richard Neville, Earl of Warwick, known as the "Kingmaker," a 15th century English magnate and the subject of Bulwer-Lytton's novel, *The Last of the Barons*, with David Garrick, the 18th century English tragedian, and Yorick, the fool, whose skull Hamlet contemplates in Act V, Scene 1 of Shakespeare's play

During the sitting of Court one of the Jurors addressing his honor stated that the jury were fatigued and dry and hoped they might be permitted to send for refreshments. His honor graciously nodded assent, and brandy cocktails were ordered. Dr. F. stated that he hoped "the court would not be left in suffering condition." After jury retiring, it was unable for a time to agree, refreshments & a deck of whist cards were sent for, in order to pass time. Fortunately we compromised the affair, and rendered a verdict in time to save our patience.

Central San Francisco-1851

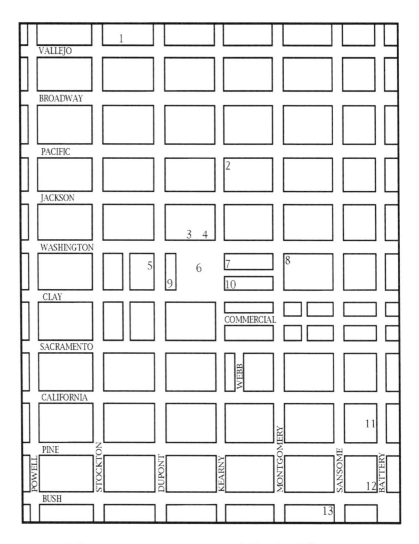

1. Jail
2. City Hall
3. Bella Union
4. New Custom House
5. Adelphi Theatre
6. Plaza (Portsmouth Square)
7. Union Hotel
8. Courier Office
9. Post Office
10. California Exchange
11. V.C. Headquarters
12. Oriental Hotel
13. Rassette House]

CHAPTER EIGHT

Delegate to San Francisco

Thursday, May 22nd.

After eating my dinner and saying "good bye" to some of my friends, I left Murderer's Bar for San Francisco. I pursued my way leisurely amid the valleys and over the plains & the mountains, drinking in at every breath a thousand sweet fragrances which the atmosphere exhaled from myriads of beautiful flowers which sprang up smilingly from every side, round every rock or moss grown stump. I could not but gaze admiringly upon the beautiful panorama of nature spread out constantly before me as I traveled onward, and my mind busied itself both with this and reflections of the past, present, and future. I wished for mother and sisters to delight with me in these scenes, but was rejoiced that my friends in a distant land experienced not the darkened side of my picture; the hard lot which has been my partner thus far; the hard pillow and harder fare. But Heigh ho, I traveled along as a Delegate to the First Whig State Convention of our State with a light heart—and a light pocket. What a curious thing is honor, and political honor at that...

After walking 8 miles I stopped for the night at Norton's, hoping to get a wagon to take me on the morrow. Norton is an old Mormon, and has a very pretty daughter, Isabel, who is *rather* uncultivated. I found she was not afraid of a young gent. like myself, for when I assayed to talk with her she met me half way; pigs and chickens, beauxes and Balls, seemed to delight her, and her tongue rattled merrily upon these subjects.

Friday morning came, but no downward bound wagon hove in sight, so I in haste departed a-foot—*hoping*. But what a thing is hope! Nothing like it to send a fellow bowling through the world or over such confounded hills as I found in my track. About once in fifteen minutes I listened in the hope of hearing the rattling of an empty wagon, but my ears were greeted with nothing but the moaning of the wind among the trees or the hoarse croaking of a solitary raven. In the course of time I found myself on the summit of a mountain overlooking the pretty amphitheatrical valley and village of Salmon Falls. On that mountain I found a convenient seat and then and there entered sundry notes in my memorandum book concerning my travels and the village which lay in the distant valley, but having lost said memorandum, those valuable annotations are among the things which are not. One hour from this time found me in the store of R. K. Berry[1] of Salmon Falls, reading the "Cincinnati Gazette," which I had purchased of an "Express man" while plodding onward. At 11 o'clock I found myself 25 miles from Murderer's Bar, and at that precise moment heard an "*empty sound*," that is to say a wagon rattling behind me, which I judged to be empty. I was soon assured of the truth of this and some little time was rolling along quite comfortably… Ate dinner at the 16 mile house, for which I paid one dollar, leaving me $35.00. About 10 miles from the city I noticed some magnificent fields of barley growing luxuriantly from the rich soil of the Sacramento Valley. Only think of over 100 stalks, each with a fully developed head of grain growing from a single grain of barley! It is a truth!!

I obtained a flying view of the American Gardens, belonging to my old acquaintance, Col. Suffron, as I neared the Brighton House. I noticed also an indication of the Col.'s taste in the wild flowers which grew here and there in spots and which had by design been spared from the attacks of the Hoe. At the "Brighton" or "Pavilion House" and Race Course a great crowd were assembled to see the races.[2] … Between the "Pavillion" and the City, the road was crowded with buggies and equestrians going to & from the Pavillion.

---

[1]Reuban K. Berry, a former stage coach operator and rubber manufacturer, came to California from New York in 1849 and settled in Salmon Falls (then called Higgins Point) where he entered the freighting business. He remained a leading citizen of this town for the rest of his life, serving as its first *alcalde*, and later as justice of the peace. Sioli, *El Dorado County*, 234.

[2]The town of Brighton was founded on the south bank of the American River in 1849 by Sacramento speculators who built the race track and Pavilion Hotel. The village prospered from 1849 to 1851, and the race course was the scene of bull and bear fights as well as horse races. In 1851 the Pavilion Hotel was destroyed by fire. The town was abandoned the following year because of land title problems. Wright, *History of Sacramento County*, 211.

At 4 P.M. I arrived in the Forest City vide Sacramento, and took lodgings at the Crescent City Hotel, with mine host Sylvester.[3] During the evening I met numerous old acquaintances, and among those Wm. Crawford, Col. Joseph C. Potter, & E. C. Cromwell of Murderer's Bar. The latter two were just returning from the Democratic Convention holden at Benecia. With these I sallied out after tea in search of adventure. Our course brought us to the place where the Loco-focos were holding their ratification meeting. I heard the Hon. T. J. Henley,[4] formerly of Madison, Ia., repeat one of his old woman's abusive Democratic stump speeches, remodeled to suit California. I heard Mr. McConaha[5] make the ridiculously absurd remark that California at the next election would give the Democratic ticket 50,000 (fifty thousand) majority. Phew. I don't believe it will receive that many votes. The "Democratic Ratification Meeting" proved rather a mixed up concern, as it turned into a Whig Jollification. R. N. Berry,[6] Alderman

---

[3]Edward Sylvester, a native of Canada, owned and operated the Crescent City Hotel from 1850 to 1852. A staunch Whig, Sylvester repeatedly made his hotel available for party meetings and celebrations, establishing it as the effective Whig headquarters in Sacramento. When he departed for the east in July, 1852, Sylvester refused to sell the hotel to a "Locofoco" at any price, selling it instead, for thousands of dollars less, to fellow Whigs. 1850 Census, Sacramento County, 169; Sacramento city directory, 1851; Severson, *Sacramento,* 98-99, 106; *Union,* August 8, 1851, June 15, July 2, 5, 1852.

[4]Thomas Jefferson Henley (1808-75) a former Indiana lawyer, banker and congressman, came overland to California in 1849 and engaged in banking in Sacramento. In 1852 he became postmaster of San Francisco, and in 1854 he was appointed superintendent of Indian affairs in California, a post which he held until his dismissal for corruption in 1859. Bickham, in a letter to the *Cincinnati Daily Gazette,* characterized Henley as "the gentleman who brought with him to our shores a headless keg full of old speeches, from the bottom of which he draws upon public occasions, and when finished with one throws it on top, thus keeping them revolving." Bancroft, *California,* 6: 674; Secrest "The Rise and Fall of Thomas J. Henley," *passim.; Cincinnati Daily Gazette,* October 25, 1851.

[5]Ohio born George McConnaha (1820-54) practiced law in Missouri before traveling overland to California in 1850. The following year he was elected city attorney of Sacramento, and later assemblyman. In 1852 he moved to Seattle, where he played a major role in the creation of Washington Territory. In 1854 he served as president of the upper house of the first territorial legislature, which met at Olympia. While returning to Seattle by canoe at the end of the session, McConnaha and all but one of his companions were drowned. Grant, *History of Seattle,* 411-13; Snowdon, *History of Washington,* 5: 300-301.

[6]Richard N. Berry (d. 1873) a native of Massachusetts, was a Sacramento auctioneer and commission merchant in 1850-51. He later moved to San Francisco, where he was a merchant and stock broker for much of the 1850s and '60s. 1850 Census, Sacramento County, 158; Sacramento city directory, 1851; San Francisco city directories, 1852-65; *Bulletin,* July 7, 1873.

Queen,[7] and several other Whigs addressed the assembled multitude amid vociferous plaudits.

California Politics, like everything else in California, are sui generis. In the States it would be considered a remarkable circumstance for the antagonistical parties to hold their meetings at one and the same place and at the same time, without discord and inharmony being prevalent. But here it is not so. They meet together and hold their discussions with perfect good feeling and bandy words with each other without manifesting the least ill feeling. Often have I seen a Whig follow a Loco from the same stand and receive as many cheers as his opponent and be listened to with the same attention. This is as it should be, and so long as it continues will the idea of disunion be driven from our thoughts. I believe the people of California to be the most eminently patriotic of any in the Union.

During the evening I called upon Mr. Lawrence,[8] Editor of the Placer Times. Do not think him a man of talent, but do think him an active business man.

Saturday at 2 o'clock found myself on board the fine steamer *Wilson G. Hunt,* surrounded by a number of Whig Delegates to the State Convention. A more intelligent company of gentlemen I have not met this many a day. I have been introduced to them all. There are 8 of us from El Dorado, viz. E. L. Sanderson & Mills[9] from Salmon Falls, S. S. Brooks[10] & Vinal Daniels[11] from Coloma, Dr. Cutler[12] from Cold

---

[7]James Queen, (d.1881) a Pennsylvania printer, came to California in 1847 as a sergeant in the New York Volunteers. After managing Sam Brannan's store on Mormon Island, Queen was elected supernumerary delegate to the 1849 constitutional convention. He became prominent as a Sacramento publisher and was active in politics. Biggs, *Conquer and Colonize,* 194 n. 9; Bancroft, *California,* 4: 785; 1850 Census, Sacramento County, 241; *Sacramento Bee,* June 23, 1881.

[8]Joseph E. Lawrence, a native of Long Island, arrived in California in 1849 and served as editor and publisher of several newspapers, including the *Placer Times and Transcript.* In 1861 he became editor and part owner of the literary weekly *Golden Era,* and gave employment to such promising young writers as Bret Harte, C. W. Stoddard, and Prentice Mulford. Walker, *San Francisco's Literary Frontier,* 119-22, 142, 145; E. C. Kemble, *History of California Newspapers,* 356.

[9]Samuel Belden Mills (d. 1871), a New York native, is listed in the 1850 census as a miner, aged 32, living on the South Fork of the American River in October 1850. During the 1860s, Mills was a lawyer and insurance agent in San Francisco, where he contributed to the local press. 1850 Census, El Dorado County, 383; San Francisco city directories 1857-71; *Alta,* September 21, 1871.

[10]Stephen S. ("Babbling") Brooks, an Ohio native, arrived at Coloma in 1849, where he operated a log store and served as first postmaster and justice of the peace. He later constructed mining ditches near Coloma and Yreka, the latter being the largest such ditch in California. During the 1860s, Brooks, a San Francisco street contractor, was involved in the southwestern extension of

Spring, Whitney[13] from Placerville and Griffiths[14] from Weber. I was introduced to all on board, the most prominent, Dr. Morse,[15] Editor of the Sacramento Union, E. J. C. Kewen Esq.,[16] Candidate for Congress, &c. Passage on the steamer, $10.50.

At 11 P.M. we arrived at the great city of San Francisco, and enjoyed an elegant promenade among her dark and dusty streets in search of Hotel quarters. Mills, Dr. Hurd,[17] and I rambled in a cold night wind until two A.M. before we were accommodated. At the time we brought up at the Rasette House,[18] and mine host I found was a Cincinnatian.

Sunday morning in San Francisco and the cold wind blustering and howling through the streets—Sand flying, noses dripping, eyes tearful, and hats going through the air like kites. Whew! "cease rude Boreas."

Market Street and the development of the Western Addition. 1850 Census, El Dorado County, 398; 1860 Census, San Francisco, 1,252; San Francisco city directories 1859-83; *Call*, September 20, 1883; BL: CB 383.2, Records of the El Dorado County Clerk; *Union*, August 15, 1885.

[11]Vinal Daniels, a native of New York, served as *alcalde* of Old Dry Diggings in 1849, and was El Dorado County judge in 1850-51. BL: CB 383.2, Records of the El Dorado County Clerk; 1850 Census, El Dorado County, 396; Coy, *County Archives of California*, 158; *Union*, February 6,1852.

[12]Dr. John Cutler was elected to the state assembly from El Dorado County later that year. Bancroft, *California*, 6: 657.

[13]Samuel Whitney, a New Hampshire native and former New York resident, is listed in the 1850 census as a 21-year-old miner living in the Placerville vicinity. *Alta*, May 27, 1851; 1850 Census, El Dorado County, 321; 1852 California Census, El Dorado County, 10.

[14]Pennsylvania-born George R. Griffiths is listed in the 1850 census as a laborer living at Weaverville, El Dorado County. 1850 Census, El Dorado County, 252.

[15]Vermont native John Frederick Morse (1815-74) arrived in California in 1849. He was a Sacramento physician, newspaper editor, and civic leader, as well as author of the first history of that city. Wenzel. "Historical Note on the Life of John Frederick Morse," in *First History of Sacramento*, 3-16.

[16]Edward J. C. ("Alphabet") Kewen (1825-79) a native of Mississippi, served as an officer in the war with Mexico, and practiced law in St. Louis before coming overland to California in 1849. He was elected the state's first attorney general but failed to be elected congressman in 1851. Kewen practiced law in San Francisco and authored the first book of verse published in California. Between 1855 and '57 he was financial agent for filibuster William Walker, and took part in Walker's Nicaragua campaigns. In 1858 Kewen moved to Los Angeles where he served as district attorney and was twice elected to the state assembly. During the Civil War he was briefly imprisoned on Alcatraz for his outspoken pro-Southern sympathies. Reinhardt, "On the Brink of the Boom," *CSHQ*, 52: 70, n. 5; Phelps, *Representative Men*, 341-47.

[17]Probably Tyrus W. Hurd, a physician, born in New York, living in Salmon Falls in late 1850 and early 1851. 1850 Census, El Dorado County, 386; *Sacramento Transcript*, January 18, 1851.

[18]The Rasette House, a five story frame building on the corner of Bush and Sansome Streets, was owned by Joseph Rassette, a native of Canada, who had come by sea to California in 1851 and erected the building soon after. It was considered one of the best hotels in Gold Rush California. 1852 California Census, San Francisco County, part I: 172; San Francisco city directories 1852-58; Soulé et al., *Annals*, 448; Millard, *San Francisco Bay Region*, 3: 103-4.

What a sad, sad prospect meets the eye on every side. Where a few short weeks ago were standing magnificent hotels and storehouses are now to be seen a heap of smoldering blackened ruins. All swept away at one swoop of the fell destroyer, fire. A stench almost suffocating rises up from the blackened mass, and the passer by knows not but the charred and blackened body of a friend may be buried neath piles of churned iron and broken crumbling brick. Yet still what evidences of the character of the Californian are presented. Energy, enterprise, perseverance. Already are many portions of the burnt district rebuilt; and men whom but a few days agone were on the verge of ruin are busy with the active scenes of the California Merchant's life, retrieving their dilapidated fortunes. Hundreds of new houses are springing up on every side, and in a few short weeks all traces will have disappeared, and the Great Fire will only be known as a thing of the past. Great country this!

After getting "barberized" I repaired to the "California Exchange," [19] the Headquarters since the destruction of the "Union Hotel,"[20] and there entered the busy throng of Politicians, Delegates, Office Seekers, &c. Introductions to this one and that, a Sherry Cobbler here, a Salop there, and a Brandy Smash with another. Well, I was introduced to most of the first Whigs of the State and one or two of the Locos. Great Guns, viz. Judge Sherwood[21] and Col. Jno. B. Weller.[22]

---

[19]In addition to serving as a gambling resort and stock exchange, the California Exchange provided facilities for political meetings and fancy dress balls. De Russailh, *Last Adventure*, 13, 30; Soulé et al., *Annals*, 665-68.

[20]The Union Hotel, the first truly elegant hotel in San Francisco, was, according to the *Annals of San Francisco*, of comparable quality to any similar hotel in the United States. After its destruction in the fire of May 4, 1851, it was rebuilt and long served as a meeting place for local politicians. Soulé et al., *Annals*, 649; Johnson, *San Francisco As It Is*, 43-45.

[21]Winfield Scott Sherwood, (d.1870) a native of New York, represented the Sacramento district at the 1849 constitutional convention, was elected to the ninth judicial district the following year, and served as a presidential elector in 1852. Davis, *Political Conventions*, 653; Bancroft, *California*, 6: 288; 1860 Census, San Francisco, 485.

[22]John B. Weller of Ohio (1812-75) represented his native state in Congress from 1839 to 1845, and served as lieutenant colonel in the war with Mexico. In 1849 he was appointed by President James K. Polk to head the International Boundary Commission, entrusted with surveying the boundary between Mexico and California, but was recalled later that year by President Zachary Taylor after having been accused of misconduct in office. Weller practiced law in San Francisco, served as U.S. senator from 1852 to '57, and was governor of California from 1851 to 1860. Melendy and Gilbert, *Governors of California*, 81-90.

Whilst standing in front of the Exchange talking with a friend, whom should I see walking past but my old friend Lucius Coffin.[23] Had one dropped from the clouds I could not have been more astonished than when I grasped his cordially extended hand. I had no more idea of his being in California than I had of flying. Truly was I rejoiced. Yet a little longer and most of those cherished old friends will all be here, and then I am content to spend my days in California...

Monday Morning, May 26th.

Convention organized at 11 o'clock. Judge Shepheard[24] called the Convention to order by the nomination of Dr. Jno. F. Morse, Editor of Sac. Daily Union, as Chn. Pro. Tem. Committees were then appointed, one from each County, to present the names of officers of the Convention. In a half hour the following names were offered and unanimously chosen as officers—Gen. Jno. Wilson[25] of San Francisco, Chairn., G. A. Griffiths of El Dorado, Vice Presdt.—Jas. B. Devoe[26] of Santa Clara

---

[23]Lucius Coffin was the son of Charles Dustin Coffin (1804-80) a congressman and superior court judge in Cincinnati. Lucius was in San Francisco, employed by the customs service, in 1850 and '51. He is listed as a clerk in the 1855 Cincinnati city directory, but at the time of his father's death in 1880, he was living in California, aged 52. Wright, *Obituaries of Cincinnatians*, 147; *Biographical Directory of the American Congress*, 998-9; *Cincinnati Enquirer*, January 12, 1851; *Cincinnati Commercial*, April 6, 1851.

[24]Philip W. Shepheard (1813-65) a native of Plymouth, England, came to the United States at age 14, and by age 21 had risen from common seaman to master of a merchant ship. He sailed with his family to San Francisco in 1849, and was elected justice of the peace the following year. In 1856 he was admitted to the bar, and he subsequently served as counselor of law for the state supreme court and deputy district attorney for the San Francisco police court. In 1863 he was elected police court judge, an office which he held for the remaining two years of his life. *Alta*, December 17, 1865; San Francisco city directories 1852-65.

[25]John Wilson (1780-1877) a native of Tennessee, moved early in life to Missouri where he was active for many years as a Whig politician and newspaper editor. He probably acquired the title "General" when serving as an inspector general of militia during the Black Hawk War. In 1849 Wilson was appointed commissioner for Utah and naval and Indian agent for California, and journeyed via Utah to San Francisco. He spent the remainder of his life as a prominent California lawyer, specializing in land cases. Shuck, *Bench and Bar*, 468; Bruff, *Gold Rush*, 734 n. 82; Rogers, *Bear Flag Lieutenant*, 75, n. 171.

[26]James B. Devoe, a New York journalist, published the *California State Journal* in San Jose in 1850-51, and the *San Francisco Placer Times and Transcript* in 1852. During the 1850s he was the proprietor of the San Francisco Machine Works. 1852 California Census, San Francisco County, Part I, 133; E. C. Kemble, *History of California Newspapers*, 218, 336; San Francisco city directories, 1850-69.

Cou., Secy., also E. L. Sanderson Esq. of El Dorado and _____
Robb[27] of San Joaquin. Another committee was appointed to draft rules
for the regulation of the Convention and ordered to report to-morow at
11 A.M. Convention then adj'd. Delegates then again repaired to Cal.
Exchange, and went through the ceremony of imbibing and electioneering. I met more acquaintances and was introduced to about 50 gentlemen.

Tuesday and Wednesday we were occupied with the election of nom-
inees, which all passed off harmoniously, although there was of course
some little dissatisfaction resulting from the defeat of favorites. The
Delegates from Yuba and Butte were displeased because of the nomination of Major Reading[28] instead of Capt. Waldo,[29] and the Delegates
from San Francisco and myself, besides some others, because of the
nomination of Col. Moore[30] of Tuolumne Co., instead of Col. R. N.
Wood[31] of San Francisco. I, however, had no personal feelings whatso-

[27]John S. Robb, a native of Philadelphia, came to California via the Gila route in 1849. He was
a prominent California journalist and writer during the 1850s, and at the time of his death in 1856
was editor of the *Spirit of the Age. Bulletin,* October 7, 1856; Bieber, *Southern Trails to California,*
159, 164.

[28]A native of New Jersey, Pierson B. Reading (1816-68) came overland to California in 1843
and was employed as clerk and head trapper by John Sutter. In 1846 Reading took part in the Bear
Flag Revolt and served in Frémont's California Battalion. He received a large land grant on the
Trinity River in 1844, where he later discovered gold. After losing the gubernatorial election of
1851, Reading devoted his later years to ranching. Bancroft characterized him as a "man of well-
balanced mind, honorable, energetic and courteous; one whose California record seems never to
have furnished material for adverse criticism." Bancroft, *California,* 5: 689.

[29]William Waldo (1812-81) a Santa Fe trader, merchant, and Missouri farmer, came to California in 1849. In 1850 he risked his life rescuing several California-bound emigrant parties, and
in 1853 he ran unsuccessfully as Whig candidate for governor. Drum, "Glimpses of the Past."

[30]A native of Alabama and resident of Texas, Benjamin Franklin Moore (c 1823-66) arrived in
California in 1848, describing his profession as "elegant leisure." He was, according to Elisha
Crosby, "the most disagreeable man" at the 1849 constitutional convention, where he "carried an
enormous bowie knife and was drunk most of the time." Moore sat for San Joaquin County in the
state assembly of 1849-51, and, despite his illiteracy, lack of legal knowledge, and fierce pro-South-
ern prejudices, was one of the most successful and certainly most colorful lawyers in early Tuolumne
County. Lang, *Tuolumne County,* 181-85, 304; Bancroft, *California,* 4: 744; Crosby, *Memoirs,* 46;
Gilbert, *History of San Joaquin County,* 26.

[31]Robert N. Wood, a native of Virginia, practiced law in San Francisco in 1850, served as assemblyman in 1852, was district attorney of Contra Costa County in 1853, and judge of that county in
1853-55. Wood was active in the nativist Know-Nothing Party, running on Millard Fillmore's electoral ticket in 1856. The following year he joined Henry Crabb's filibustering expedition to Sonora,
Mexico, and was killed by Mexican troops at Cavorca. CSL- Information card catalogue: sketch from
letter of 4/8/1954 from A. L. Stall; Bogardus, *San Francisco and Sacramento Directory,* July 1850; *Alta,*
May 14, 1857; Bancroft, *California,* 6: 651, 657; Hurt, "Know Nothings," *CHSQ,* 9: 42, 100, 103.

ever to gratify while in Convention. I sought for those whom I considered best qualified and most available. Thursday our Principles for future guidance were presented to Convention and unanimously passed—We then adjourned, the best possible feeling prevailing.

During the sitting of Convention I made many valuable and pleasant acquaintances, and moreover my admiration for the population of the Eureka State was greatly increased, and my intention of making her my home more strongly confirmed. The citizens of San Francisco I peculiarly fancied, so affable, courteous, and hospitable, reminding one at once of those true Western gentlemen whom I delighted to meet at home. I was afforded opportunities for judging of the characters and qualifications of many of the different leading men of the State. One circumstance pleased me much, that the young men were most powerful and have the power to will and minds to do. Thought I, old Political tricksters who emigrate hither for the sake of office will find themselves egregiously disappointed. I am totally opposed to countenancing in any manner whatever the designs of these old office seekers. Happily for the Whigs, they have very few of that class among them. All of our Candidates are either young men or those who were never before known in [the] Political World.

Sunday, June 1st, 1851.

Another windy, dreary, cold day. What a place for excitement is this. Nothing but excitement day in and day out. The very air we breathe is of that nature. We have no calm, social fireside or evening amusements with friends in the ladies' parlor or family circle, and unless one engages in exciting amusements, he becomes melancholy—has the blue devils &c. One cannot read anything of a calm, reflective, or philosophical nature, but must snatch up a paper, dash into politics or money making schemes, and then away. And a great place is it too for studying human nature. In one and the same hour one meets citizens of all the nations of the world, each shadowing forth their national and personal peculiarity.—There's the ingenious Chinaman, the Industrious and reflective German, the selfish John Bull, the gay and volatile Frenchman, the Sedate Spaniard, the witty Irishman, and thrifty son of Scotia, with Kanakas, Mexicans, Hottentots, Bengalese, Chileans, and South Americans generally, and fifty other representatives of other nations all overtopped and surpassed in each and every of their peculiarities by the representatives of the Universal Yankee Nation. The finest specimens of Masculine humanity I have ever met have been my companions and acquaintances in this Country, as well have I seen the queerest and poorest in physical proportion. Such universal energy of character and persevering determination the world never before has seen, and indeed such universal intelligence. We also have the most depraved and wicked of the human species of both sexes. Few indeed of virtuous women have we in our midst. They truly are like angels' visits. The French have almost taken the place but also almost all if not every one of the females are *"Sans vertu."* But it's as "good as a play" any day to go into the streets and note the different characters one meets.

CHAPTER NINE

Inspector of Customs;
The *Anne McKim*

Thursday, June 5th, 1851.

My friend, Col. R. N. Wood, yesterday gave me a letter of introduction to Dr. Brent of the U. S. Marine Hospital,[1] desiring him also to apply to the Collector of Port, Hon. T. Butler King,[2] for a commission in the "Customs" for me. The Dr. acquiesced and to-day called upon Mr. King and at his instance [I] was made "Inspector of Customs" at a salary of $6.00 per day. I had business in Sacramento and obtained leave of absence to go. In the afternoon I took passage on the Confidence and had a pleasant trip.

Friday rec'd two Gazettes from home. Saw a number of friends and at two o'clock took return passage on the Senator... Had a pleasant passage, &c.

---

[1]Dr. William T. Brent, who had practiced medicine in New Orleans during the 1840s, came to California via the Gila route in 1849. In the spring of 1851, Collector Thomas Butler King contracted with Brent to provide medical care to sick mariners in a building at the corner of Broadway and Dupont streets. That same spring Brent was chosen by the state legislature to be one of the two visiting physicians attached to the State Marine Hospital. *Journals of the Legislature of the State of California at its Second Session,* 449, 1769-71; Bieber, *Southern Trails to California,* 167, 176, 194, 210; New Orleans city directories, 1842, 1849.

[2]A lawyer, planter, and Whig congressman from Georgia, Thomas Butler King (1800-64) was sent to California by President Taylor in 1849 to investigate the statehood movement. In 1851 Taylor's successor, Millard Fillmore, appointed King collector of customs in San Francisco. This office gave King considerable patronage which he used to build a powerful political machine and establish himself as leader of the California Whigs. He ran unsuccessfully for the U.S. Senate in 1851. The following year he resigned his collectorship and returned to Georgia, where he died of pneumonia in 1864. Steel, *T. Butler King of Georgia. passim.*

Saturday Morning reported myself at the "Barge Office" ready for duty, but no ships arriving, I was, of course, compelled to wait.

Tuesday, June 10th, 1851.

Weather very pleasant for this place. Day passed away in pretty much the same manner as others. I became acquainted with several more brother officers. Those with whom I have met seem to be very clever gentlemen.

At ten o'clock retired and at twelve was awakened by the solemn toll of the bell on the Monumental Engine House. Thinking at first that there was an alarm of fire, I went to the window and listened. A confused noise, as of men running and talking hurriedly, struck my ear, and in a few moments the solemn tolling of the midnight bell again sounded awfully solemn. After the lapse of a few moments, all was silent as the grave. I retired to my bed with a species of fear upon my heart, why I could not tell, but there are moments when fear or a feeling of awe will steal upon the heart of man, particularly at night, and depress his spirits far more than the presence of immediate danger. It appeared to me as though something terrible had happened or was about to take place, and my most powerful efforts failed to relieve my mind of the burthen.

Wednesday morning early, I learned that a fearful tragedy had followed the tolling of the midnight bell. My fears proved to have too great foundation. A man from Sydney named John Jenkins[3] had been caught stealing an Iron Safe from a citizen and had been arrested, tried by a jury of citizens, condemned and hanged by the crowd.—This was the cause of the confusion and tolling of the Bell. For a long time past the cities of California, & particularly the City of San Francisco, have been infested by hordes of scoundrels, robbers, murderers and incendiaries, and they when arrested, owing to the loose manner in which the laws have been administered, have almost universally escaped punishment. The People have had their city destroyed five times through the agency of these hellhounds, and every night some have been robbed and murdered. They

---

[3]John Jenkins, alias Simpton, was described by Barry and Patten as a "low, brutal, foul-mouthed villain of hurculean frame with thick coarse red hair and beard." According to one acquaintance who had known him in Australia, Jenkins was "a very bad man" who had been transported from England at age 12 for housebreaking. In San Francisco he "kept a notorious crib on Dupont Street called the Uncle Sam," and was suspected of murdering a man whose wife he desired. Barry and Patten, *Men and Memories*, 143; BL: C-D 198; Mullen, *Let Justice be Done*, 163-4.

had borne with this state of affairs until patience had ceased to be a virtue and, despairing of remedy at the hands of the Courts of Justice, took the matter in their own hands and meted out a terrible punishment to one caught in the act of stealing, as a warning to others. Among the many outlaws who infest our city, escaped or released convicts from the Penal Colonies of Great Britain stand prominent for bold and murderous outrages, and this circumstance added to others, such as fire, loss of life and property, is what has so exasperated the people. A number of our best citizens associated themselves in a body for the purpose of meeting out justice to such as should be proven guilty upon trial before a "Secret Tribunal." The[y] are sworn to defend each other with life and property, and on the night of Tuesday, June 10th, the first terrible execution took place...

In the afternoon a meeting was called for the purpose of ratifying the proceedings of the "Secret Committee." The great portion of [the] community responded "Aye!" to the execution, though there was quite a number, headed by lawyers, who endeavored to create, and, in fact, succeeded in creating, great excitement. David C. Broderick,[4] last winter Speaker of the Senate, was the leader and endeavored to rouse a spirit of Indignation against the Committee. This, I honestly believe, was done not upon honest principles. I believed he hoped to make party capital out of the affair. He had assembled around him a lot of "Empire Club bullies" who applauded all he did and endeavored to confuse the proceedings of the meeting. The chief objection to the execution was that the tribunal which (consisting of 100 men) condemned him was "Secret." Mr. Loco-Foco Broderick did himself little service. The almost universal voice of the community upheld the Tribunal. The papers were, without exception, in favor. To be sure, all deplored the circumstances, yet they acknowledged the necessity of the proceedings.

Those in the Atlantic States will doubtless comment with severity upon this action, but as they do not appreciate our situation, it will make but little difference. Californians know what they are doing and ask not the aid or opinion of the world in these matters.

---

[4]The son of an Irish stone mason who had worked on the national capitol, David C. Broderick (1820-59) was active in New York's Tammany Hall before coming to California in 1849. By 1851 the austere, ambitious Broderick was president of the state senate and one of the most powerful political figures in California. In 1857 he achieved his lifelong goal of election to the U.S. Senate. Two years later he was killed in a duel by California Chief Justice Terry.

Sunday, June 15th, 1851.

After waiting a week at the "Barge Office," I this morning was so lucky as to get on board the Ship Ann McKim[5] from Valpariso, 500 tons, laden with Flour, Nuts, Sweet Meats and apples. I presume I shall remain on her 40 days. The Captain and Mates *appear* like clever fellows, and my accommodations are as good as I wish for. As soon as my apples, Nuts, &c. are discharged, I shall have a fine chance for reading and writing. I cannot leave my vessel without permission from Head Quarters. My brother officers tell me I can take a *sly trip* ashore after locking up hatches. I shall not wish to go very often. Where! But the wind blows fiercely in the Harbor and it's cold as a day in December. I weary for a letter from Home, and suppose I shall weary for some time to come.

Sunday, June 22d, 1851.

At 11 o'clock this morning, whilst promenading on the decks of the Ann McKim, I was suddenly startled by an alarm of fire in the City. Some distance up Pacific Street I observed a dense volume of smoke ascending from an [sic] house, and vast numbers of people rushing through the streets. The wind was blowing quite briskly from the S. West, carrying the fire in such direction as endangered the greater portion of the city. The flames spread rapidly down toward the Bay and toward the N. W., and soon a large section of the city was under the influence of the devouring element. The fire spread with inconceivable rapidity owing to the combustibility of the house materials. The adjacent hillsides and streets were soon crowded with men, women, and children, and every conceivable species of Mdse. I watched the progress of the flames for several hours with mingled feelings of sorrow, horror, and awe. From the ship's deck a mile from the fire I could distinctly hear the crackling and roaring of the flames mingled with repeated explo-

---

[5]The 494 ton *Anne McKim* was built in 1833 for Baltimore merchant, Isaac McKim, after whose wife she was named. The *Anne McKim* is often regarded as the first American clipper ship, and in her prime was considered the fastest merchant ship afloat. After McKim's death in 1837, she was purchased by Howland and Aspinwall and served during the next decade in the South American and China trades. In 1847 she was bought by Chilean owners and made several trips between Valpariso and San Francisco. In September 1851, she left California for the last time under Captain Van Pelt, and was dismantled in Valpariso the following year. Howe and Matthews, *American Clipper Ships*, 1: 11-12.

View of the Last Great Conflagration (Courtesy, The Bancroft Library)

sions from powder. About 3 o'clock, the flames were stayed by the citizens blowing up houses and covering the roofs, &c. with wet blankets. That portion of the city which has here-to-fore escaped fire was nearly all destroyed. The old city hall, a very large frame building, presented a magnificent spectacle when the flames were at their height. This makes the fifth awful conflagration within less than two years.

Monday 23rd.

During the progress of the flames, hordes of thieves were prowling about, gathering plunder and setting fire to different houses. Two scoundrels were shot dead in the street by a Police Officer. A Mr. Lyon of N. York, recognized by a ring on his finger, was found in the street, dead; burned to death. Mr. Bach of the firm Bach, Barnett & Co. was burned to death. Others were slightly, and some severely, burned. Whilst the patients were being removed from the City Hospital, one of them, who had long been sick, turned over and died.

The scene in the Plaza during the fire beggars all description. Mdse. of all descriptions were piled up indiscriminately in huge masses. Men were running about in wild haste, shouting and swearing, women looked pale and frightened, and children were screaming. When Washington Street on the Plaza took fire, large portions of these goods were consumed, and the scene presented of the owners was terrible, sorrowful and often amusing.

Deeds of heroic daring were frequently accomplished during the fire by different citizens. Every man felt it his duty to labor, and few idle ones could be seen. All in truth worked desperately.

Attempts were made to arrest the flames by blowing up houses, but owing to the scarcity of powder little good could be accomplished. Thos. Tuite[6] from Cincinnati was blown from the top of his house to the opposite side of the street and lit upon the ground standing, meeting with very slight injury. Seymour[7], a Cinti friend of mine, was again burned out, making the 2d time in the last two months.

Several persons, some "Sydney ducks," were caught plundering and

---

[6]Probably Thomas Jessup Tuite (1824-72) a native of Ireland and a Cincinnati resident, employed as a bookkeeper and post office clerk. *"Old Woodward,"* 295; Cincinnati city directories, 1843, 1846, 1849.

[7]George T. Seymour had arrived in San Francisco by November 29, 1850. He was a furniture dealer in that city for much of the 1850s. *Cincinnati Enquirer,* January 12, 1851; San Francisco city directories 1852-58.

were immediately taken to the quarters of the Vigilance Committee Rooms and placed under guard. The voice of the people was almost unanimously in favor of giving all the rascals to the Committee, and united in keeping off the Police. The excitement against these offenders was terrible. Some who were innocent were dragged before the committee but were instantly set at liberty and remunerated for their loss in the mob. In a day or two I presume we shall have act second of the Jenkins tragedy.

The scene of the city on fire was one of the most awful I have ever witnessed. Dense volumes of smok[e] rose and obscured the sky, the sun shining through with lurid glare and looking almost like a bloody ball of light, the flames whirling and soaring like a hurricane and sounding, as they gathered the buildings within their folds, like the noise occasioned by the tearing of the sides of the houses by a thousand hands. Explosions, cries, yells, ringing of bells, men running to and fro, women wringing their hands in despair, and children screaming, whilst the carmen were whipping their horses into speed, carrying Mdse. and furniture beyond the reach of flames. T'was terrible indeed.

Some of the wretches owning carts, drays, &c. made the fire the occasion of rapid money making to themselves, charging $20, $25, $50 and $75.00 per load. In one instance a scoundrel compelled a poor woman to give him $250.00 for carrying 3 loads. She had but $50 but gave him that and gave her note for the balance. The "committee" arrested all of these upon whom they could lay their hands.

The present loss is estimated at three millions of dollars. The prospective loss must be far greater. The loss unfortunately falls upon many poor families who are burned out of everything. The fire has hitherto missed that portion of the city. One good thing, however, results from yesterday's conflagration. The neighborhood contained the most dissolute and depraved characters of the city, and they are thus driven away for a season. The poor will generally be provided for. W. C. Canfield,[8] my friend, lost his baggage and room furniture. I lost all my shirts.

Sunday Night, about 9 o'clock, a horrid murder was perpetrated on Merchant St. below Kearny. A man by the name of Gallagher shot a Mr. Pollock through the head on account of a woman to whose favor G.

---

[8]William C. Canfield, a former Cincinnati druggist, was employed as a druggist in Sacramento in October 1850. Cincinnati city directory, 1849-50; 1850 Census, Sacramento County, 144.

claimed the exclusive privilege. G. was immediately arrested and handed over to the authorities to stand his trial.[9]

One would almost think the judgment of Heaven was upon this city for its wickedness. Six awful conflagrations almost destroying the city each time, all within 18 months.[10]

Wednesday, June 25th.

Yesterday and to-day were favored with weather which seldom falls to the lot of San Franciscans. It was really delightful. It is quite refreshing to have pleasant days occasionally. The wind is in the habit of playing us daily somewhat fantastic tricks. Out in the harbor it is cold, and in the city one is constantly rubbing his eyes to wipe out the dust which accumulates therein in perfect banks. When the wind gets on a "bender" there's no use trying to dodge it. It blows up street, down street and across. Where the deuce don't it blow! A fellow is compelled to keep one hand on the lapells of his coat to keep it from blowing off, the other [on] his hat to keep it from taking flight, and then to navigate, one has to take a quick survey of his course, marking a particular object for which to run, then close his eyes and foot it for dear life; this course followed, a man stands some chance of getting *somewhere*. But a woman, whew! A prudish old maid has no business here. Her ancles are in constant danger of being exposed as high as her knees. It requires a woman of considerable nerve and muscle to navigate. Capital place for a fellow to make survey of a pretty foot...

---

[9]The son of a New Jersey clergyman, Samuel Gallagher served with distinction in the war with Mexico and was later employed by a mercantile house in New York. In 1849 he came to California where he became a gambler. Louis Pollock, a native of New York, first arrived in California in 1837 and worked for merchant Nathan Spear. In 1840 he was expelled, along with other U.S. citizens, by Governor Alvarado. Pollock returned in 1849 and, after mining on the Mokelumne River and keeping a hotel in Stockton, moved to San Francisco where he, like Gallagher, took up gambling. Pollock and Gallagher were at first on friendly terms despite sharing the favors of prostitute Jane Hurley. The quarrel ending in Pollock's death began during the June 22 fire when Pollock publicly called Gallagher a coward. After fatally shooting Pollock outside of Jane Hurley's bedroom, Gallagher was arrested by the Vigilance Committee who, refusing to take cognizance of a crime of passion, surrendered him to the regular authorities. He was tried for murder the following August, but the jury was unable to reach a verdict. After a second trial in November, Gallagher was found guilty of manslaughter and sentenced to three months in prison plus a $500 fine. He was pardoned by Governor McDougal the following month. *Alta*, June 23, November 11-14, 18, 1851; *Herald*, June 23-25, August 8-9, 11-13, 1851; *San Francisco Daily Evening Picayune*, December 6, 1851; *Union*, July 2, 1851; Shuck, *Bench and Bar*, 80-81; CSL Information Catalogue under "Pollock, Lewis."

[10]The fires of December 24, 1849, May 4, June 14, September 17, 1850, May 4 and June 22, 1851.

This evening I went ashore for an hour without leave of the "powers that be" to obtain to-day's papers. I discover from them that the citizens are again agitating the question, "Which is the best possible plan for the preservation of the city from fire?" A dozen different methods are proposed. I believe the best would be to pass an ordnance prohibiting the erection of frame buildings over 10 feet in height. First, however, I would pass a law requiring Masters of vessels from foreign ports to enter into bond guaranteeing the good behavior of all passengers whom they may land here from a foreign nation for a period of 2 years. I opine these "Sydney Ducks" would be kept out by this means.

The citizens, nothing daunted by the conflagrations, are already rebuilding. I noticed to-night a house being put up by candle light. Fast country. Fast People. Deserve success!...

Monday, June 30th.

What a disagreeable change in the weather since Saturday—from calm to storm, from delightfully warm weather to a chill, damp atmosphere and clouded skies.

This morning Col. George Torrence, an old friend from Murderer's Bar, now on a visit to the Bay City, came out to see me just as I was preparing to go "ashore" to have my monthly settlement with Uncle Sam. The Col. brought me tidings from John, who is his partner, which proved agreeable. He remained in house and then repaired with me to the city, where we called upon some "auld acquaint" and enjoyed ourselves the while. How delightful 'tis to meet with kindred spirits and esteemed friends in this land!

About 12 o'clock I left the Col. to attend to business. I repaired to the Custom House and drew the value of my check, paid $10.00 for the advancement of the Whig cause, and then "made tracks" for the Post Office where I rec'd a letter from John, and one from "old Chabarnneau" *[sic]*. The former pleased, the latter amused. The old Indian is every inch a man, and a noble one too, notwithstanding his quaintness. He congratulates me on my position and tells me not to forget my friends and subscribes as follows, "Remember, Remember, Remember. Your Friend, J. B. Chabanneau." *But no letters from home!* However, a note I received informed me that should I call at the "Spring Valley Laundry, at the Lagoon," I would find a "package" from home. As soon as I had eaten dinner with Col. T. and a friend whom I had invited to dine with me, I repaired to the Laundry, two miles distant, and met a Mr. Hawley, who handed me a package sent from home, conveyed by a Mr. Northop. Upon opening it, what should I find but a most precious treasure, the very thing I should have asked for, the memorial of a sister's love, the four miniatures of four sisters, Emma, Angie, Lida and Ella[11] ... One letter, too, from Yeat,[12] the first he ever wrote—That amused me more than anything I have met with for months. My friends here envy my good fortune...

Wednesday, July 3d, 1851.

Old Boreas still on a "spree," cutting more fantastic shines than ever imagined by the king of pantomimists. Cold, dreary and unpleasant it is, and the waters of the bay chase each other in rough blue waves, their white caps lashing each other, appearing like a parcel of sheep gambling in their pastures or leaping one after another over a stile. Little sail-boats whiz past like a swiftly fleeting white cloud. Ships glide along gracefully into the harbor or make a bold front towards the "Golden Gates." The black hulks of ocean steamers rush by like some dark spirit or fierce thunder cloud, vomiting forth dense volumes of smoke which darken the already murky atmosphere. Occasionally the sun peeps forth and brightens the world for a moment, but it's like the cold, icy smile of the cynic or misanthropic spirit. Whew, how the wind whistles through the rigging and the waves dash against the side of the Ann McKim, but here I sit in the cabin jotting down nonsense to pass away the time and occa-

---

[11]Bickham's youngest sister, Mary Ella, was approximately five years old in 1851. In 1870 she was still living in the family home in Riverside, but in 1872 she married Abram D. Wilt, the principal and proprietor of Miami Commercial College in Dayton, and moved to that city. 1870 Census, Cincinnati, Ward 21, 702; Conover, *Dayton and Montgomery County,* 274-5; *Dayton Daily Journal,* March 28, 1894.

[12]Bickham's youngest brother, Thomas H. Yeatman Bickham, usually known as "Yeatman," was about nine years old in 1851. Ten years later he was employed as an assistant city auditor in Cincinnati. During the Civil War, Yeatman served as a first lieutenant in the 19th U.S. Infantry, was captured at Chicamauga, and incarcerated in Libby Prison, Virginia. During much of the 1870s he lived at the family home in Riverside, and worked at various times as assistant U.S. marshal, clerk at Fleischman and Co., and co-proprietor of the Queen City Copper Works. By the early 1880s he had moved to Findlay, Ohio, where he subsequently purchased the Findlay Gas Light Company and manufactured carriage bent-work. Cincinnati city directories: 1860, 1861, 1872-77; *War of Rebellion,* Series I, 30: 323; Series II, 6: 1005; 1870 Census, Cincinnati, 21st ward, 702; DMCL Bickham collection, "Sketch," 3-4; *History of Hancock County, Ohio,* 575, 625.

sionally bothered by the *nonsense* of Capt. Van Pelt. Our mates are busy experimenting with the boat, having just made a new set of sails.

I pass my time on board sometimes writing letters, sometimes in study, and occasionally pick up a trashy novel, (though only occasionally). When I get tired of study, I take a cigar and promenade the decks, taking in that time a view of what's passing in the Bay or taking a peep through the spy glass at a lassie who is cooped up a short distance from me in the Ship Marianna.[13] Don't I sympathize with her in her imprisonment? I don't know whether she is the Captain's daughter or not; she looks like a single woman, and it will be a little singular if I don't find out. Who would lead a bachelor's wife [sic] if he could help it? ...

But how unpleasant 'tis in this harbor, and how disagreeable in the city. No society nor much enjoyment. Only think of it, I know but two ladies in the city, one married and the other so busy in the house that a fellow can't have five minutes chat with her. She's an Irish girl and sometimes "blarneys" me, but I'm up to such tricks.

Yesterday, Mr. Wm. H. Graham, one of the Custom House officers, had a street fight with a Mr. Frank Lemon and got the side of his face with four teeth shot away. Graham fired 3 times and did no damage. Lemon fired 5 times and hit G. twice, once in the left arm. The street was crowded at the time, and one poor fellow had his arm broken by a pistol ball. Cause of Difficulty—something in Graham's family affairs.[14]

---

[13] The 379 ton ship *Marianna* arrived in San Francisco under the command of Captain E. J. Rassiter on May 23, 1851. The lady Bickham saw may have been the captain's wife who, together with their child, accompanied her husband on this voyage. Rasmussen, *Passenger Lists*, 1: 108; BL: C-A 169, part II, reels 2, 11; Bates, *Incidents on Land and Water*, 82-83.

[14] William Hicks Graham, a small but feisty Philadelphian, was characterized by fellow customs clerk, Caspar T. Hopkins, as "the hero of three duels and numerous street fights." Prior to his conflict with Lemon, Graham had wounded William Walker, the future filibuster, in a duel. George Frank Lemon, a native of Troy, New York, came to California with Stevenson's New York Volunteers and saw action in Baja California in 1847. He was a member of the San Francisco legislative assembly in 1849 and served as city assessor. The quarrel between Graham and Lemon, who had previously been friends, resulted from Lemon's dalliance with Graham's wife, whom Lemon, himself, had introduced to Graham. On the previous Sunday evening, Graham had attempted to provoke a duel by throwing the contents of a glass of water into Lemon's face, but friends intervened. The following Tuesday, Graham had a card printed in two morning newspapers calling Lemon a "scoundrel, liar, villain and poltroon." Later that day, the two met in the Plaza where the gunfight occurred. Both men were examined by courts of law but neither was punished, and Graham, when he recovered from his wounds, challenged Lemon to a duel. Hopkins, "California Recollections," *CHSQ*, 25: 336; Thrapp, *Encyclopedia of Frontier Biography*, 2: 578; Biggs, *Conquer and Colonize*, 167, 169, 219; Myers, *San Francisco's Reign of Terror*, 49-50; *Alta*, July 2, 1851, December 19, 1862; *Herald*, July 1, 2, 26, September 14, 1851; *Union*, July 3, 4, 1851; Below 231.

Since the fire, owners of property have been busy re-building, and over one hundred houses are now finished and occupied. Business *seems* brisk as ever, and citizens do not *appear* to have been troubled, but yet there is an undercurrent which runs strongly and deeply. There's distress and growing dissatisfaction in many an unfortunate's heart...

A few days ago a British ship arrived from China with two hundred and twenty-three passengers; two hundred and twenty-one of the number were shoe-makers, one a lawyer, another a Doctor. Huzza for the "sons of St. Crispin."[15]

If a stranger should land in our city at night and take a stroll up Commercial Street, I would wager not a little that his first impressions were that he had made a mistake and landed in Paris instead of in an American city. How the Messieurs and Mademoiselles do congregate amid the fantastic barrooms and gambling saloons in that street! What a picture of animated life is nightly presented! There is the Frenchman at the gambling table, his whole soul seemingly wrapped up in the game, and yet he talks on as merrily as a magpie. There's "Rouge et Noir" and "Lansquenet," and at these games the French are adepts. At yonder table sit a quartette of Monsieurs drinking claret and chatting with great vivacity, meanwhile gesticulating with terrible energy, yet always most courteously. There's another party playing at Billiards, and they are as noisy as a flock of blackbirds. But there's a bevy of Mademoiselles dressed in most complete Paris style, and every look a sweet smile, every gesture seductive. They are politeness itself. A Yankee may chat for a half hour in his own language with them and never suspect for a moment that they are as ignorant of what he is saying as would be an Arab. How sweetly is the "Oui Messieur" whispered from their inviting lips. How the whole battery of their charms are brought to bear on a fellow through the medium of their eyes, which flash like meteors in the sky, or melt into tenderness in a minute. The[y] sip a grass of wine with such grace and manner charmant as almost throws him off his balance. Oh these French women are d—ls. By daylight is nothing to be seen, the street all deserted and lonely; at night lights flash from many a dark eye, and all is animation and enjoyment. They all gamble, and losing or winning are ever the same.

---

[15]The patron saint of shoemakers.

The California Exchange and Union Hotel are the places of general evening resort for merchants and gents and until 10 o'clock are crowded. There associates meet and pass their time in talking over the topics of the day or reverting to old times, seasoning their discourse with an occasional glass of wine and smoking cigars. Such a thing as a public library is not known in San Francisco, and until we are secured from fires it is useless to attempt the organization of a Library Association.

The pleasantest method of passing an evening here is visiting the room of a friend and taking a hand at whist.

There are numerous churches in the city but Custom House Officers cannot leave their duties to go. I have not entered a Church since I left New Orleans, and when I do I shall note it as something out of the ordinary course of things in California.

Friday, July 4th, 1851.

Seventy five years ago this day was promulgated the ever memorable Declaration of our Independence, that glorious instrument which gave unity of sentiment and action to our ancestors, and around which they assembled in patriotic bands to deliver their country from tyranny and oppression. To-day how changed is all! The proud rivals in everything, the superiors in most, of our former oppressors! The proudest people on the face of the globe! This day, too, is one of [a] thousand in this our Pacific Coast. Not a cloud to mar the beauty of the Heavens, and the sun beams with added brilliancy. Every thing conduces to the enjoyment and celebration of the nation's holliday. The winds which usually detract so much from our comfort to-day are lulled, and a gentle breeze is wafted through our streets. Thousands are decked in holliday attire and are preparing for the different classes of celebrations, processions, orations, pic-nics, &c. The cannon are roaring, and ten thousand star spangled banners are floating proudly o'erhead. The shipping in the harbor of all nations is decked in their national drapery, while the proud American ensign is waving among the glittering flags as if conscious of its superiority.

My ship is resting in the bosom of the harbor, but her custom house officer is enjoying himself on shore among brother officers and other friends. One year ago I was among the mountain fastnesses of El

Dorado with a little patriotic band under far different circumstances from the present, busy celebrating the holliday.

The amusements of the day consist of the grand procession and oration, in which the different interests of the city took part; citizens generally, firemen, boatmen, draymen, military, Free Masons and Sons of Temperance. The draymen mounted on their horses, about 200 in number, made the fairest appearance. They were a body of the finest looking men I have ever seen, and their stock being of a superior order and in excellent condition. The boatmen, numbering 80 on foot, looked extremely well. At their head was a long row boat, carrying three boys dressed in character, with banners upon which were engraved various pretty mottoes. The company had some half a doz. other very beautiful satin banners with inscriptions and mottoes. One I noticed presented the painting of a row boat propelled by oars, while above was the motto "With the Oar for the '*Ore.*'" Another with this inscription, "The girls we left behind us, and those we've got around us." The firemen did not turn out so strongly as usual, yet their portion of the procession was very beautiful. They were dressed with their Fire hats, white shirts with red drawn over, and black pants. Their apparatus were finely decorated. The "Masons" were distinguished by a crimson ribbon in the button hole of their coats. The Sons of Temperance by the insignia of their order. That which pleased me most was a procession of children, perhaps about fifty.

The procession formed in the Plaza and marched through the burned district, bringing up at the Monumental Engine House, which was finely decorated with flags and evergreens. At this place a dense mass of citizens were congregated to hear the Oration, delivered by Andrew Williams.[16] The Declaration of Independence was read by the Hon. T. B. Van Buren.[17]

----

[16]Colonel Andrew Williams (d. 1876), a native of Cherry Valley, New York, practiced law in San Francisco in the early 1850s. He married the mother of author Bret Harte, and served as mayor of Oakland in 1857 and '58. According to the *San Francisco Daily Evening Picayune,* Williams' hour-long Independence Day speech, which "recalled the minds of his auditors to the dark and gloomy days of the Revolution,.. was repeatedly and earnestly cheered throughout, and at the conclusion the audience seemed for several minutes transported out of themselves." Merwin, *Life of Bret Harte,* 18-19; Johnson, *San Francisco as it Is,* 172-75; *Alta,* January 20, 1876.

[17]Thomas B. Van Buren, a native of Clermont, New York, arrived in California in 1850. He was elected senator from the San Joaquin district later that year, and practiced law in Stockton and San Francisco. After returning east he served as U.S. commissioner to the World Exposition in Vienna and as consul-general to Japan. *Call,* October 14, 1889.

View of the Plaza of San-Francisco (Courtesy, The Bancroft Library)

The Boys, as usual, enjoyed themselves with shooting crackers, pistols, &c., making terrible noise.

The ladies of the Episcopal Church held a fair over the California Exchange which was largely attended by the gents of the city. I was so busy with friends I did not go. I have thus far lived in California without female acquaintance, and as I am desirous of making money, I think it best to keep clear of them, knowing that an acquaintance with the dears would cause expensive outlays of money without much real enjoyment. At all events my pocket at present will not justify my engaging in these affairs, particularly as I wish to keep even with the first of my gentlemen friends.

Quite a numerous party went to Benicia to see the "Bull Fight," and many went to Sacramento upon a pleasure excursion. Thousands went to the races out at the "Mission," but the majority passed their time drinking wine and chatting with friends.

The Sons of Temperance held their celebration in the Baptist Church, but the "turn out" was rather slim. The oration was delivered by Mr. Taylor,[18] a young lawyer. I heard only the closing portion. The composition was very good but the delivery imperfect. Music by a French orchestra very good.

The children of the city had a celebration of their own at the Methodist Chapel, but I was too busy to attend it. The little fellows appeared as happy as birds on a May morning.

W. C. Canfield, W. H. Woodyard[19] of Cincinnati, and myself took a stroll through the burnt district and finally "brought up" at the Plaza, where W. H. W. bought two packs of Shooting crackers in remembrance of boyhood sports. One bunch he distributed to the urchins around, and the other he set fire to, repeating in the meantime the first verse of the song,

"O Would I were a boy again."

I wondered what to-day would be the course pursued by my friends on the Ohio. Pic-nics, rides, and a meeting of the "Moonlight Club" at night. My own enjoyment was not very great, consisting in nothing but excitement. I met many old friends and many recent acquaintances of the city.

The myriads of Frenchmen who throng our city entered with as great zest into the celebration as Americans themselves. I heard one burly grenadier looking chap, who was as happy as happy could be, cry out terrifically, "Hurrah for ze, ze Fourth of July!" Poor fellow was just about "tight" enough to feel patriotic. Another one I heard say, "Ze Americans is von grand peoples!"

---

[18]Edward W. Taylor, a native of Michigan, represented San Francisco in the 1855 state assembly after being nominated by both the Whig and Know Nothing parties. He held no other political office and practiced law in San Francisco until his death, aged seventy, in 1897. Hurt, "Know Nothings," *CHSQ*, 9: 29; 1860 Census, San Francisco, 804; *Great Register of San Francisco, 1867*; *Call*, February 12, 1897.

[19]Apparently *H. W.* (Henry Wellington) Woodyard, a native of Kentucky, who served as customs inspector in San Francisco from 1849 to summer of 1851. Woodyard practiced law in San Francisco during the later 1850s and early 1860s. He died, aged 41, in April 1864. BL: C-A 169, Part II, reel 11; San Francisco city directories, 1856-63; 1860 Census, San Francisco, 437.

I had quite a pleasant little tete a tete with a pretty German woman, whose husband keeps a fine Saloon on Commercial st. She tells me to call and see her, and she will learn me to speak "Ze German and ze French, if I will teach her el Anglaise." To be sure I will go.

I heard not of a single accident during the day, although I was in constant terror lest some of the many rockets and squibs which were burned should set fire to the city...

Wednesday, July 9th, 1851.

Went ashore this morning to report expiration of time for discharging the Ann McKim... Met several friends and passed the compliments of the Day. Procured a file, consisting of 30 or 40 papers of the Cincinnati Daily Commercial, and then proceeded to Long Wharf to meet the McKim's boat. While waiting for her, I met an old acquaintance, that erratic genius, W. J. Sperry,[20] whom I had not seen since parting with him on board the steamer Webster at the Cincinnati wharf in April, 1849. Sperry had on his shoulders and in his pockets sundry Surveying Instruments, and he informed me that he had been carrying them since the winter of '49. He is Dep'ty County Surveyor. He looked as natural as a young horse. Says he's never going to the States 'cept on a visit, that when he does travel, 'twill be further West.

At 4 o'clock the Captain came for me, and as we returned we called on board the barque Vesta, and had quite a pleasant time with a Mrs. Anderson who was present... The conversation turned to ladies' dress, which was introduced by way of a critique on the new style a la Turk which has just made its appearance.[21] Several Englishmen who were

---

[20]William J. Sperry (1823-56) a native of Monmouth County, New York, moved to Ohio in 1840 to attend Oberlin College. He became a Cincinnati journalist, took part in the anti-slavery movement, and authored a poem lamenting the fate of the Iroquois Indians. In 1849 Sperry came overland to California, where he served as deputy surveyor of San Francisco from 1850 to 1856. In December of 1856 his body was found in San Mateo County where he had gone several days earlier to survey a piece of land. The cause of his death was unknown. Martzoleff, *Poems on Ohio*, 62; *Cincinnati Enquirer*, March 28, May 8, 1849; Haskins, *Argonauts. of California*, 399; San Francisco city directories, 1850-56; *Alta*, December 8-9, 1856.

[21]This was the "Bloomer" style, popularized by feminist editor Amelia Bloomer. It consisted of a loosely fitting costume with knee length dress and Turkish style pants buttoned at the ankle. This style generated considerable controversy in San Francisco when displayed in the window of Mrs. S. E. Cole's millinery shop. It attracted still more attention when Mrs. Cole wore bloomers on the street, looking, according to the *Alta California*, "exceedingly neat and pretty." Lotchin, *San Francisco 1846-1856*, 307; *Alta*, July 8, 9, August 12, 1851.

present took part on both sides [of] the question. The lady supported her sex with that ability usually displayed by women when on the subject of dress. She was really eloquent. I held that ladies had a perfect right to arrange affairs belonging peculiarly and appropriately to themselves. The whole subject of dress, ancient and modern, was canvassed quite freely, and bustles as well as multitudes of petticoats were handled quite cavalierly; long waists, short waists, balloon sleeves, hoops, tight lacing, long trains, and flouncing came in for a liberal share of praise and abuse. In the end the "New Style" was triumphant.

In the course of the conversation, I alluded casually to Cincinnati, and after we had finished the discussion "on dress," Mrs. A. made enquiry if I hailed from thence, and being answered affirmatively, began to ask me questions concerning various citizens and old acquaintances of mine. I learned that she had resided there with her husband a few years ago, and I was quite delighted with my good fortune in meeting her. More particularly was I pleased as she was the first *lady* of intelligence I have conversed with in California. Our conversation was quite lively, and I was very happy to meet a lady who knows so many of my acquaintance... Mrs. A. is a fine, healthy looking young Englishwoman, who seems to know very well what she is about, and is quite happy in administering to the entertainment of gentlemen in her company.

The Captain of the McKim was anxious to return to his vessel, and I was fain to accompany him, but I was exceedingly loth to quit the "Vesta." The husband of Mrs. A. has been in the Custom House employment, but lately rec'd his discharge. Col. Collier[22] gave him his appointment, it is said, on account of his pretty wife, the old Col. being quite a gallant gentleman.

The "new style" of Dress, which yesterday made its appearance, has created quite a flutter among the females of San Francisco, and no little stir among the hombres. Hundreds flocked to the store of Miss Cole to see how it looked, and though it appeared odd on account of its novelty,

---

[22]A lawyer, politician, and veteran of the War of 1812, James Collier (1789-1873) was appointed collector of the port of San Francisco by President Zachary Taylor in 1849. Collier served in that office until 1851, when he was replaced by Thomas Butler King. Although charged with several malpractices, Collier was vindicated by the U.S. Supreme Court. Ernest de Massey, a French gold-seeker, characterized Collier as "a heavy-set busybody" and a "rapacious rascal." Forman, *The Adventures of James Collier, passim.;* Massey, *Frenchman in the Gold Rush,* 27.

it was generally admitted to be quite "the thing." It is really beautiful if one would not notice the violent contrast. The ladies pronounce it the best thing yet started for California. It is handsome, luxurious, and seductive. Unfortunately it is suitable only for the beautiful; those having pretty forms, feet and ancles. Tall women will not look well in it, and dumpy ones, oh!...

Friday, July 12th.

This morning at 9 o'clock the "Committee of Vigilance" hanged Jas. Stuart, with half a dozen aliases.[23] He has several times escaped from the hands of the police, but this time he got into hands where there was no escape for the guilty. He made a confession in which are some most astounding disclosures, evidencing what we have long suspected, organized bands of desperadoes in our midst, who have regularly prepared plans to rob, murder, and burn. Also implicating in most dishonorable transactions some of the first men of the State...

Strange and deep excitement prevails throughout the city. One party, very respectable in numbers and ability, bitterly condemn and oppose the action of the V. C., but by far the greater number side with them. The Mayor[24] this morning issues his proclamation calling upon all good citizens to support the law in the endeavor to disorganize these persons styling themselves the V. Committee. The friends of the "V. C." are highly excited by the Confession of Stuart, and seemed determined to support it in ridding the country of the desperadoes who infest it. The sternest and bitterest feeling is aroused against those law[y]ers and judges mentioned in the Confession. Heaven only knows where it all will end.

---

[23] A native of Sussex, England, James ("English Jim") Stuart was transported to Australia at the age of sixteen for forgery. He was pardoned six years later and arrived in California in 1850. After attempting to make a living by mining and various small enterprises, he returned to a life of crime, committing numerous robberies and at least one murder. Returning to San Francisco, Stuart became the principal leader of the "Sydney Ducks," a gang of ex-convicts from Australia whom he led in a series of robberies. He was captured by the Vigilance Committee on July 1, 1851. Williams, *Committee of Vigilance*, 252-59; Stewart, *Committee of Vigilance*, 143-84.

[24] The mayor at this time was Charles James Brenham (1817-76) a native of Kentucky and a former Mississippi riverboat captain who, upon coming to California in 1849, became captain of the Sacramento river steamboat *McKim*. During his term as mayor of San Francisco from May 5 to December 30, 1851, Brenham opposed the Vigilance Committee and mob violence in general. He was mayor a second time from 1852 to 1854, and earned praise for his economy measures. Heintz, *San Francisco Mayors*, 10-15.

How strange it appeared at the moment of execution that the vast crowd assembled should have, as if by one mind, uncovered their heads. It was awful in the extreme. Stuart did not appear to show the least fear, save that his really fine and intellectual countenance was slightly pale. After the guard was formed, Stuart stepped forth with his hands manacled and said, "here I am, gentlemen, in your power, you may hang me if you choose!" In accordance with his wish, his face was left uncovered. As he was drawn up, he lifted up his hands and eyes to heaven and died without a struggle.

July 13th, 1851.

This morning Judge Campbell[25] in his charge to the jury, characterized the hanging of Stuart as "deliberate murder," and the Committee with the spectators as "guilty of Murder," and called upon them to assist in bringing all whom were possible to be taken to justice. His "charge" altogether was exceedingly able and well written, but in the opinion of the great portion of the community, very inappropriate, or at least in bad taste.

The coroner's jury gave in verdict according to facts.

The Confession, to me, does not seem to agree in its different parts, there being several inconsistancies, yet it wears an air of truth and implicates many who have hitherto been above suspicion in most dishonorable transactions. It tells us plainly that our courts are corrupt and our officers unfaithful. What must be the feeling of that community which is betrayed by the very persons to whom it has looked for protection? The contempt of all good citizens will [be] visited upon the traitors.

July 14th, 1851.

This morning being Sunday, I assumed a liberty and went ashore, where I passed the day with some friends. Whilst there I heard of the Murder of Don San [sic] Francisco Guerrero, an old native Californian, on the road to the Mission, in broad day light. How it is possible for men

---

[25]Alexander Campbell (1820-1912) a native of Jamaica, practiced law in Brooklyn, New York, before moving, in 1849, to San Francisco, where he was elected county judge. Campbell presided over the Court of Sessions at the time of the first Vigilance Committee, and despite his opposition to that body, was respected by some Vigilance Committee sympathizers for his honesty and ability. Shuck, *History of the Bench and Bar*, 1901, 514-18; Daggett, *Scrapbook of California*, 3: 76.

directly in the face of ignominious death [to] commit a crime so revolting, and so soon, too, after an execution but two days before for a less offence, is one of those mysteries of human nature which I cannot understand. A Frenchman is suspected of the crime.[26]

But why should I enter in my journal these details of crime committed in our midst? Not a day passes but the papers from all sections of the State bring accounts of horrid murders, robberies, rencontres, executions, &c. Vigilance Committees have been formed all over the State, and not a day rolls around without bringing accounts of executions. Last week a Spanish woman was hanged by the authorities for stabbing a man to the heart who had insulted her the night previous. The poor fellow had come to apologise when she plunged a knife into his heart. She adjusted the rope on her own neck, having gracefully removed two heavy, glossy, black locks from her shoulders to make room for the fatal cord. She then mounted to the scaffold fearlessly and in answer to a question "if she had anything to say against her sentence" said, "Nothing, only I would do it again if I were so provoked."[27]...

July 17th.

Seldom do I read works of fiction, but to-day, feeling disinclined to useful studies, I indulged an humor and read "Queen Joanna, or Mys-

---

[26]A native of Mexico, Don Francisco Guerrero (c. 1811-1851) come to California in 1834 with the Hijar-Padrés colony. He served as *alcalde* and *juez de paz* of San Francisco from 1839 to 1844, as sub-prefect 1845-6, and again as sub-prefect under American rule in 1849. Guerrero was, according to the *Alta California*, "celebrated for his kindness and hospitality, particularly among the Americans to whom he was always a warm friend."

When Guerrero was found dead on the Mission Road, foul play was suspected, although some believed he had died from an accidental fall from his horse, and François Le Bras, a mentally disturbed French sea cook who had been seen riding with Guerrero, was arrested by the Vigilance Committee. The coroner's inquest, at which Le Bras was present, found against him, but the Vigilance Committee refused to surrender him to the sheriff until they had investigated the case and found the evidence insufficient for conviction. When Le Bras was tried by the district court the following November, he was acquitted, but some contemporaries continued to believe that he had murdered Guerrero, suborned by parties involved in the litigation over the Santillan land grant, in which Guerrero would have been a key witness. *Alta,* July 14-16, 24, November 16, 1851; *Herald,* July 14-15, 1851; *San Francisco Daily Evening Picayune,* July 15, 23, 1851; Davis, *Seventy Five Years in California,* 115-16; Williams, *Committee of Vigilance,* 317-18; BL: C-D 94: 80.

[27]The "Spanish" (probably Mexican) woman, usually known as "Juanita," was hanged in Downieville on July 5, 1851, after a summary trial. She was the only woman known to have been lynched during the California Gold Rush. For an interesting account of this tragedy, see Stewart, *Committee of Vigilance,* 154-62.

teries of the Court of Naples," by _____ Reynolds.[28] I do not like his style. His work appears forced and stiff and is altogether too marvelous even for fiction. The plot is even not well founded.

Late in the afternoon I went ashore to put a letter in the post office, and whilst rambling, I dropped into the "Courier office" where I met Col. Kewen, our candidate for Congress, on an electioneering visit to our city. The Colonel appears quite sanguine and gives a good account of the State as far as he can judge from his own observations.

On my return to the Wharf for the boat, I found the Capt. with several old English Ship Captains in a jolly state of inebriety. We accompanied Capt. Love[r]ing[29] to his ship, where we remained a short time and discussed a bottle of ale. I was much amused during my visit, noticing the characteristics of Englishmen which they showed in eminent light while feeling so gloriously hilarious. They were decidedly more sociable in this state than even Yankees. Like all others of their countrymen, they think the U. S. not half so great as she really is, and though they speak well of her, they cannot imagine that she is anything like Merry England in point of worth. One thing is certain, that most of these old English Captains are well read gentlemen. Many of them speak with critical acumen upon the merits and works of authors...

I have noticed a peculiarity in the character of Californians which exists in no other country. Their *seeming* want of hospitality and their carelessness upon meeting individuals whom they are in the habit of terming friends. It is caused by the nature of the situation in which they are placed. Being constantly roving from one point to another, strangers comparatively in a strange land, and if not actually engaged in business, the very air the[y] breathe is so impregnated with excitement that they are constantly hurried from one thing to another and cannot feel contented to demean themselves as they were wont to do at their appropriate homes. One meets an old acquaintance, shakes him warmly by the hands, asks him a few hurried questions, invites him to "join him in a glass," says he will be pleased to see him at his office, excuses himself,

---

[28]A radical English politician and journalist, George William MacArthur Reynolds (1814-79) was the author of a long string of lurid novels very popular with nineteenth century British workers. *DNB.*

[29]Apparently Captain E. Lovering of the 252-ton British bark *Enterprise*, which had arrived in San Francisco on May 5, 1851, after a fifty day voyage from Valparaiso. BL: C-A 169, Part II, Reel 11.

and away he flies. The Californian thinks not of paying the same attention to a friend as at home, for there the cit. would be looked on as a boor
if, upon meeting an old acquaintance, he did not administer to his com-
forts and pleasure in numerous ways; here, however, it is not expected,
but the stranger just landing on our shores thinks very strangely of us.
He is not here three days before he becomes thoroughly imbued with the
same spirit, and may be seen flying through the streets like a comet.
When a party does meet, glasses must glisten on the board, cigars show
themselves, and conversation be of an exciting nature, or cards produced, else alas for pleasure. Excitement, Excitement, Excitement!
Therefore will the citizen of California when he returns to the East be
discontented, therefore will he in a short time return, therefore is he
foolish for thinking of returning to the east without the wherewithal to
keep up excitement, and therefore will most of those who visit here take
up permanent residence. My own heart is warm and opens with a
thrilling bound towards a friend upon meeting him, but I am a Californian, and to save me I cannot help acting as all others. How uneasy I
am in one place, chatting with a friend. I must stir, stir, stir!!!

If one is solitary, he is lonely indeed. If surrounded by friends, he feels
as though something were wanting, and what that is he cannot tell.
Excitement is necessary to keep him from being miserable... Many mistake in deeming that excitement is *the* pleasure; it simply is the shield of
unhappiness. It drives away melancholy thoughts, and we live in ficti-
tious element. It is a morbid, unwholesome pleasure which we experience and I much fear will undermine the future happiness of this life.
Contentment cannot dwell in the minds of those placid walks of life at
home where one has been schooled in the academy of highly wrought
excitement. There are then those who were miserable here who return
home to be more miserable. There are those who live an excited life here,
who must remain to keep alive the feeling of morbid pleasure or happiness. And all this is for the pursuit of wealth and happiness! Of wealth
as necessary to happiness, Of ambition as necessary to happiness!
Strange world; inconsistent Man! And I too am thus!

July 18th.

I have just been thinking of the inconsistency of those who have
adventured to California in the pursuit of wealth. Those who at home

were discontented with their condition, their comparative poverty, and who came here determined to better their condition. I have noticed this inconsistency in the mines, have myself experienced it. I need not, Sisters, write a long essay upon the matter but will explain in a few words. Young men at home would imagine that those who were here would when certain of making some three, four or five dollars by *working* a half day, not fail of applying themselves. I once thought so. But here have I many a time, as well as others, when being able to do thus much, refused it, and have gone to immense trouble and some expense to prepare for a fishing excursion. Then have gone and fished all day without getting a "bite." Else have gone on some other foolish expedition, never without expense. Now does it not seem great inconsistency to complain of our hard fortune when we will thus neglect opportunities? I really cannot explain this inconsistency of human nature. Is it not thoughtlessness?

About dusk I went ashore to hear Col. Kewen's speech. The California Exchange was much crowded, and the Col. enchained their attention for an hour and a half in an eloquent and powerful address. He, however, appeared much worn by previous efforts in the South. The Whigs were quite enthusiastic. I noticed Hon. T. Butler King, his black eyes glowing like coals of fire, seated on the platform as Chairman. The Whig Editors of the city officiated as Vice Chairmen, and my friend, Col. Wood, was Sec'y.

San Francisco is the most lonely place to me I have found in California. I have a decided preference for my ship, where I can read and enjoy my thoughts or fancies undisturbed. I walked around and listened to music in the different Gambling Saloons & at 11 o'clock came back to the Ann McKim.

July 19th.

This morning I had quite a discussion with Captain Van Pelt with regard to California, her present condition, her wealth, agricultural and mineral, and her future destiny. I contend that she will speedily assume her position as one of the first states in commercial *and* agricultural importance in the Union. That in her mineral lands, her large, fertile agricultural domain, her splendid climate and geographical position, are the elements of unbounded prosperity and greatness. That that class of people who have immigrated hither are the most intelligent and worthy citizens at home. That their enterprise and energy is of the greatest, and that from these causes of necessity become a great people in a great state. The Captain, with many others who know nothing of the subject, contends that but a very short time will suffice to exhaust our placers, our surface diggings, and that soon will mining cease to be unprofitable [sic] to individuals. I have observed that this idea prevails only with those who have never been practical operators and form their conclusions upon a basis which cannot stand. My own opinion is that individual mining will prove profitable for a century to come.[30]

July 20th.

This morning arrived the Pacific Mail Steamer Tennessee 19 days from Panama, bringing dates from Atlantic States June 14. I went ashore and amused myself during the morning reading the Delta & Tribune. Could obtain no Cincinnati Papers. Felt dull and discontented and at 3 P. M. returned to the Ann McKim, having succeeded in borrowing from Capt. Love[r]ing of Br. Barque Enterprise Lamartine's History of the Gironidsts, 3 Volumes.[31] I brought with me the 1st volume of Dumas' Louise la Valliere, being the 1st of the Conclusion of the series of novels beginning with "The Three Guardsmen."[32] There is much attraction for me in Dumas' writings, yet I become almost worried out of my life with his interminable descriptions of character and *new* characters which he constantly introduces. That which makes the attraction of a work of fiction is entirely wanting in all his writings, viz: a pleasing *conclusion*. All his novels either end sorrowfully or terribly, and this is anything but satisfactory to a reader as they are read for the pleasure afforded to the imagination and as a pastime. I shall read no more of them...

---

[30]Van Pelt was correct. By the mid-1850s the surface placers were largely played out, and mining had become a task for big business rather than the individual miner.

[31]Alphonse de Lamartine (1790-1869) the earliest of the French Romantic poets, was an active political figure, a champion of social reform and the author of a history of the moderate Girondist Party during the French Revolution.

[32]*Louise de Valliere* forms one portion of *The Vicomte de Bragelonne*, the huge third novel of Dumas' trilogy beginning with *The Three Musketeers* (which Bickham refers to as *"The Three Guardsmen"*) followed by *Twenty Years After.*

Lamartine's History, so far as I have read, is anything but a Narrative or mirror of the past. It is a beautifully written historical Essay, not possessing the interest of history, yet more agreeable on account of the pleasant manner in which it is presented. It appears to me that he constantly strives to produce and *exhibit* original ideas without giving arguments in support of opinions regarding the true opinions of the nation during the Revolutionary period. He talks of passions, of anarchical feelings, &c., not in historical manner but as a metaphysician or essayist.

Health not good—severe cold—pain in chest—bad humor—cross—dissatisfied, &c. I wish I could hear from home.

Well, I am lonely!!

Having become wearied with my long sojourn on the Ann McKim, and accommodations with the association of the Captain proving disagreeable, I concluded to go ashore and spend a portion of the afternoon and the night. I went to the "Courier Office" and looked over the list of Exchange papers, selected such as I wanted, and then wandered about to see what was passing. I came to the conclusion that, notwithstanding the crowds of people passing and repassing, that San Francisco is the most lonely place I have yet seen.

I read all the city papers from the column editorial to the conclusion of "marine news," noticing the action of the different political parties in various parts of the State, news from the Placers, Quartz diggings, tidings from the Indian Wars, and City gossip, and thereby received "of course" a vast deal of enlightenment. At bed-time I went in the unsuccessful search of lodgings to various Hotels, &c., and was about coming to the conclusion that I would save myself unnecessary trouble by returning to the Ship, when, to my great astonishment and joy, I was tapped on the shoulder by an old acquaintance, Hubbard Stone,[33] a fel-

---

[33]Hubbard Stone, an Ohio native, is listed in the 1850 census as a 24-year-old miner living in Stockton. By 1856 he had returned to Cincinnati where he had become a commission merchant. During the Civil War Stone, at age 35, joined the Ohio Volunteer Infantry as a private. He rose to the rank of captain by the time of his discharge in October 1864, having served at Shiloh, Vicksburg, and Atlanta. 1850 Census, San Joaquin County, California, 303; Cincinnati city directory, 1856; *War of Rebellion*, Series I, 38, part 3: 213; *Official Roster of the Soldiers of the State of Ohio in the War of the Rebellion*, 5: 129, 141, 153.

low townsman, who left home shortly after my departure, but whom I had not before met in California. He had been in the city about one month, arriving here from Trinadad, where he has been engaged for two or three months working at his trade on his own account. He informed me that he made about $1,000. Is now working here for $8, 10 and 12 per diem. We passed several hours in talking over old times, and I felt more contented than for many a day past. I lodged with him between two blankets on the floor of the establishment where he is engaged.

July 25th.

This morning I had a difficulty with Captain Van Pelt on account of the fare he endeavors to force on me. I desired him, very coolly, to do better for me or he would be compelled. He was "werry" much excited and told me he knew "*my* rights on board his ship." I desired no discussion on those points as I was not aware of his having any business with me farther than to attend to my advice in time. He soon cooled down, and to-day I notice a change for the better…

I am getting quite deeply into Lamartine's "History of the Girondists," and am much interested and pleased with his facility in writing and his graceful style. A fault with him however, being a graceful man himself and charitable, he imparts too great a gracefulness to those characters he describes. He seems to think the inspirations of Liberty cover over those dark spots in the character of some of the bloodiest minded fanatics that have ever lived. Like all Frenchmen he is continually harping upon the string of *"ideas,"* and not unfrequently gives a mere fancy the importance of an "idea." And no less does he prate upon those supremely French "ideas," "Fatality" and "Destiny," without once deigning to give the reader an "idea" of his meaning of the ominous words. I have often acknowledged the justice of his deductions, yet frequently have noticed the introduction of many truisms which are as old as Methusalem but which he claims for original. He is certainly not a profound historian, however meritorious he may be as a Poet. I would prefer one of Macaulay's works to a half dozen of his. There's no comparison between them as Historians. McCaulay [*sic*] in profundity of thought, acuteness in deductions, depth of research, is as far superior to him as Bulwar to Dumas in fiction.

July 27th.

To-day I am decidedly in an ill humor. Cause—Dissatisfaction with the Captain who has gone off with the boat and is making a stay beyond all reason and his promise to be back soon, thus leaving me on the ship with a dirty shirt when I wish to go ashore for a clean one. Another reason is brooding over disappointment in not receiving letters from home.

At 3 o'clock I got ashore and was not long in getting shaved and putting on that indispensable article to my comfort, a clean shirt. After doing this, I found H. Stone and took a walk with him away out Stockton Street and back to Happy Valley. We saw over a dozen drunken men during our rambles, one of them vowing to the crowd that he was a bona-fide "poet." We had a specimen of his rhymes, and, moreover, the bright flash of circumstance revealed to our view in an upstairs window the countenance and form of a pretty lady. She beamed out like a brilliant star from 'neath a dark cloud, then suddenly retreated, leaving all dark again, we looking in vain for another glimpse of beauty. Just before sun-set, "Judge" Coffin joined us; we then turned our course to the Mission road which we followed beyond the toll-gate, and came to dead halt upon meeting a mire of sand which was in our way. Returning took the last resort, viz: went to the Bella Union, seated ourselves in huge armchairs, smoked and chatted away the evening, and at 11 o'clock, like peaceable and worthy citizens, returned our way to bed, there to dream of fortunes [and] of home.

Thursday, July 31st, 1851.

To Day is a great Holliday for the Inspectors, it being General Settlement Day. I repaired to the Custom House early and there met quite a crowd of brother officers, all rejoicing in their *wealth*(?) What was not particularly pleasing, however, was the idea of being tapped on the shoulder just about the time of receiving the oro & putting in pocket, and requested to fork over $10.00 towards assisting the great Whig Party. "Them as dances must pay the fiddlers." Just about 6 per cemtum. This is the 2d time in 2 months—next month 'twill be the same...

Sunday, Aug. 3d.

This morning arrived the Pacific Mail Steamer California. I went ashore to see the excitement attendant upon the landing of her passengers. These occasions are always amusing and interesting. Amusing to see the new adventurers clad in their tall heavy boots and regular California suits, hastening to leap to the quays as though they saw the gold glistening from the declivities of Telegraph Hill; or delighted beyond measure to escape from their ocean prison to terra firma. How many of the poor fellows will wish they had not been in such hurry to leave pleasant homes. It is deeply interesting to witness the meetings of old friends, of husbands and wives, sisters and brothers, fathers and mothers. I observed a number of returning Californians who stated that they found it impossible to remain in the old states.

The occasions of the arrival of Mail Steamers are glorious ones for the newsboys. They rush precipitately from a thousand directions to the different Express Offices and there await with noisy impatience the opening of the Newspaper Packages. One after the other, as they are served, the[y] rush for the streets, flying from this corner to that, from one public house to another, crying out as loudly as they can yell the different periodicals they have for sale, shoving a paper into the hands of this one, into the face of that, extending a hand for the anticipated "quarter." Such a noisy uproarious set as are these boys. Men might learn lessons of perseverance and industry from them. Most of them are acute at driving a trade and turn many a penny to their pockets. I generally purchase the Delta, Tribune, Herald, and Cinti. Gazette, and the Washington papers when they are to be procured.

Aug. 8th...

This is another foggy, damp, unpleasant morning, but such as we frequently have here. It is very oppressive and certainly cannot be conducive to health, as it assuredly has a tendency to destroy the equanimity of one's temper. I am to-day decidedly ill-humored and cross-grained. Part owing to the atmosphere.

I presume I shall leave the Ann McKim about Sunday as I have orders to make my "Return." I have now been on board 55 days and have not enjoyed myself as I might on a different craft. I have finished Larmartine's History of the Girondists, and all I regret is that it was not extended.

CHAPTER TEN

Politics and Death

Monday, Aug. 11th, 1851.

This morning left the Ann McKim and made my "Return," having been on board 57 days. Reported at the Barge Office and..[illegible]..the day without getting on board another vessel.

At 8 o'clock P.M. met with the young Whigs of the city composing the Young Men's Whig Association of San Francisco; transacting in the evening the business which devolved upon our body. We received a strong accession of strength to our body in the persons of many young men, among the number E. W. Taylor Esq., whom I imagine at some future day will rise to eminence among his fellow men. He is the same who, in the 4th of July, '51, delivered an oration before the Sons of Temperance in this city. He is quite a young man and appears to be a young gentleman of fine abilities. He is quiet, dignified, and self-possessed. I understand that he is a candidate for the office of District Atty., subject to the decision of the Whig Convention soon to be holden.

The Young Men's Whig Association has ever its object the purification and unity of the party; intend acting in concert with the Gen'l Whig committee. We are a secret body, each member pledging himself to secrecy in the affairs of the body. One of our constitutional articles reads as follows:

"Resolved—That all successful stratagems are honorable."

I only became a member on Saturday night, Aug. 9th. Considerable jealousy is manifested toward us by the Old Hunkers[1] of the party, and

---

[1]The term "Hunker" stemmed from the Dutch word "hunkerer" or self-seeker, and referred to politicians who "hunkered" after office. This term had previously been applied to the conservative wing of the New York State Democrats, but it is here used by Bickham to designate the old guard of his own Whig party.

more particularly by the *Old Office Seekers*. Mr._____[2] heard of our organization and, being fearful that the association might interfere with his ambitious schemes, sent a polite invitation to meet him. He made some explanations, expressed a desire to become a member, and broke the necks of several bottles of Champagne with his "young friends." There is a manifest desire in his whole course to make political friends among all parties in order to accomplish his views, and many of his efforts are not such as a good Whig could commend, although all must close their eyes and ears to reports and facts, as in him rest our chances of success.

Tuesday, Aug. 12th.

This morning I boarded the splendid Clipper Ship Witchcraft[3] frm. New York, 127 days from port to port, running days, 103. Having touched at a foreign port, an officer was required. I found no foreign cargo on board, and left immediately; however, was put on board the British Barque Francis[4] from Hobart Town, Australia, laden with Potatoes and Onions. Very small cabins, tho' clean and neat. In the afternoon I went ashore to attend the Primary election of the Whigs for the County Convention.

Whilst attending the polls I gained more new political ideas, being enabled to see in some manner the working of the wheel within wheels. The old Hunkers manage things pretty much to suit themselves. This will be stopped before another election shall take place.

One idea which I especially dislike, viz.: on the last day of each month the Officers of Customs draw their pay; ere we get outside of the House, each is asked to *"Contribute* $10.00 for party purposes." This is all very well, and I, as a good and true Whig, willingly and freely bestow my mite, but the manner in which this contribution is taken is what I do not

---

[2]Probably Thomas Butler King, the leader of the San Francisco Whigs.

[3]The 1,310 ton clipper ship *Witchcraft*, built in 1850, left New York for California on April 4, 1851. On May 9th she lost most of her spars in a storm and was forced to put into Rio de Janeiro for 21 days refitting. After a 62 day passage, she arrived in San Francisco on August 11, having made record time. The *Witchcraft* made five other voyages from the East Coast to San Francisco before she was wrecked off Cape Hatteras in April 1861. Howe and Matthews, *American Clipper Ships*, 2: 724-27; Rasmussen, *Passenger Lists*, 2: 189-90.

[4]The 216 ton British bark *Francis*, commanded by Allan Christy, arrived in San Francisco on August 12, 1851, after a 110 day voyage from Hobart Town. BL: C-A 169, part II, reel 11.

commend. It is seemingly a voluntary gift, but the very moment an officer should presume to decline payment, that very moment he would lose his office. Thus though it is asked as a contribution and is in the nature of a free gift, it is really an exaction which if resisted is punished with loss of office. I will bear these things in mind.

Another circumstances I shall not forget. Mr. _____, hoping thus to make political capital and friends among the opposing party, bestows his favor upon some of them. A Mr. Frank Ball, who was formerly an employee in Clayton's drinking Saloon, composed a pasquinade ridiculing the gentleman for the part which he took in the removal of deposites from the burned Custom House. The song was obtaining great celebrity, crowds of persons visiting the saloon nightly to hear it. It is now heard no more; Ball is an Inspector. Mr. _____ was seen to enter Clayton's, and there are good reasons to suppose that B. was bought off.[5] Ridicule is a terrible weapon in any society, but it seems preposterous that a man who aspires to the dignity of U. S. Senator should condescend to buy off an individual who would descend to such ridicule as was contained in the song. The vote of no sensible man could have been cast into the opposite scales for a mere song, and those who compose the mass, uneducated and subject to the domination of passion and prejudice, never entered the saloon. The gentleman's warmest friends condemn this action.

The Election was conducted with earnestness, and much good humored rivalry and excitement prevailed. If the Whigs but work as hard on election day, they will obtain a magnificent victory. Jack

---

[5]"Mr. _____ " was Bickham's superior, Collector Thomas Butler King. On May 28, 1851, King, with the aid of thirty armed men, transferred the deposits from the old Custom House, which had been largely destroyed by the May 4th fire, to the new Custom House. King's manner of transferring the deposits, "marching like a proud drum major at the head of a miniature grand army," struck many observers as excessively pompous. Frank Ball, a Mexican War veteran and member of the Vigilance Committee, who often entertained habitués of Clayton's saloon with comic songs which he composed himself, satirized King in a song entitled "The King's Campaign." He had a large number of copies of the song lithographed with a caricature print of the procession, and sold 500 of these copies in a single night at one dollar each. King, as Bickham relates, bought Ball off with a customs post. On another occasion Ball's satirical gifts had a less happy result. When he composed a song about the hanging of John Jenkins, he was brutally assaulted by "Dutch Charley" Duane, a pro-Broderick "shoulder striker" and a friend of Jenkins. Soulé et al., *Annals*, 334-38; Stewart, *Committee of Vigilance*, 219-23.

Moses[6] was a defeated candidate. The vote he rec'd was, however, a very flattering one to him. He was *only beaten* by a *very popular gent some 30 votes.*

Glory—I have rec'd two letters from home, the first in four long months. I'm happy as a clam at high tide. Mother, Sisters, and friends all well. But how long the letters have been in transit. From March and May until August…

Aug. 15.

The Steamer leaves this evening; last night I wrote to _____ _____, but did not finish and must therefore send it unfinished. Beautiful weather, health good, spirits flowing, and tolerably contented. The *Frances* not a very nice craft, although Capt. tries to make me comfortable.

Aug. 17th.

It has been trying all day to rain, and at the present time the drops patter slowly on the Barque's decks. The weather is warm and no wind. I have been passing the day with O. Stokes, a brother officer, on board the Barque Sacramento hard by. He has a nice vessel and enjoys himself finely.

I have just returned from a short trip to the "Village" where I have been conversing with Mrs. Canon of the Barnum House.[7] She is a strong-minded, sensible woman, although rather eccentric. Has decidedly an eye to business. I have considerable pleasure in her company as

---

[6]A native of South Carolina, Andrew Jackson Moses was a San Francisco grocer, commission merchant, and customs inspector before moving to Washington Territory, where he served as district court clerk in the early 1860s. By the end of that decade he had moved to Portland, Oregon, where he was employed as a real estate intelligence and collecting agent and later as an attorney. 1852 California Census, San Francisco County, Part I: 26; San Francisco city directories, 1852-57; 1860 Census, Thurston County, Washington Territory, 219; Withington, *Yale University Library; Catalogue of Western America* #390; 1870 Census, Multnomah County, Oregon, 270; 1880 Census, Multnomah County, Oregon, 248; Portland city directories 1869-95.

[7]The Barnum House restaurant on Commercial Street was founded by Adam Cannon, together with two other Cincinnatians, in 1850, and continued in operation into 1854. At the time of the 1870 census Adam Cannon, his wife, Marion, and three children were living in Alameda County, California, where Adam was dealing in real estate. *Cincinnati Enquirer,* December 25, 1850; San Francisco city directories, 1852-54; 1870 Census, Alameda County, 39.

she, contrary to the generality of women, says what she thinks, speaks what she feels. Our conversation is often of a metaphysical nature, friendship, virtue, reputation, character, &c. She is matter-of-fact enough in all conscience. She is quite a mother or sister to the young gents from Cinti. She is, as are women of her character, very kind hearted, although she seems not to be so. She talks very plainly of the little peccadillos of gentlemen and lectures those of her circle of friends quite soundly. A woman's privilege…

Wednesday, Aug. 20th.

This morning I was roused at an early hour by the tolling of bells in the city, the dread signal of the "Vigilance Committee." Being aware that there has been in their power two culprits, McKenzie and Whittaker,[8] both escaped Sydney Convicts, and both figuring extensively in Stuart's Confession, and both having lately been tried and confessed to diabolical crimes, it struck me at once that the tolling of bells was the signal for their execution. I, however, soon learned that it was for the purpose of calling the Committee together. This was 3 A.M.

It appears that the report had been bruited abroad that the two convicts were this morning to be executed. The report reached the ears of Gov. McDougal, who happened to be in the city, and forthwith he sought out the Sheriff, Col. Jack Hays,[9] obtained a posse of police,

---

[8]Samuel Whittaker, a native of Manchester, England, was transported to Australia at the age of ten for housebreaking. He came to California in 1849 after receiving a conditional pardon. Whittaker shared with "English Jim" Stuart the leadership of the Sydney Ducks and, possibly, the favors of boarding-house keeper Mary Hogan. One colleague considered him to be "the smartest thief of the whole gang," and Vigilance Committee member G. W. Ryckman characterized him as being "as brave as a little Caesar, the only man whose execution I regretted."

Robert McKenzie, alias McKinney, a native of Cumberland, England, moved to New Orleans at age 13, and lived there until coming to California. After a period as a coastal shipper and an Indian fighter, he joined Stuart's and Whittaker's gang. Ryckman characterized McKenzie as "a low, groveling creature, who could not appreciate anything, with no refinement in his composition." Stewart, *Committee of Vigilance,* 212, 245; Williams, *Committee of Vigilance,* 279-80; Williams, *Papers of the Committee of Vigilance,* 463-88; BL: C-D 196: 10, 12.

[9]A former Texas ranger and veteran of the war with Mexico, Col. John Coffee Hays (1817-83) served as sheriff of San Francisco from 1850 to '53. He was later appointed surveyor general of California, and in 1860 he commanded a volunteer force in the Pyramid Lake Indian War. Hays spent his later years in the real estate business and played a major part in the development of Oakland. Greer, *Colonel Jack Hays, passim.*

repaired to Judge Norton[10] and from him obtained a writ of Habeas Corpus and, accompanied by the Mayor and city Marshall in addition to those already mentioned, proceeded to the Vigilance Committee rooms and captured the prisoners. The Committee was taken completely by surprise, and there being but four of their number present, they were unable to effect a rescue, and before a sufficient force could be collected, the prisoners were placed in jail.

An immense crowd immediately repaired thither, expecting an attack would be made by the Committee for the purpose of regaining prisoners. An intense excitement prevailed. The vast majority of the crowd denounced in violent terms the action of the Authorities. The latter in the meantime were frightened at their own temerity, the Governor in his terror sending an order to Gen'l Addison[11] to order the Howard and California Guards under arms; expresses were sent to the Præsidio to look after cannon, and all sorts of foolish thoughts and schemes entertained. Some one of the number proposed that the Cap't of the Vincennes, Sloop of War, should be requested to bring his batteries to bear upon the city. Dr. Robinson of Sacramento Squatter Notoriety[12] on the other side made a

---

[10]A native of Vermont, Myron Norton (1822-86) practiced law in New York State before coming to California in 1847 as a lieutenant in the New York Volunteers. He played a major role in the constitutional convention and was superior court judge in San Francisco in 1851. Not long afterwards he moved to Los Angeles, where he served on the city council in 1852 and later held office as county and municipal judge. Norton practiced law until 1874 when he was stricken with paralysis. Warner et al, *Historical Sketch of Los Angeles County*, 35; Biggs, *Conquer and Colonize*, 184-5; Bancroft, *California*, 4: 755; Crosby, *Memoirs*, 45; *Los Angeles Daily Herald*, April 17, 1886.

[11]John E. Addison, a Washington, D.C., lawyer, and the son of the mayor of Georgetown, was characterized by journalist John Nugent as "a man of magnificent presence, and a rare specimen of manly beauty," without whom no party in the nation's capital "was considered complete." In 1849, Addison came by sea to San Francisco, where he served as county clerk and as brigadier general of the California militia. In later years he suffered so severely from gout that in 1874, fearing another attack of that ailment, he took his own life. Nugent, "Scraps of Early History," *Argonaut*, Vol. II, no. 14: 3; Bancroft, *California* 6: 217; 7: 455; *Alta*, September 4, 1874.

[12]Bickham confused Dr. Charles Robinson, the leader of the Sacramento squatters and future governor of Kansas, with Dr. David G. ("Yankee") Robinson, theater owner, playwright, performer and satirist. In his correspondence with the *Cincinnati Daily Gazette*, Bickham correctly identified the latter of the two Robinsons as the one who made this speech. A native of Maine and a Yale graduate, David G. Robinson arrived in California in 1849 and operated a drugstore on Portsmouth Square. A major figure in the theatrical life of early San Francisco, he was manager of the Adelphi Theater at the time of the first Vigilance Committee. Robinson was well known for his satirical verses on famous people of his time, and for his burlesque of Lola Montez. His popularity was such

fool of himself. He harangued the excited crowd and stated that, although "he had neither the pleasure or honor of being a Vigilante, yet considering that the courts were wickedly corrupt, and the officers of the law notoriously inefficient, he endorsed the actions of the Committee and would spill the last drop of his blood to assist the Committee in regaining possession of the two prisoners." He appealed to the crowd to know "if they would assist." An unanimous Yes was the response. The Dr. then retired, stating he would be with them again in a moment, but several hours elapsed without his making his appearance. In the meantime the Committee met and came to no determination save that they had been betrayed by some of their number, and that the authorities had acted not only extremely injudiciously but wickedly, as they [*sic*] course they had pursued tended to produce a collision between authorities and citizens.

Great excitement prevailed all day among those on the side of the Authorities, they appearing to be expecting and exceedingly fearful of a collision. The Vigilantes, however, were exceedingly cool; indeed, though angry and indignant at being the victims of mean trickery, they appeared to be highly amused at the consternation betrayed by his gallant excellency *Governor* John McDougal. The Governor issued a proclamation exceedingly intemperate in tone, calling on good citizens to array themselves in support of law and order against an unauthorized organization styling themselves the Vigilance Committee of San Francisco. In fact it called in substance upon the citizens to fight against *themselves* and their own interests...

During the day Judge Crane[13] of the Morning Courier issued an

---

that he was elected alderman in 1850, and was a candidate for mayor in 1851. In 1856 he sailed for the eastern states in order to produce a pageant on California, and died of yellow fever in Mobile, Alabama. *Cincinnati Daily Gazette*, October 13, 1851; Estavan (ed.) *San Francisco Theatre Research*, 2: 72-108.

[13]A native of Virginia, James M. Crane moved to California in 1851 at the request of President Taylor for the purpose of founding the *Courier*, the first Whig newspaper in California. Bickham, in a letter to the *Cincinnati Gazette*, characterized Crane as "a worthy, honorable gentleman and a good Whig," who wielded "a pen more plausible than powerful," but who published "as good a paper as any in the corps." In 1852 the *Courier* failed, partly because of Crane's quarrels with his co-editor, F. W. Rice, and partly because of the decline of the Whig party. Crane spent the next several years researching the early explorations of the Pacific Coast. In the late 1850s he was twice delegated by the inhabitants of present-day Nevada to request Congress to separate their region from Utah Territory. He died of apoplexy in 1859. Kelly, *First Directory of Nevada Territory*, 28-31; E. C. Kemble, *History of California Newspapers*, 104-7; *Cincinnati Daily Gazette*, July 14, 1851; Mack, *Nevada*, 79-81, 175-76, 183.

Extra in true Marat style, abusing and ridiculing the governor in sound terms, and unfortunately as injudiciously under the influence of impulsive feelings, and through eyes which see all public questions through a political telescope, endeavored to throw odium upon the Locofoco party because the Gov. happened to be of that faith. Men of all parties condemned it, but here again the Governor betrayed his meanness and weakness. Arming himself and taking with him a comrade, he went to Judge C.'s office and insulted him. The Judge was unarmed and was compelled to bear it. In the afternoon George McDougal,[14] a brother, with another person, both large men and both armed, entered the editorial room of the Judge and hastily demanded if he were the editor. "Yes," replied he. "Well, Sir," retorted George McD., "you are a scoundrel and a liar," following up these words with a slap of the hand in the Judge's face, and placing his right hand on a pistol. The Judge, a small man and unarmed, said, "Sir, this is an unfair attack, two large men and armed entering to attack me without giving me warning. It is cowardly." "That's a fact," said McDougal, and immediately with his associate shot out of the room. . .

Thursday, Aug. 21st.

The last 4 days have been supremely beautiful, warm and genial without clouds, fog, or wind. Atmosphere perfectly clear, and sky blue as sapphire. No Dust either, which is by no means an unimportant item.

Papers this morning filled with accounts of the Yesterday's Excitement, with editorial notes accompanying. The Alta, the Courier, and the Herald came out manfully in opposition to the proceedings of the Authorities. The two former papers claim to be independent, though in reality are Locofoco papers, the latter Whig. The Herald and Alta therefore deserve great commendation for their real independent expression of sentiments. The Post, Whig, as much as I am ashamed to say it,

[14]George McDougal, the governor's brother, came to California with the Swasey-Todd party in 1845 and entered the lumber business near Santa Cruz. In 1846 he accompanied Frémont's California Battalion, although he did not officially join that force. During the early 1850s McDougal profited from real estate and trading, but by 1853 he had tired of civilization and spent much of the next two decades living among Indians, first in the western United States, later in Patagonia. In 1872 while pursuing a lawsuit in Washington, D.C., he committed suicide. He was, according to historian H. H. Bancroft, "an eccentric but brave and popular man," of "herculean proportions." W. F. Swasey, *Early Days*, 177-79; Bancroft, *California*, 4: 723, 6: 645.

endeavors to ride both sides of the pole and can't stick to either. It is a trimmer, and by no means accomplished in the art. The Pacific Star, Locofoco organ, makes a defense of the Governor and authorities though a poor one.

The two Conventions, Whig and Loco, met last night and made a few nominations. They meet to-night to complete their tickets. It is amusing to watch their manoeuvering. Both are endeavouring to have their opponents select their candidates first, as it's an object to know who are to be beaten, who are strong and whom are weak, that the nomination of either party may be made strong. If one candidate is wanting in one requisite, the opposite party will nominate an opponent possessing the qualifications which the other lacks. The Whigs have generally out-generalled the Locos in such instances. Jack Hays is the nominee of the Locos for Sheriff and I believe will be elected.

Sunday, Aug. 23d…

The Whig County Convention last night completed its nominations, and the party is generally pleased with the ticket. One fact, however, strikes me with peculiar force. The gentlemen honored are all young men but, with perhaps one or two exceptions, have no more idea of what are to be their duties than a Hottentot the value of freedom. They have sought the nomination for the honor, that their names may return to their homes beyond the Sierra Nevada bolstered up with this new importance. I am better pleased, however, that young men should have been chosen because their youth is sufficient guarantee that they will be actuated more by patriotism than should old selfish political hucksters and office-seek[er]s, selfish place hunters. A young man's feelings are enlisted on the side of his country and party, whilst old men, having greater experience in the selfish world, are apt to be governed by princi-ples or motives which may conduce to their personal welfare. The latter would just as surely adhere to their party because in faithfulness is their only salvation, but they would be governed by such motives as would render everything subservient to their own clique. I judge of young men from my own sympathies. I have seen too much of party trickery, too much of wheels working within wheels, and although I am desirous of honors, —as what honorable young man is not?—yet I despise this play-ing from one hand to another and would contribute my little mite to the purification of my party from these impurities. The mass of California population, the mass of the Whig party here, is composed of young men, and they have their power, if they *will* only exercise it, to rebuke those broken down old politicians who have come here from the Atlantic slope for the sake of office. At the present time young men *seem* to direct, whilst in *reality* old men have the helm and manage in such manner that all circumstances subserve their intentions. I dinna like it! I see who governs, *one man;*[15] I see what is his machinery; power to patronise; his tools, certain old office-seekers who build up an influence by obtaining the best offices while dividing the inferior ones among young men....

Yesterday, being the time appointed by the courts of Sacramento for the execution of Robinson, Thompson, and Gibson for the robbery of Wilson in the streets of the city about 6 weeks since, it appears witnessed an intense excitement among the people. At the proper hour the prisoners were taken possession of by the Sheriff and proceeded to the place of execution, followed by an immense crowd, many persons of which had arrived from the country for the purpose of witnessing the execution of a Judicial sentence. From the scaffold a reprieve from execution of Robinson by the Governor was read; immediately the indignation of the crowd burst forth; fierce cries of "hang him! hang him!" thundered in the ears of the prisoner who appeared paralyzed with fear at the outbreak. A meeting was held at the Orleans Hotel, and there it was resolved by the people that the culprit should die by their hands. He had been left, after reading the reprieve, in the hands of the military, and [was] afterwards by them, accompanied by the excited throng, taken to the place of execution, where after making confession, which he strung out as if to gain time, he was hanged at 15 minutes before 5. Public tranquillity was then in a measure somewhat restored.[16]

---

[15]Apparently a reference to Thomas Butler King, the leader of the California Whigs.

[16]On the afternoon of July 9, James Wilson, a miner from Volcano, was assaulted and robbed on the outskirts of Sacramento by three recent acquaintances who had lured him there with the promise of introducing him to some "señoritas." The three assailants, William B. Robinson *alias* Hepperd, an American, James Gibson *alias* Hamilton, an Irishman, and John Thompson, *alias* McDermott, a native of Manchester, England, were promptly arrested. A hastily formed vigilance committee demanded the prisoners from the authorities, but dispersed when a speedy trial was promised. All three suspects were condemned to death, but after sentence was passed 231 persons, including members of both the grand and trial juries, petitioned Governor McDougal to spare

What description of man is Governor John McDougal? We find him soon after the Execution of Jenkins by the Vigilance Committee just organized promulgating a pusillanimous proclamation, weak in all its points, suggestive of methods by which the evils of society might be allayed, expressive of fears that collisions might occur between the Committe[e] and constituted authorities, advising them in the tone of a communication from a private citizen to disband; and *not* standing upon his authority and dignity as Governor of the State of California. In the next place, he is found desiring an introduction to the Executive Committee of the V. C., and after being gratified, unexpectedly to them and voluntarily stating that they, the "V. C.," had done much good, and hoping that they may continue to act in concert with the constituted authorities, and if a Judge should be found not fulfilling his duties, to *hang him,* and *he would appoint another!* Again with the inconsistency of a weak or a drunken mind, it is hard to tell which, or the hypocrisy of a Judas, he concocts a scheme, the effects of which, if carried out, is the very thing to produce that which he so much feared, and against which he spoke, a collision between the Committee and authorities. *Now,* not content with having kindled a revolutionary flame here, by pursuing a course which was his duty in the first organization of the Committee, by rescuing from them a brace of notorious villains, condemned to death for their crimes and richly deserving of it too, he proceeds to reprieve a criminal in Sacramento, condemned to death after a fair trial before the regular State and County Courts! Poor weak humanity!

The citizens are indignant and irate. They look upon John McDougal with scorn and contempt. Privately and Political[l]y he has signed his own death warrant. He could not here, outside of a few associates, receive 10 votes for street cleaner. He is but a sample of the beauties of Locofoco administration in this State since the promulgation of our Constitution and the election under it...

At 11 P.M. I have just returned to the Frances from the city where I

Robinson. They may have been influenced by Robinson's American nationality, by his brave bearing during trial, or by his claim to be a Mexican War veteran. The governor granted Robinson a 30 day reprieve "to allow further time to produce anything for or against him," but the Sacramento mob, as Bickham relates, seized Robinson and put him to death on the same day as his fellows. *Union,* July 12, 16, 1851; *Herald,* August 25, 1851; *Alta,* August 29, 1851.

have been marching in Whig Procession with the Reading Rangers.[17] This is but the beginning of the excitement and as such will do very well. I heard several addresses from young Whigs at our meeting in the California Exchange, among the rest C. S. Biden,[18] one of the editors of the Picayune, Mr. Flower,[19] and E. W. Taylor, our candidate for District Attorney. On Monday night we are to have another turn out which I prognosticate will be a lively one.

Previous to coming on board, I spent an hour with Taylor in his room talking over some of our old affairs, experiences &c. He hails from Detroit, Michigan. I was, during the evening, introduced to Frank Soulé,[20] our candidate for State Senate. A man of good strong sense and of fair ability, natural and acquired.

Sunday Evening, Aug. 24, '51.

I have just witnessed a most awful scene! I have just been present at the execution of two human beings! I have just beheld two men hanging by the neck in the presence of a vast concourse of excited and angry people! I have beheld one of those fearful and horrible scenes which seldom falls to the lot of men to witness. Two men, tried, convicted, and condemned, have received the penalty of numerous outrages and infamous crimes in the presence of the people, with their consent, at their instance, with their assistance, with their unanimous and heartfelt con-

[17]The Reading Rangers were a politico-military organization formed by some of the younger Whigs on August 23. Their declared purpose was to "use all honorable exertions" to achieve Reading's election and the Whig victory. *San Francisco Daily Evening Picayune,* August 25, 1851; *Herald,* August 26, 1851.

[18]Printer and editor Charles S. Biden, a native of New York, was active in the Young Men's Whig Club, of which he was president in 1853. In 1860 Biden served as president of the San Francisco Fire Department, and he was a member of the Board of Supervisors from 1860 to '62. San Francisco city directories 1858-66; 1860 Census, San Francisco, 846; *Sacramento Union,* April 21, 1853.

[19]A native of Louisiana, Samuel Flower arrived in California in 1849 and remained ten years, during which he worked as a reporter for the *Herald* and represented San Francisco in the 1853 state assembly. In later life he served as subtreasurer of New Orleans. *San Jose Pioneer,* 1897, vol. 12, # 1: 11; Bancroft, *California,* 6: 675; Kimball, *Directory,* 45; Parker, *Directory,* 54.

[20]A Maine-born newspaperman, Frank Soulé (1810-82) gained his greatest fame as co-author of the *Annals of San Francisco* (1855) the first detailed account of the city's early history. Although he more than once ran for public office, his election to the state senate in 1851 was his only political success. Soulé et al., *Annals,* xiii-xix

Tremendous Excitement! (Courtesy, The Bancroft Library)

currence!...Whittaker and McKenzie are no more. They have expiated their crimes on the scaffold. They have felt the vengeance of a long outraged people, the people whose wrath is terrible when excited. Pray God that theirs may be the last sacrifice of the people long subjected to depredations, robberies, and murders; the last execution by the people who have found no protection in those whose duty it is to administer the laws faithfully and justly.

The circumstances of the execution may be found to originate in the course pursued by Gov. John McDougal on the morning of the 20th, when he basely and hypocritically, when the city laid in slumber, stealthily abstracted from the possession of the Committee the two prisoners, in order to place them in the hands of the law.

The Committee, justly indignant at this, particularly since it has been demonstrated so clearly that the law or its administrators are inefficient, resolved if possible, without disturbing the public peace or bringing on collision, again to obtain possession of the prisoners [and] execute the sentence it had already passed [after] a fair and impartial trial. This afternoon about..[torn].. o'clock this opportunity presented itself and they *[sic]* Committee availed itself of it, and were successful in their endeavors. Divine service was being held in the prison; some three or four members of the "V. C." managed to obtain entrance; their friends and assistants to the number of 36 had prepared a carriage, which was standing behind the corner of the street—Dupont and Broadway—out of sight of the jail. Themselves they were waiting in different positions from without. They wished not to interfere with the service and did not. The solemn Amen was pronounced by the Minister; the signal was given in a second; a rush against the door from without forced it in, it having been opened a little distance by some one from within; the prisoners, Whittaker and McKenzie, who by some strange chance had not gone into the service room, were seized and hurried out. Several pistol shots were fired from the jail, one from a watchman it is supposed was without a ball, drew upon him from the Committe[e] a dozen revolvers, which however were not fired, as the fellow exclaimed, "For God's sake, gentlemen, don't fire, I will not." The culprits were then hurried with terrific speed into the coach, followed by as many members as could get in, all armed to the teeth; whip was plied to the horses which flew like lightning, with the coach attended by two outriders, down Dupont Street to Clay where the[y] whizzed round like a meteor, running upon two wheels and almost upsetting; turning the corner again from Clay to Kearny st., out Kearny to California, down California to _____ and up to the Committee Rooms where the prisoners were hurried up stairs by other members in waiting.

In the meantime that dread Alarum bell on the California Engine House had sounded the fearful and well known peal. The citizens seemed electrified, stopped suddenly to listen, thinking it for a moment to be that equally terrible alarum, Fire—then catch[ing] at once the idea as if by inspiration, rushed madly in immense crowds toward the Celebrated Rooms. Members who had heard the alarum in common with other citizens could be seen ..[torn]..-ing with the crowd with their revolvers strung [to] their sides or held in their hands. But few people were really aware of the cause of the excitement until within a square of the "Plaza de execution," and on every hand were heard enquiries of the cause, whether the Committee had really gotten the prisoners. The carriage coming back, the driver, waving his hat, assured them of the fact. Tremendous cheers and waving of hats in return greeted him, showing the gratification of the immense throng.

Soon fully ten thousand people were thronged together in a dense mass in front of the Committee Rooms. The wide street was filled with people from California St. to _____St. The roofs of adjoining houses were covered with cheering spectators. The masts of the shipping in the harbor directly in front were alive with men; the piazzas of the Oriental Hotel were crowded with anxious citizens. Hoarse cries of "Hang them! "Hang them!" "Let them swing!" ascended with deafening echo every now and then. The windows & doors of the Committee room upstairs were flung widely open, the entrance door was guarded by a strong guard of stalwart, determined men. Soon some one from the windows, in answer to the crowd, cried out, "All right, this time boys, we have them." A tremendous cheer from below was the response, a terrible sound to the prisoners. In a few moments two of the members climbed out of the doors by assistance from within to two beams overhanging, to which were attached reeve blocks, and running lines through, again descended.

Now was there a certainty of death to the convicts! A few moments were passed in drawing up by the ropes from the street into the Room different members who arrived on the spot, and then for an instant a slight movement was visible, McKenzie appeared, pale and the image of terror; Whittaker, tall, well proportioned, and rather well looking, stepped forward at the other door, determined to die bravely! A quick jerk and both were launched into eternity! One deafening prolonged cheer, the spontaneous outbursting... up and indignant feeling, seeming as if affording... the immense crowd now rent the air a terrible [dea]th knell to the wretched criminals.

The horror of that...moment can never be effaced from my memory; and yet my heart told me that it was just. But it is the nature of man to pity suffering, even though that suffering be the meritorious punishment of crime. I felt that it would have been divested of half its terrors had it been the work of the constituted authorities; my principles of justice, my reverence for law, my partiality to law and order seemed for a moment to awaken in me a deep regret, but yet I could not but feel its justness. All of that vast throng of my fellow citizens loved law as well as I, but yet they responded *cheerfully*! aye cheerfully to the executions. Cheer after cheer, huzza following huzza rent the heavens. A terrible Sabbath afternoon! terrible indeed! And what is the reason of this terrible disposition existent among and manifested by the people? It is not contempt for law for they reverence and cherish that. It is not because the law is inefficient. No! it is because of the base and incorrupt administration of the law. It is because of the contempt shown by the citizen known by our constitution as the first citizen of the State, Governor John McDougal, and those whom he has appointed or who administer the laws under him. It is because those to whom the people look for protection are found corrupt and unfaithful. They have no other alternative, no other security, than to take the law to themselves, to the source from whence it emanated; they have no resource but in themselves, [an]d the rights, the peace, the security, the majesty of the people must be assured and protected. Thus is it that they execute without the forms of legality those sentences commensurate with the crimes of bad men. Thus is it they hang in the face of day after fair and impartial trial, granting every opportunity for defense, those whom they have convicted of felony, incendiarism, burglary, highway robbery and murder. It was the people who to-day executed the sentence of Death upon Whittaker and McKenzie or McKinnie.

The condemned died without a struggle. W[hittaker] clenched his fists as though he had concentrated... powers in one last effort to die bravely and with[out strug]gling. After hanging full ten minutes, he crossed one foot over the other. McKenzie on being launched grasped at the rope, but the impetus given by his body as it swung loosened his hold. The horror which was depicted on many countenances gradually died away as the scene became more familiar; people passing and repassing congratulated each other with smiling, laughing visages, with remarks similar to "Quick work wasn't it," "That's the way to do it," "Served them right," "I am pleased to see it," &c. At the end of 20 minutes the bodies were drawn in and examined to see if life were extinct. A physician pronounced them not yet dead, and they were again launched.

The blood had now settled in their hands and countenances, and their open mouths with tongues sticking out, their teeth glittering, was a ghastly sight indeed.

Soon after they were relaunched, Samuel Brannan,[21] who was one of the prime movers in the organization of the Committee, made his appearance and delivered an eloquent and powerful address, appealing from and in the name of the Committee to the people. He stated that "the organization had ever been actuated by the sternest sense of duty, that they were sworn to it by their lives, their fortunes and their sacred honors, and that they would fulfill that determination and trusted to be supported by the people so long as they were right." His remarks were received with deep enthusiasm and a clear endorsement by the people of the actions of the Committee. Dr. Robinson of the Athæneum, not a member, was called upon by the multitude to address them. He responded to their call in an earnest and glowing address sustaining the Committee in toto, and asked a vote on the question. *Aye*, was the unanimous shout which greeted the question, "Are you satisfied that the Vigilance Committee is right?" Dr. R. referred to Gov. John McDougal, and the name was greeted with three furious groans. He said, "It was not the Governor against whom their indignation was aroused, but that it was the man." When he ceased speaking again was he cheered, and if there were any in that immense concourse who were totally opposed to the Committee and disposed to allow the Courts to proceed, even if there were continued maladministration, he was sufficiently discreet to remain silent. Stephen Payran, Chairman of the Executive Committee of the Committee of Vigilance,[22] next addressed the People. He spoke earnestly of the evils of the administration, and declared the principles by which the Committee are governed, and there *[sic]* determination to continue in the course they had been following.

---

[21]A printer, businessman and apostate Mormon elder, Samuel Brannan (1819-89) was one of the most spectacular figures of early San Francisco. He played a major role in the formation of the 1851 Vigilance Committee, and served as its first president, but by July his unstable character and heavy drinking had led to his replacement.

[22]Stephan Payran, a professional copyist from Philadelphia, served as president of the executive committee of the 1851 Vigilance Committee during its most active period. Although a heavy drinker and inclined to be autocratic, Payran proved an able administrator and interrogator. Williams, *Committee of Vigilance*, 201-02; Stewart, *Committee of Vigilance*, 146-47.

The Members of the organization during the whole affair were perfectly calm, cool, collected, and determined. But theirs was the determination which is fearful. There was not the slightest confusion or embarrassment. The crowd, too, though cheering and deeply excited, were calm, but theirs was the fearful calm which spreads into the terrific storm if their wishes are opposed. Countenances looked earnest, yet strange to say were smiling. For my own part, I felt calm, but it was such a calm as chilled my blood.

Whittaker was a tall, fine-looking man with a most cunning expression of countenance. He would have been taken for an adroit scoundrel in any company. He had, too, something sinister in the expression of his eyes and his upper lip, which spoke of determination to succeed in his undertakings at any hazard. A more rascally countenance than that of McKenzie I never before saw. His hair was very black and grew down upon his temples and so low as to leave but a very narrow forehead; his eyebrows seemed to melt and mingle into each other, forming a continuous black line clear across his countenance. His eyes were of that dark, sullen cast which speaks of cowardliness and murder, and with these a peculiar expression of the mouth betokened a low, groveling, murderous disposition. His skin was dark, his person short and rather heavy, though not chunky. His dress, unlike that of W., was dirty and ragged, himself dirty.

A short time before sun-set they were taken in to be placed at the disposal of the coroner. Some fellows cried from the crowd to "send for the Governor to come and see his friends."

The Sacramento Papers contained detailed accounts of the execution and Confessions of Thompson, Gibson, and Robinson. Also of the proceedings of the citizens after the execution of the latter. A vote of the citizens in meeting was taken and it was unanimously "resolved that Governor John McDougal be requested to resign his office." Afterwards *His Excellency* was hanged in effigy and burned amid the jeers of the people. I doubt not he would have been lynched had he been present in that city on Friday last, and to day if he had been here he would have been in dangerous quarters. I noticed one of his Proclamations posted on the Corner of Montgomery and Clay streets, and just over it in large letters surrounded by thick lines of black, the Printer's sign of mourning, "When the wicked rule, the people mourn!"...

Thursday, 28th, upon going ashore to the P. O., to my surprise I found a thick letter from home. 'Tis certain that I felt overjoyed. I opened and read [as fast] as I can. "All's well," sounded as sweet to me as to the Mariner at sea. One long one from Sister Emma, one from Lida, and one written by her for little Nell. I have been very busy during the week writing for the Gazette. Subject, the Execution of Sunday. I am heartily fatigued with it. I have in the meantime written to my friend, Tom H. Foulds,[23] to Mother and Lida.

Friday, Aug. 29th.

Rec'd my month's salary to-day—and upon going to the P. O. rec'd a letter from John and one from Charbonneau, both at Murderer's Bar. I am pained to hear that John is doing so poorly.

The Independents,[24] holding their mass meeting this evening, and the Locos, forming their procession, rather interfered with the Reading Rangers. The Whigs looked and felt disheartened, but I think they will cheer up again before election day. I never knew of an Independent organization of parties which did not militate against the Whigs and generally defeated them too. I have my fears in this case but shall only labor the harder for success...

Monday evening attended the Whig ratification meeting. The Locos turned out in great strength. There seemed for a period a want of unanimity among us, but in a short time we got a tremendous crowd into the California Exchange, and with speeches from candidates and songs from our singers we got up a capital excitement. The word to Rally was given, and though we had but two drums and a fife we formed and had an immense line. We marched all over the city, and finally, passing up

---

[23]Thomas H. Foulds (1829-91), a successful flour and grain merchant, built the first grain elevator in Cincinnati and served as postmaster of that city. Greve, *Centennial History* 2: 575-77.

[24]The Independent ticket, organized by Vigilance Committee members, included some Whigs, some Democrats, and a few nonaligned candidates. While none of the non-partisan candidates were elected, all of the Whigs and Democrats endorsed by the Independents were. The Independent movement proved more harmful to the Whigs than to the Democrats. Stewart, *Committee of Vigilance*, 291-92; Williams, *Committee of Vigilance*, 323-28.

Clay along side the Plaza, we fell in with the Locofoco procession, which, thinking to outnumber us, marched alongside. A regular Babylonian confusion of tongues ensued, a perfect pandemonium of shoutings, hootings, and groans. We beat 'em and give them tremendous defiant cheers. The Whigs were almost crazy with delight. We marched and counter marched and finally brought up at Jo. Clements,[25] our headquarters, where we had more speeches, more songs, and more jollification. T. B. K. [Thomas Butler King], Col. Fellows,[26] and all the old Whigs in town were present and seemed in as glorious humor as any of us. We have them! Hazzah! Huzzah! huz— to morow night is the grand torch-light Rally! Huzzah!

The Steamer Tennessee left this evening with the mail for Panama. Gold Dust in freight to the Amount of $1,800,000.

Tuesday, Sept. 2d, 1851.

I went ashore early this evening to prepare for the "procession." Having been trying for several days to have a stuffed coon prepared, I determined that this evening it should *surely* make its appearance. I accordingly procured it.[27] At an early hour in front of Joe. Clement's the Whigs began to assemble; the Marshalls attired in sashes with their horses, the music, a carriage with 10 white horses, and a boat on wheels, decorated with transparencies &c., drawn by 4 white horses. At 7 o'clock the procession began to form. The boatmen, draymen, &c. began to come up in large numbers. I brought my "tame old coon," and heard the

---

[25]Joseph Clement (1810-93) a New York native and long-time Alabama resident, arrived in San Francisco in October 1849. He invested in real estate, served as deputy county recorder in 1852, and spent his remaining years as a searcher of titles and records and a school director. *Call*, March 30, 1893.

[26]Hart Fellows (1798-1878) a Massachusetts native, served in both the War of 1812 and the Black Hawk War. He was a lawyer, recorder and probate judge in Illinois before moving to California in 1851. Soon after his arrival, President Fillmore appointed him surveyor of the port of San Francisco. At the end of Fillmore's term, Fellows returned to private law practice, eventually moving to Placer County, where he served as county judge for two terms. At the time of his death in 1878, he had been receiver of public moneys at the U.S. Land Office in Sacramento for twelve years. *Alta*, December 28, 29, 1878.

[27]The raccoon had been a symbol of the Whig party since the "log cabin" campaign of 1840 when the Whigs had presented wealthy candidate William Henry Harrison as a rough frontiersman. Remini, *Henry Clay, Statesman for the Union*, 564.

animal greeted with 3 hearty cheers. We began to move up Washington street; as we progressed on our march masses of Whigs rolled in, and we soon gathered such force as ne'er before was seen in procession in San Francisco. It seemed as though Whigs never would stop rolling in. From one end of the city to the other we marched with our music, hundreds of transparencies, some torch lights, banners, &c. We Whigs were in glorious mood. The "Independents" also had a large meeting on the Plaza, but not comparable to ours. After we had marched and counter-marched sufficiently to show our strength, we halted at our stand on the Plaza about 75 yards from the Independents, and then listened to a number of short, decisive speeches. At 11 o'clock adjourned, and many of us repaired to Jo Clement's where we had more speeches, more songs, and a good many "b'hoys' got somewhat inebriated.

Wednesday, Sept. 3d, 1851

This is "Election Day," quite early in the morning. The first Political State battle is to be fought in California. The Whigs have two enemies to fight, and if we hold our own with them we shall do gloriously. The weather is warm, and I suppose the excitement will be much heightened by this. Doubtless some rows will occur. I must work for the "Whole Whig Ticket."

Evening—and I am almost worn out. I have electioneered all day. Talked until my tongue will scarce wag. Talked with some "hombres" like a father all about the good Whig cause. I have seen lots of sport but heard of no rows. Very strange. All parties have had their wagons and carriages plying the streets to pick up voters. Down long Wharf, down California Street, down Pacific Street &c. The result is doubtful... The Whig State ticket will have a large majority. If we had had a clean field the Locofocos would have been sadly in the minority. Not one of their candidates would have been elected. Vast numbers of illegal votes were polled. Money flowed like water, and Whigs worked like heroes.

Thursday, Sept. 4

The Returns as far as heard from look badly for the Whigs. We shall probably elect 5 out of 7 Assemblymen and Soulé for Senator. Sac. City & county are Loco Foco.

Sunday, Sept. 7

The P. M. S. Northerner, 22 days from Panama, arrived this morning with the Mail and dates 28th July from New York. I purchased a Gazette. I passed to day perambulating the streets with A. B. Moses[28] and Sterling. I did intend to go to church, but it was 12 M before I got ready.

Tuesday, Sept. 9th...

It is now almost certain that the Locofocos have carried the State. Hell, it cannot now be helped. The Hurly burly's done. One side must always rejoice whilst the other mourns...

My mind is altogether unsettled. Politics have occupied so much of my attention of late that I cannot bring my mind firmly to the consideration of any other subject; notwithstanding I am wearied with the constant din of Whig and Loco Arguments, trickery, electioneering, &c. I cannot say that I have any particular desire to be a politician as such a profession is terribly harassing. Particularly unpleasant is it when one is of the defeated party. I see, however, where and how we were defeated, and I stated my fears to friends and candidates previous to the election. It did no service.

Col. Moore, whose nomination I opposed in State Convention as a candidate for Congress, as I felt then convinced would not at all be suitable to the miners, proved a perfect drag on the ticket.

I was correct in my belief, and in one other affair of which I spoke to Col. Weller I am proven to have been correct. The Locos claimed El Dorado Co. by from 3000 to 5000 majority. I laughed at the Col. and told him that it was exceedingly doubtful whether she were Whig or Loco, and that in any event the Latter ticket would not receive over 500 majority. It now promises to be about 300.

After the County Nominating Convention in July, I stated my belief that Frank Stuart, Whig, would in all probability be elected one of the

---

[28]A. Benton Moses, a native of Charleston, South Carolina, and the brother of A. J. Moses (see above 207-208) served in the Mexican War before coming to California, where he took part in an expedition against the Southern California Indians. He later moved to San Francisco, where he served as deputy to Sheriff Hays. In October 1851, he accompanied his brother, Collector Simpson P. Moses, to Puget Sound, and in 1853 he was appointed surveyor of the port of Nisqually. He was killed by Indians in 1855. Bancroft, *History of Washington, Idaho, and Montana*, 56, 62, 119.

Senators, and that W. R. Hopkins of Murderer's Bar would go into Assembly. The latter is elected. The former not yet in minority. Murderer's Bar went Whig, quite contrary to the expectation of my Loco friends there residing. I told them how it would prove. My young head had figured more than their old and crafty ones. I do not know what Col. Potter now thinks. He laughed quite merrily when I called the first Whig meeting on the Bar, which, by the way, was the first ever called in El Dorado County. I wish I could meet him. I'd banter him on his $250 banner.—Good for old El Dorado.

Aug. [September] 10th.

I have just returned, 10 PM, from a visit to the city. I left the *Francis* early in the evening with my friend Gibbs, and wended my course to the Merchants Exchange, Whig Head Quarters, in order to learn the news of the day. It is still a matter of considerable doubt as to whom is elected Governor... The Locos think they are successful throughout, having a large majority in the Legislature. To-night, expecting Col. Bigler[29] down on the Sacramento steamer, they repaired in large numbers in procession with a band of music to Pacific Wharf for the purpose of escorting him up. Arrived at the steamer, they enquired whether Gov. Bigler was on board; some genius answering, *"Yes,* he is *not,"* and they hearing merely the affirmative response, gave three hearty cheers. They were compelled to return without his company; he doubtless deeming it yet too soon to rejoice, wisely refrained from paying us a visit. I fancy the Locos are crowing to[o] soon, for it is quite probable we will be the exultants.

I ascertained that both my friends, W. R. Hopkins and Dr. Cutler, are elected to the Assembly from Eldorado County. Frank Stuart lacks but 50 votes of going to the Senate. Milt. Elstner, Whig, formerly of Cinti., is elected, and Jo. Gordon, County Clerk. Huzzah for El Dorado! Wonder what Col. Potter now thinks of the "banner county."[30]

Since the first beginning of the Independent movement in this city, a newspaporial correspondence of a not very friendly or creditable char-

---

[29]A Pennsylvania printer and lawyer, John Bigler (1805-71) came overland to California in 1849. He served two terms in the state assembly before being elected governor. After two terms in that office, he was defeated for reelection in 1856 due to his failure to solve the state's financial problems. Melendy and Gilbert, *Governors of California,* 50-65.

[30]Stewart and Elstner were not elected, although Hopkins, Cutler and Gordon were.

acter on the part of one at least, has been carrying on between A. C. Russel,[31] Ed. of the Evening Picayune, Whig; and Capt. J. L. Folsom,[32] one of the prime movers of the Independent nomination. Russel charged the latter with attempting to bribe the Whig convention into the nomination of Mr. Gilman[33] for Judge of the Superior Court. Folsom denied and pronounced R. a "liar and scoundrel." The latter, in the Alta Californian of next morning, published his final card, reiterating his charge, and retaliated in strong language upon the insult of the other. Folsom challenged him, and just before dark, with their several friends, they repaired to the "Mission" to take a shot at each other. "Pistols at ten paces, and to fire between the word *fire* and one, two three," were the terms. The first two shots were exchanged, nobody damaged. Jack Moses, who was present, informed me that Folsom, though a "fighting man," was a "little shakey." Russel was cool, calm, and determined, but in his haste threw his pistol too much out of line. The word was the third time given. Russel had dead aim for the neck of his antagonist, but the cap of the latter's pistol snapped. The former had the right to take advantage, but bravely and magnanimously refused, stating that he "wished to give his opponent a fair chance." The seconds then interfered because it was growing too dark. Russel wished to fight it out by moonlight, but the affair was finally settled amicably and satisfactorily to all. *Farce!*

---

[31]A native of Tennessee, Andrew Campbell Russell was among the best-known journalists in Gold-Rush California, where he published and edited newspapers in Marysville, Sacramento, Stockton, San Francisco, and Los Angeles. He was more than once physically assaulted by enemies and dueled with ex-Governor John McDougal in 1852. At the time of his death in 1891, Russell, aged 71, was working as a journalist in Stockton. Johnson, *San Francisco as it Is*, 16-18; *Union*, September 29, October 1, 1894; *Call*, September 30, 1894.

[32]Joseph Libby Folsom (1817-55) arrived in California in 1847 as quartermaster of the New York Volunteers, and served as collector of the port of San Francisco from 1847 to 1849. He became wealthy by purchasing property belonging to the William Leidesdorff estate. Bancroft, *California*, 3: 742; Soulé et al., *Annals*, 754-57.

[33]Charles Gilman (1793-1856) a native of New Hampshire and resident of Baltimore, arrived in California in 1849 where, after a period of mining on the Yuba River, he practiced law in San Francisco. According to A. C. Russell, J. L. Folsom offered to pay the Whigs $5,000 for Gilman's nomination as judge of the superior court, and to spend another $5,000 towards his election, in the hope that Gilman as judge would help Folsom gain control of the Leidesdorff estate. In 1853 Gilman lost a leg when serving under filibuster William Walker in Baja California. He later joined Walker in Nicaragua, where he died of cholera in 1856. Stowell, "Bound for the Land of Canaan, Ho!" *CHSQ*, 27: 368 (n. 9); Oehler, ed. "Nantucket to the Golden Gate," *CHSQ*, 29: 169, 171; Kimball, *Directory*, 501; Morgan, *Directory*, 24; Parker, *Directory*, 52; Scroggs, *Filibusters and Financiers*, 39-40, 115-56, 182; Soulé et al., *Annals*, 824.

CHAPTER ELEVEN

Autumn in San Francisco

Aug. [September] 13th. [1851].

Joys are none the less sweet because delayed. I experienced this in a most vivid sense this morning upon visiting the city. I had given up all hope of receiving any tidings from home in the last mail, and consequently was quite disconsolate. Had been in melancholy mood during the whole week. Upon glancing at Gregory's letter list, I discovered my name. I rec'd a letter, a long letter full of tidings from Home, written my own kind mother. I was repaid a thousand fold for the many sad moments I had experienced during several long, long days...

Saturday Evening found me ashore. After taking a warm bath and dressing myself cleanly, I repaired to the Adelphi Theatre, being desirous of seeing Stark and Mrs. Kirby[1] in the "Hunchback."[2] I did not *really* wish to go, but I felt rather lonely and could find none of my associates, and moreover, having nothing to engage my attention, and having not visited a theatre but once before in California, I thought I would indulge myself. I found quite a number of friends there before me, Sam

---

[1] James Stark and Sarah Kirby, both students of the famous William Charles Macready, were among the first major actors to perform on the West Coast. They played opposite one another in a variety of roles, and were co-managers of the Jenny Lind Theater before its destruction by fire in May 1851. They married in June of that year and remained popular in California throughout the 1850s. Koon, *How Shakespeare Won the West*, 33-46.

[2] This popular drama, written in 1832 by Irish playwright James Sheridan Knowles, concerns the romantic problems of Julia, an innocent country girl in 17th century England, brought up by the noble hunchback, Master Walter, who, at the play's end, is revealed to be her true father and an earl.

Jones[3] among the rest. Some few ladies and also a few *females*. The piece, so far as Stark & Mrs. K. were concerned, passed off very well, better than I had expected. But those who have seen Macready[4], Murdoch,[5] Anderson,[6] Booth,[7] &c. as Master Walter; and Mrs. Mowatt,[8] Julia Dean,[9] or Eliza Logan[10] as Julia would have considered it rather tame. I felt no better satisfied after the performance than before entering the Theater doors...

[3]Possibly the Samuel Jones listed as a carpenter in the 1846 Cincinnati city directory. Jones set out across the plains in 1849 as secretary to a party of 51 gold seekers. After the party split at Fort Laramie, he contracted typhoid fever, and was left by his mess mates in the care of a Mormon couple at Fort Hall. In November 1849, Jones was reported to have recovered and arrived in California. He was mining in the Yuba River region the following summer, and by November 1850, he had moved to San Francisco and taken employment with the customs service. He was still in California in February 1853. *Cincinnati Daily Times,* November 27, 1849; *Republican,*April 11, 1849; *Cincinnati Enquirer,* September 1, 1850, January 12, 1851; *Cincinnati Commercial,* April 26, 1851, April 4, 1853.

[4]The arrogant and hot-tempered William Charles Macready (1793-1883) one of the leading tragedians of nineteenth century England, performed in America on three occasions. During his third visit, in 1849, Macready's feud with the American actor, Edwin Forrest led to the Astor Palace Riot. Boardman, *Oxford Companion to the American Theatre,* 452-53.

[5]James Edward Murdoch (1811?-1860) a member of a prominent Philadelphia family, was a noted actor and teacher of elocution. He performed in San Francisco and Sacramento in 1853-54. Boardman, *Oxford Companion to the American Theatre,* 494; Gagey, *San Francisco Stage,* 49.

[6]Possibly David C. Anderson, a prominent character actor born in New York City, who came to California in 1850. Koon, *How Shakespeare Won the West,* 148; *San Francisco Chronicle,* September 28, 1879.

[7]After achieving fame as an actor in his native England, Junius Brutus Booth (1796-1852) moved to America in 1821, where he became the most noted tragedian of his day. Among his offspring were the famous actor Edwin, and the assassin, John Wilkes Booth. In 1852 Junius, together with his sons Edwin and young Junius, performed in San Francisco. Soon after his return to the eastern states, Junius died while on a steamboat to Cincinnati. *DAB* .

[8]Anna Cora Mowatt (née Ogden) (1819-70) the daughter of a well-to-do New York merchant, was established as a poet, novelist, and playwright before embarking on an acting career in 1845. She remained on the stage until 1854 and was praised by Edgar Allen Poe for her "ease and self possession" and her "rich and voluminous voice." *DAB;* Boardman, *Oxford Companion to the American Theatre,* 491-92.

[9]A daughter and granddaughter of theatrical performers, golden-haired, blue-eyed Julia Dean (1830-68) achieved great popularity as an actress during the 1840s and 1850s. One of her most popular roles was "Julia" in *The Hunchback.* During the late 1850s and 1860s Dean performed in California, Nevada, and Utah, where she was a particular favorite of the Mormons. *DAB;* Koon, *How Shakespeare Won the West,* 119-123; Boardman, *Oxford Companion to the American Theatre,* 190.

[10]Eliza Logan (1830-72) the daughter of playwright Cornelius A. Logan, began acting at age eleven. During the 1850s she was a major theatrical star in the southern and midwestern states, and her acting was praised as "impulsive, electric and at times singularly impressive from the power she throws into a few brief words." Boardman, *Oxford Companion to the American Theatre,* 437.

Sunday I passed in company with some friends; I was again too late for church. I took my promenade, as usual, with A. B. M. [A. B. Moses], and finally adjourned with him to take tea at his Boarding House. Here I had quite a pleasant chat with the landlady and a Miss Gilmore, a boarder. Shortly after 8 P.M, passing down Commercial Street, the French part of town, I saw quite an amusing fight in a Saloon between four or five American B'hoys and a room full of French. The latter poor fellows did not know the "ropes" and got "slayed" right and left. All the windows in the room were smashed as well as sundry bottles, glasses, &c. Passing from this, I went to George Ensign's[11] room where I wrote a portion of my letter to the Gazette. *Passing from this,* I passed into the arms of Morpheus—2 A.M.

Monday 15th.

The mail steamer departs to-day, and I am very much in haste. I have Emma's birth-day letter to finish suddenly, as also that for the Gaz.

This morning I learned that a duel was yesterday fought at Benecia between Frank Lemon and Wm. H. Graham of this city. Distance 10 paces, "revolvers" the weapons. Seven shots were fired before execution. The 7th struck Lemon in the right shoulder, making a severe and painful wound. Graham ought never to have given the scoundrel such a chase for his life. Anyone else would have shot L. without giving him warning. I think I have noted the cause in a former part of these papers. G. will yet kill him, I hope.[12]

---

[11]A San Francisco lumber dealer during the 1850s, George R. Ensign helped found the Spring Valley Water Company in 1851. He later invested heavily in the Lake Tahoe Co., created for the purpose of building an aqueduct from Tahoe to San Francisco. San Francisco city directories: Kimball, *Directory,* 42; Parker, *Directory,* 52; Wheat, "Bantam Cock," *CHSQ,* 9: 283, n. 97; Pisani, "Lake Tahoe Scheme," *CHSQ,* 53: 354-55.

[12]See above 185. After Lemon recovered from his wound, Graham challenged him again, but mutual friends intervened and the quarrel ended.

In 1855 Lemon served under General Juan Alvarez in his rebellion against President Santa Anna. Returning to the United States, Lemon operated a steamer between New York and Port Richmond. During the Civil War he joined the 32nd New York (1st California) regiment of volunteers, and was mortally wounded at the battle of South Mountain.

In the mid-1850s Graham joined the California bar. In 1862 he followed the Comstock rush to Nevada and eastern California, where he killed two men in gunfights. Tiring of his violent career and reputation, Graham retired to Los Angeles where he died peacefully in 1866. *Alta,* June 18, 1855, November 6, December 19, 1862; *Union,* January 3, 1856; Truman, *Field of Honor,* 315-17; Thrapp, *Encyclopedia of Frontier Biography,* 2: 578.

Well, my letters are in the P. O., and I am once more at leisure for study. Politics and Vigilance Committee no longer disturb me. I sent papers to different parties and letters to the amount of 50 pages to Emma, Morris Johnston and to the *Gaz.* 12, 20, 18 = 50 pages. The exercise is improving in addition to the pleasure I experienced.

I borrowed from G. E. [George Ensign?] to-day a new book to me, Metaphysical Book old to the world, one which I never had studied. For weeks I shall be immersed in the theory of "ideas" and "essences," sensations, perceptions, &c. Strange I should have never read the works of the Stagyrite.[13]

This evening the Brigantine Columbus came in hard by and cast anchor. I discovered on board quite a number of Señoritas. Immediately I went over and made myself acquainted with my brother officer, R. Langdon[14] of North Carolina. (We always are sociable in S. F., particularly U. Sam's hombres). Of course he invited me to call back, after I had taken tea, to see the ladies and hear them sing. They then were ashore. Accordingly, after tea I repaired to the C. and, upon entering the cabin, was no less astonished than pleased to see seven elegant and handsome Mexican ladies, their dark eyes flashing diamond like as L. and I proceeded to go through the formalities of introduction. Neither of us could speak more than half a dozen words of Spanish, nor they more than two of our language. We said "Buenos Noches," however, with our blandest smile and most killing bow, (We are "some" at the latter as we have taken lessons from the pines of our mountain forests). Upon recovering from our embarrassment consequent upon such an extensive introduction, we began to look around us to see where we should begin. Of course I immediately singled out one as the object of my admiration. Like all of her countrymen, her complexion was brunette. I liked her appearance decidedly. She was not beautiful. Her features were rather plain, but

---

[13]Aristotle, so called because he was born in Stagirus, Macedonia. The book Bickham borrowed was apparently the *Metaphysics.*

[14]Richard F. Langdon of North Carolina is listed in the 1850 Census as a 22-year-old merchant living at Stockton. He served as a customs inspector from the summer of 1851 to the fall of the following year. During the Civil War Langdon served in Virginia as quartermaster of the 3rd North Carolina Regiment CSA. BL: C-A 169, Part II, reel 11; 1850 Census, San Joaquin County, 306; Manarin, *North Carolina Troops 1861-65, A Roster,* 3: 191, 488.

there was in her expression something so sensible I could not help being attracted. There was a dignity in her demeanor, and withal a vivacity, which would please any sensible man. Her eyes were large, dark as night, and seemed swimming in stars of beauty. Brow intellectual. Mouth tempting, and teeth white as pearls. I was not "Struck," oh no. I thought of *other dark eyes* and sensible expressions and merely compared. I was pleased. Stature above medium. Langdon was taken with one who was decidedly pretty but looked like a "vixen" to me. The Captain of the Vessel was there and interpreted for us occasionally. I desired to know something of the family. He stated that the name of the old Senor was Ainsa. That he had two or three sons living in Stockton. That he was very wealthy and was just removing with his wife and family (The old lady had been the mother of 18 children, thirteen now living, eleven with their parents in the Columbus) from Mexico to Stockton. So I was "posted up."

After blundering through my stock of "Castillian" as well as possible, I finally got the ladies to singing, my "dulce amiga" playing the Guitar and singing, five sisters accompanying her. I was constantly watching and frequently gazed deeply into dark eyes which seemed always ready to meet my own. (Vanity, but Spanish girls will attract a fellow as a snake does a bird, and will look at him, particularly if his complexion is fair & eyes blue)—Langdon was dark skinned, and I had the advantage. Their first song, which rang upon my eagerly listening [ears] with melodious, deep harmony, was scarce finished when who should make their appearance but my friends, Ward and Gilmore. They had also seen the Senoritas and were attracted back. This was quite an accession to the party. I still kept up my mute conversation with "mi dulce amiga" and soon got her to sing again. The captain then sang. I was now called upon, and as Spanish ladies love attention, I believe, more than any on earth (and all do love it) I could not decline. I was in an embarrassing situation. I never had opened my mouth to sing alone in the presence of any woman, and to attempt it in the presence of such a bevy of bright-eyed, merry, musical girls as these required a degree of bravery sufficient to enable a man to withstand a charge of cavalry. I would sooner have stood face to face with a revolver and bowie knife. However, my pride as an "American" depended, and catching a look from a pair of black eyes, I gained courage and made bold. Whew! I was astonished at myself. I do believe I sang very well. I thought so, for I vow I never before, when singing to myself on the deck of the ship, had found my voice so smooth. However, I resolved not to try again for fear I should lose my dearly earned laurels. The girls liked the tune if they did not the singing for they wished to learn it. Ward being a singer, he was now called upon and gave us several songs in excellent voice. Black eyes do inspirit a fellow. He said he never before did so well. Langdon and Gilmore did not essay.

At 12 o'clock, after spending the most delightful evening I have yet experienced in California, we arose to depart. But we had our compliments to offer the ladies for their entertainment they had given us. Fortunately there was in company a young Spanish gentleman who acted as interpreter when pantomime would not answer our purpose. Many gallant things were said, and the ladies gave such responses as only Spanish women know how to give. The old Senor gave us all a pressing invitation to call at his home in Stockton. As the last sound of the midnight bell sounded, we bad them *"buenos noches,"* ourselves perfectly delighted with our visit. They depart to-morrow; Miserable! but I shall be on board the Columbus bright and early... These girls are all disengaged, so says the Captain. The eldest is 22. "Ma amiga."

Tuesday, Sept. 16th.

After breakfasting this morning I went to *see Langdon*—certainly it was Langdon I went to see—I met with the Señoritas and joined them in a glass of wine and ate with them an orange. Was most bewitchingly pressed to take breakfast with them, &c. After they had breakfasted, we went on deck for a promenade. Langdon and myself assembled around us the whole seven and commenced receiving and giving lessons in "Castiliano." It was rare fun on all sides. Sometimes we would mutually forget and express our meaning in our own vernacular, and of course a laugh would ensue. However, we learned the Spanish for heart, love, blue eyes, black eyes, &c., while they learned the Americano. Sometimes, again, here would result some pleasant passages. The girls had taught me so assiduously, and my intellect being brightened, I learned fast. I could understand. They could look and say "no entiende." "Si Signorita," responded I. I made one "point" which considerably amused them. Ma Dulcie was teaching me the Spanish terms for brow, eyes, nose, mouth, &c. She got to the mouth, placing her fingers on her lips to signify, when, quick as thought, I made a loop and exclaimed *"bonita"* (pretty). The girls took the cue, and Dulcie blushed smilingly. It was awkward, but still it was a point. I managed to get five of them to write their names on a piece of paper for me.[15] That of my favorite is Josepha (pronounced Hosapha), Langdon's, Dolores or Lola, the others, Belen (Balahn), Filomena, Adalida. The others I did not ask. The endearing term of Josepha is Sopha or Josephita (Hosiphetah).

At 12 o'clock they left for the steamboat, bidding a kind "adios," thanking us for our attention, inviting us to call and see them, and waving their scarfs until the boat which bore them away had vanished. Now we felt right lonely, but dinner time being close at hand, we passed the time very well, determining to go and see the girls previous to 4 o'clk, the boat not starting until that hour. Before that time, however, we were called upon by the two Yankee girls on the *"Ganges"* to escort them to another vessel some distance away. We did so of course, and upon taking them whither they wished, we went to see the Ainsa family once more. I was amused at finding Ward in the cabin. He was as much taken as we. We also met a friend of Langdon's, a young married man who could speak (abla) "Castiliano" and who interpreted for us. Fifteen minutes time passed, and we bade them a final farewell, not leaving them until the latest tapping of the bell. Senor Ainsa (Aheen-sah), for bringing such a family into California, deserves the gratitude of the Country and should receive from Government for each member a donation of a half section of land. The girls are very accomplished and quite intelligent. Usually the immigration from Mexico is of a miserable character, but this is a God Send. Quite a chapter on Signioritas. I fancy I shall again see the fair Josepha about Christmas times. What a deuce of a titivation these bewitching, black eyed brunettes kick up with a "fellow's

---

[15]This piece of paper still survives among the Bickham family papers in the Western Reserve Historical Society Library, Cleveland, Ohio.

feelinks." But I'm safe. I have proof against her wiles and arrowy charms—*Aye, haven't I?*[16]

The papers of this morning make the statement that the celebrated Committee of Vigilance has disbanded in a manner. They are to remain organized for the purpose of assisting the authorities and, if necessary, by giving a signal assembling all the old members. When the mind maturely reflects upon the principle of this organization, it is naturally shocked. It so militates against all those institutions which we have been taught to respect. It so tends to produce a contempt for established customs and constituted authority, for Law which we all reverence and in which consists not only our personal security but is the bulwark of our liberty. The question presents itself even under the consideration that the passions of the people are armed with principle, if we had as assiduously aided the authorities and upheld the law as the Committee has supported its character, would it have been necessary to resort to such strange and startling defenses of our property & persons? I fear we have been governed far more by passion, by revengeful feelings, than we should. However, it is time for the Committee to disband. There is strong opposition in the field.[17]

Wednesday, Sept. 17th.

This morning Hamilton of Murderer's Bar visited me. I rec'd tidings from John, learning that he is now doing very well.

About 3 P.M. Vanderbilt's steamer Independence, Capt. Wakeman,[18]

---

[16]The Ainsas, a family of wealthy Manila Spaniards, settled in Sonora, Mexico, during the late colonial period and invested in mines and landholdings. After Mexico achieved independence, the family was persecuted by local authorities because of its prominence under Spain, and Don Manuel Ainsa, the head of the family, together with his wife and most of their offspring, moved to California where they established a mercantile house in San Francisco and Stockton. Filomena, one of the Ainsa daughters, married Henry Crabb, whose ill-fated filibustering expedition into Sonora was partly motivated by the desire of his in-laws to recover their property. In 1856, Bickham's favorite, Josefa, married Dr. T. W. Talliaferro of Alabama, a member of the state legislature. In 1860 Josefa, her husband, and two children were living in San Francisco near her parents, brothers, and sisters. She died in 1868. J. Y. Ainsa, *History of the Crabb Expedition,* 2, 8; Morgan, *Directory,* 10, 158; 1852 Census, San Joaquin County, 171; 1860 Census, San Francisco, 774-75; Bell, *Reminiscences of a Ranger,* 218-19; *Bulletin,* January 26, 1868.

[17]The 1851 Vigilance Committee never formally disbanded, and its executive committee met occasionally throughout 1852, but September, 1851, marked the end of its active period. Stewart, *Committee of Vigilance,* 297-301.

arrived from San Juan del Sud—making the passage in 16 days, bringing dates to 16th August. News from Cuba, which is now all interesting, of a contradictory though encouraging nature. Speaks of the departure from New Orleans of Gen. Lopez with 800 troops, 7 ps. artillery, on the steamer Pampero.[19] Spanish Consul sent after him the Cincinnatus. Simpson P. Moses and Lady of Cincti.[20] arrived passengers. I have not seen them...

Thursday Morning, 18th...

Hamilton took dinner with me to-day, and afterward I took a short trip with him into the city. Finally bade him adieu, giving him a letter and papers for John.

The Sacramento Steamers are now having quite a merry opposing

---

[18]Edgar ("Ned") Wakeman (1818-79) a Connecticut-born merchant sea captain, commanded the Vigilance Committee's water police and officiated at the hangings of Jenkins and Stuart. Williams, *Committee of Vigilance*, 196-97; Newall, *Paddlewheel Pirate, passim.*

[19]A Spanish officer born in Venezuela, Narciso Lopez (1799?-1851) fought against Simon Bolivar during the Latin American Wars of Independence, and later took part in the Carlist civil wars in Spain. After moving to Cuba in 1839, he became dissatisfied with the Spanish colonial regime, and plotted its overthrow. When his plans were discovered, he fled to the United States where he gained the support of Southern expansionists who wished to annex Cuba as a slave state. Lopez made three further attempts to overthrow Spanish rule. In 1849 he was prevented from sailing to Cuba by the intervention of the U.S. government, and in 1850, after landing in Cuba, he was defeated by Spanish troops. On August 3, 1851, Lopez again sailed for Cuba accompanied by 44 Cuban exiles, some 20 Germans and Hungarians, and 354 American volunteers. Brown, *Agents of Manifest Destiny*, 42-47; Caldwell, *Lopez Expeditions*, 43-92.

[20]Simpson P. Moses, a native of South Carolina, and the brother of Bickham's friends A. J. and A. B. Moses, served in the war with Mexico, and was a Cincinnati exchange broker in 1849. In May 1851, he was appointed customs collector of the Puget Sound district and arrived at Olympia in November after a short stay in San Francisco. As collector, Moses angered the Hudson's Bay Company by seizing several of their ships for alleged customs violations, causing one H.B.C. employee to call him a "contemptible little Jew." In November 1851, Moses, on his own authority, outfitted an expedition to ransom a party of gold seekers held captive by Haida Indians on Queen Charlotte Island. Treasury Secretary Corwin reprimanded Moses for exceeding his authority and refused to recompense him for the expenses of this expedition, but the territorial legislature successfully asked Congress to reimburse him. Moses was removed from office by the Pierce administration in 1853 and was charged with various acts of mismanagement, but these charges were never proven. By 1860 he had moved with his family to Washington, D.C., where he worked as a claims agent and lawyer until his death in the mid-1880s. His wife, Lizzie, was a Washington, D.C. native. A. A. Graham, *History of Richmond County, Ohio*, 300; Cincinnati city directory, 1849; Snowdon, *History of Washington*, 3: 137, 139-41, 165; BL: P-A 83: 17; 1860 Census, Washington D.C., 4th ward, 59; 1870 Census, Washington, D.C., 2nd ward, 242; Washington, D.C., city directories, 1862-86.

time. There are 5 daily lines, and [they] are carrying passengers for nothing and for $1.00. Charging for meals, however, from $1.50 to $2.00. The Confidence and New World are continually racing. Last night the former came in 30 minutes ahead. To-night one of the line, I presume the *Senator*, came in very early, and since that time there has been great cheering. I presume she made a quick trip. It is 11 P.M. I have been reading and shall read an hour more. Quantum Suffict.

Sunday, Sept. 21st.

Sun crosses the line to-day. I presume we shall soon have the Equinoctial storm. This morning is more pleasant than any we have enjoyed for 10 days. I do not feel very well. Reason, want of rest—Why don't I rest? Because the fleas are so troublesome. During the daytime they retire to their hiding places. About 10 P.M. they issue forth in small squads, all converging to one center where they seem to hold general parlay. Suddenly, as if by mutual agreement, they separate into small foraging parties and traverse from a fellow's shirt collar to the heels of his socks, presenting their bills at different points and filling their knapsacks with the richest blood which flows from the heart. The bloody minded varlets leave the imprint of their seal in beautiful pale red blotches wherever it may happen to suit their fancies. Sometimes they seem to have regular jumping matches among themselves, and they always take good care to stick a peg as a mark of their activity, to denote the extent of their leaps. San Francisco, what a place art though![*sic*] But few "lassies;" a devil of a wind, and dust constantly blowing in a fellow's eyes; fires; Sydney Coves; Vigilance Committees; rats and Fleas! Oh!

I went ashore this morning after breakfast and after "barbarizing," bathing, shirting, putting into my face a fragrant Habana, I essayed forth to meet my acquaintances. It was too late to go to church. I passed the compliments of the morning with sundry individuals, and finally meeting with A. B. & Jack Moses, went with them to see their brother, Simpson P., the new Collector for Puget's Sound, whom with his lady have just arrived in California from the Atlantic States. I passed some time at their hotel very agreeably. SPM's wife is a very pretty woman, but if there's anything in physiognomy, she has a temper of her own. She seems a very quiet, unassuming little body. SPM is very proud of his position as Collector. About 3 o'clk A. B. and myself started on our usual Sunday afternoon walk. The wind blowed so fiercely we did not extend it to the usual degree. After leaving him, I went to see Anna—what's her other name?—O'Neil—the Irish lassie who lives with Mrs. Canon. Anna is a fine looking, sensible woman and it's quite a treat to talk to her.

I had scarce gotten on board the Frances this evening and lighted my candle before I heard a terrible hubbub on deck. Rushing up, I found the Capt. (who had just been reading his Bible) and his second mate locked in firm embrace and tumbling about over the decks, trying to pound each other. I tore them apart and tried to make peace when again they went at it. I tore them apart again, but in the meelee got rolled on to the deck myself, receiving a scratch on the countenance and a pretty severe kick in the side from the Capt. (my ribs ache now). All accidental, however, as the kick and scratch were meant for the combatants. I got a little mad, however, particularly as the Capt. picked up a billet of wood and struck at the mate, and collared them both, commanding peace or else I'd make it. Result of the combat. Severe threats from both sides; mate's face somewhat bruised and bloody; Capt's face and hands scratched; my phiz marked slightly, and the fourth rib damaged. I wish I had let 'em fought*[sic]* it out. Never mind, they will to-morrow…

B-y-e the bye, I saw Sam Ayers to-day. Sam's come back to try brick laying again. If he'll stick he'll make money, but I'm afraid there's little of the adhesive in his character.[21]…

Tuesday, 23d.

The weather has changed from lively to serene. It is to-day decidedly pleasant, clear and sunshiny. No news afloat. Nothing to "dot" in my Diary save that last night I had a glorious sleep, the fleas not distressing me by their usual caracollings and playing at "pussy wants a corner;" that it is now a settled point that John Bigler and the rest of the Loco ticket

---

[21]Ayers proved more successful at bricklaying than Bickham predicted. In 1854 he moved to Los Angeles where he became a member of the firm of Mullaly, Porter, and Ayers. In 1855 this firm built the first flour mill in Los Angeles and it constructed many other brick buildings in that city. By 1858 Ayers and his partners were annually producing two million bricks. Warner et al., *Historical Sketch of Los Angeles County*, 63.

are elected, and ourselves a defeated party; that my anticipations of receiving several letters are grievously disappointed, the mail failing to bring any whatever. "Better time coming."

Wednesday, 24th.

Went ashore this morning with the captain to act as witness in the case Mate vs. Captain. Mate sued him for assault and battery. He supposed my testimony would be of advantage to him, where as it would have condemned him at once. Luckily for my patience, the Mate's lawyer persuaded the Captain to settle the vexed question without trial.

Whilst standing by the Union Hotel about 10 o'clock, talking with several of our defeated candidates who had just arrived from up the country, somebody caught my arm and started off down street with me. Upon looking to see whom the hombre might be, lo and behold, Col. Jo. Potter from Murderer's Bar appeared. To make a long story short, I was glad to meet the Col. as I always am to see any old friend. I took a walk with him to Happy Valley, from thence to Clarke's Point, and back again to the Union. The Col. dined with me at 3 P.M. and then started for Sac. City…

I understand that numerous Custom House men to-day rec'd discharges. Shouldn't wonder. What an uneasy situation it is for many. I feel quite safe myself, but it looks badly to see discharges and new appointments every day.

25th Sept.

The weather to-day very delightful. Clear, warm, pleasant. I passed a portion of the day reading and writing a letter to mother, but really did not feel in proper mood to enjoy either employment. After tea I visited mon amigo, Langdon, on board the Columbus. We passed the evening until ten o'clock discussing the pleasures vs. the miseries of California life, finally turning to political questions, slavery, and North and South. At ten o'clock we were roused by the booming of cannon, report following report in quick succession. Immediately we started ashore to learn the cause, ourselves supposing it to be the announcement of the arrival of the Steamer North America with news from Cuba. Bah! It was nothing but the glorification of the Locofocos welcoming the arrival of

Gov. Elect John Bigler, who came down from Sacramento on the Confidence. To be sure we Whigs did not feel inclined to rejoice with them. I saw the old, fat Colonel in the four horse coach as he was drawn along through crowds of exultant Democratasie, and certes a more pleased expression of countenance than his presented, I have not seen in many a day. L. and I proceeded to the "Union," where we found a small band of Whig friends talking earnestly ab[out] our "lickin" and offering sundry "good" excuses therefore… We took a cup of coffee, smoked a fragrant cigar, and wended our way to our several vessels, cogitating upon "numerous" questions.

27th Sept.

I always go ashore in the mornings to peruse the newspapers, this habit being almost as necessary to my contentment as taking a cup of water when thirsty; this morning, as I stepped upon the wharf, I met Ned Rigsby from Murderer's Bar who gave me a letter from John. John states that at last he "has found good diggings and will probably remain in the mines all winter." It's time he had found something, and I feel quite rejoiced and only hope he may not soon exhaust the "lead." I have been trying to collect my ideas for epistolary duty to day, but only succeeded in finishing my letter to mother. This I posted, made a quarterly report to the Custom House, and returned to the *Frances,* went to my bunk, and threw myself into the arms of Morpheus. I've just eaten supper.

28th Sept.

Beautiful weather. Went ashore to-day and met with several old friends, among the rest Kemp Anderson Esq. of Murderer's Bar, who was instrumental in having me sent here to the State Convention. Such friends as he has proved to me are valuable. During the Day was introduced to the Governor Elect, John Bigler. He seems in a glorious mood. Thinks the State Democrat by 10,000 majority; *if the Locofoco strength could only be brought out!* Bah! Called in afternoon to see S. P. Moses Esq. and Lady. Sim has a very pretty wife.

29th Sept.

Have been quite busy to day writing letters to the *Gazette*. Have not felt in the mood for epistolary duty. Went ashore in the evening to call upon S. P. Moses & Lady. Met there Gen'l Anderson of Tuolumne Co., formerly U. S. Senator from Tennessee, recently elected to our State Senate from the aforesaid County.[22] About 9 PM. the General, Sim, Jack Moses, and myself went to the Magnolia[23] to eat a "crab" supper. The old Gen'l unbent himself to his young friends and related to us a page from the history of his youth. He referred to some of the great men of the age, and also some of the women, whom were young with him, and particularly .. [illegible]... the case of Judge McL. of Ohio, and his Lady while she was Sarah Belle L., after she was Mrs. G., and still further after she was Mrs. Judge McL.[24] I rather fancy that the old gentleman was formerly more interested in Sarah Belle than he wishes others to know. He touched upon the theme delicately, but being in love myself, I have pretty sharp eyes and judge from the tone of regret, pathetic too, with which he referred to her brilliant youth, that her "tactics" had mastered him. The Gen'l said her first husband was a good and sensible man, but was not polished. That her peculiar character rather frightened polished men, though there were any number of them revolving around her. I made a very good impression upon the old gentleman, and myself was pleased with his affability and social qualities, though really I cannot say I believe him to possess more than the ordinary abilities of an educated man. He aspires to the U. S. Senate of California—Nota Bene. He suffers Mint-Juleps to loosen his tongue in the presence of young and ambitious men. I am a Whig so pray be careful. What is said in the social circle must not be said outside, but the relations of a politician in a pub-

---

[22]Alexander Outlaw Anderson (1794-1869) a native of Tennessee and veteran of the Battle of New Orleans, practiced law in his home state, served as superintendent of the U.S. Land Office in Alabama, as government agent for the removal of Indians from Florida and Alabama, and as U.S. senator in 1840-41. In 1849 Anderson led an overland party to California via the Gila route. He practiced law in Sonora, Tuolumne County, and was elected to the state senate in 1851. In April 1852, Anderson was appointed to the state supreme court, and served on the bench until the general election later that year. In 1853 he returned to Tennessee, where he died in 1869. He was, according to Elizabeth LeBreton Gunn of Sonora, "the most refined and gentlemanly person" whom she had "yet seen." *Biographical Directory of the American Congress*, 780; Marston, *Records of a California Family*, 148-49.

[23]Thomas Harris's Magnolia Saloon was located at 62 Kearny St. Morgan. *Directory*, 107A.

[24]John McLean (1785-1861) congressman, U.S. supreme court justice, and frequent presidential hopeful, is most famous for dissenting from the Dred Scott decision of 1857. His second wife, Sarah Bella, whom he married in 1843, was the widow of Col. Jeptha D. Garrard, and the daughter of Israel Ludlow of Cincinnati. *DAB*.

lic bar-room are not considered sacred. Honor would keep a private conversation secret, but political revelations through the influence of wine are sometimes the destruction of one party, valuable to another. That which *I* learn in this manner I shall not forget. The General is much pleased with Evans,[25] Sim Moses's Secretary. He endeavors to flatter him, I think hoping to win him. Evans is sharp as a steel trap. He, too, is taking notes. After we had paid our bill, we returned to the Munfrey Hotel[26] and sate until eleven when Dr. Satterlee[27] and Evans with myself went to Mrs. Whitney's[28] and took "two stews and a fry!"...

Oct. 1st.

Beautiful day. Finished my letter to the Gazette and dispatched it by the P. O. Also sent to Mother the San F. News Letter, a wood cut of Big Bar on the Middle Fork of the A. M., [and] the Sac City Times and Transcript with view of Coloma. Sent copy to J. B. and one to Louis C. H.[29] of Cinti. Returning from the P. O., I met Thos. Beatty[30] of Grass

---

[25]Elwood Evans, a native of Philadelphia, served as deputy clerk to Customs Collector Simpson P. Moses until February 1852. Evans practiced law in Olympia and Tacoma, and was active in the politics of Washington Territory, serving as territorial secretary during the 1860s, and as acting governor in 1865. He was one of the first historians of the Pacific Northwest. BL: PB-9-v-1; Snowdon, *History of Washington*, 3: 156-57, 4: 140, 142, 184; Bancroft, *History of Washington, Idaho and Montana*, 54, 219, 273.

[26]William Munfrey, a native of Ireland, kept a hotel at 37 Webb St. from 1850 to 1852. San Francisco city directories, 1850-60; 1852 California Census, San Francisco III, 35; 1860 Census, San Francisco: 1,318; *Bulletin*, August 18, 1862.

[27]A native of Cayuga County, New York, John Satterlee (d. 1876) arrived in California in 1849 and was elected judge of the Superior Court of San Francisco in September 1851. Gardiner, *In Pursuit of the Golden Dream*, 326-27.

[28]Mrs. H. B. Whitney's Commercial Street Saloon featured "a specimen of ice cream manufactured at her establishment," which the *Alta California* pronounced a "very palatable compound." *Alta*, April 16, 1851; Parker, *Directory*, 103, Morgan, *Directory*, 62.

[29]Louis Cheesman Hopkins (b. 1828) a native of New York State, moved at age 16 to Cincinnati where he worked as an errand boy at a dry goods store. By the 1860's he had become one of Cincinnati's leading dry good merchants. After the failure of his dry goods business, he became a life insurance broker and moved to New York City, where he was still active during the first decade of the twentieth century. Cincinnati city directories, 1849-82; 1850 Census, Cincinnati, 4th ward, 409; 1860 Census, Cincinnati, 2nd ward, 219; 1870 Census, Cincinnati, 11th ward, 586; Cincinnati and Hamilton County Library: *Newspaper Clippings on Cincinnati*, 1: 167; New York city directories, 1884-1905.

[30]Thomas Beatty, a native of Ohio, is listed in the 1850 census as a 32-year-old trader living in Grass Valley. During that year he erected Beatty House, one of the first hotels in Grass Valley, which Alonzo Delano characterized as a "capital house... equal to any in Sacramento." 1850 Census, Yuba County, 274; Wells, *History of Nevada County*, 64-65; Delano, *Pen-Knife Sketches*, 51.

Valley, also Col. Potter and Wm. R. Hopkins Esq. of Murderer's Bar; the latter recently elected Whig Representative from Eldorado County. Hon. Edwd. C. Marshall[31] departs to day on the P. M. S. Oregon for the Atlantic States. The Oregon takes $2,000,000 Gold Dust in freight.

October 2d.

The Steamer North America arrived to day from Panama having made the trip in 13 days running time, the quickest on record. She brought Atlantic dates to the 28th August. The astonishing intelligence of the Execution of Lopez and the defeat of the Cuban Expedition, coupled with that of the consequent excitement on the subject, produced among us an intense sensation.[32] Every man's heart leaped with emotions of revenge or throbbed with pity, although we could not deny the right of the Spanish authorities to punish the invaders with death.

October 4th.

The Independence, Capt. Ned Wakeman, departed this afternoon from Long Wharf, crowded with passengers for the Atlantic States via San Juan del Sud. Among them were several acquaintances, Col. Hart Fellowes, Surveyor of Port, Ned Marshall, M. C. elect, E. L. Sanderson Esq. of N. York, Col. White[33] for Cuba, Wm. Swimley[34] and W. H.

---

[31]Edward C. ("Ned") Marshall, a lawyer, Mexican War veteran, and member of a well-known Kentucky family, came to California via the Gila route in 1849 and settled in Sonora, where he practiced law. After serving in Congress from 1851 to 1853, Marshall moved to Marysville and ran unsuccessfully for the U.S. Senate, after which he returned to Kentucky. He moved back to California twenty-one years later, practiced law in San Francisco, and served as state attorney general from 1883 to 1886. Lang, *Tuolumne County,* 36-38; *Biographical Dictionary of the American Congress,* 1,503; Gardiner, *In Pursuit of the Golden Dream,* 326.

[32]Lopez landed some sixty miles west of Havana on August 11-12. Although he won several skirmishes against Spanish troops, the Cuban people failed to rise in his support, and on August 28 he was forced to surrender. Lopez was publicly garroted, and fifty of his American followers were executed by firing squads. Anti-Spanish rioting broke out in New Orleans, and the Spanish consulate was sacked, but the Fillmore administration, which had no sympathy for the expedition, limited its response to securing the release of the remaining American prisoners. Brown, *Agents of Manifest Destiny,* 77-93; Caldwell, *Lopez Expeditions,* 91-115.

[33]A native of Ireland, Col. George W. White (d. 1853) served in the Texas navy and took part both in the U.S.- Mexican War and the Caste War in Yucatan before coming to San Francisco where, in 1851, he edited the Democratic newspaper, *Pacific Star.* When he left California in 1851, White, a supporter of Narciso Lopez, hoped to raise a body of fighting men and lead them to Cuba, but nothing came of this plan. *Alta,* October 5, 1851, March 27, 1853.

Woodyard for Cincinnati. By the latter I sent my Daguerretype and a letter to Mother.

Oct. 6th.

Arrived yesterday the P. M. S. California with a large Mail, bringing same dates as North America. This morning I had the pleasure of receiving a letter from Mother, from Angie, and from Charley Hayback. As usual I experienced those unpleasant feelings which have so frequently possessed me whilst conscious of the neglect of other friends—Morris Johnston particularly. Some persons do not know how to appreciate the value of truthful friendship. I rec'd a *Gazette* containing my letter of the 28th June, descriptive of the 22d June fire.

Oct. 12.

During the past week we have been favored with most delightful weather, weather corresponding in measure with our Indian summer at home. The nights have been gorgeously beautiful, being clear and moon-lit. I have, as usual, experienced sad emotions which I cannot describe. Until yesterday evening I have been "In[spector] in aid of Customs" at the C. S. Barge office. About 4 o'clock I got on board the schooner Laura Bevans,[35] Capt. N. Pierce,[36] laden with Bananas, Melons, Pumpkins & Potatoes. I am quite well pleased with her and shall be pleasantly situated for a fortnight. A new order was yesterday issued from the Custom House, viz. "Inspectors in Aid" are expected to stand guard by turns at night upon the different wharves! I don't fancy this.

---

[34]William Franklin Swimley had been one of Bickham's fellow passengers on the *Falcon* in 1850 and arrived in San Francisco in June of that year. By late November he had settled in Sacramento, where, at the time of the 1852 census, he was working as a druggist. He was proprietor of the Cincinnati Restaurant in Sacramento during the 1850s and '60s, and was later employed as a saloon keeper and a wine and liquor salesman. *New Orleans Daily Picayune,* March 16, 1850; *Cincinnati Enquirer,* August 21, 1850, January 12, 1851; 1852 California Census, Sacramento County, 81; Sacramento city directories 1853-81.

[35]The 97 ton *Laura Bevan,* built in Maryland in 1849, had arrived on the West Coast in August 1850, and since then had plied between San Francisco and Hawaii. She later sailed the California coast, and was reputed "a staunch and safe vessel," but in April 1858, was wrecked by a heavy northwester with loss of life to the captain and twelve passengers. BL: C-A 169, Part II, reel 2, 11; *Alta,* May 27, 1858; Van Nostrand, "Thomas A. Ayers," *CHSQ,* 20: 275, 278.

[36]Nelson Pierce, who was master and part owner of the *Laura Bevan* in 1851, later became a San Francisco shipping and commission merchant and proprietor of the Southern Dispatch Packet Company. San Francisco city directories, 1858-87; *Alta,* May 11, 1865.

Great excitement has prevailed during the last 3 days among the clerks &c. of the Customs. Mr. Hopkins, the Assistant Collector, and Mr. Taylor, one of the Appraisers, had a difficulty. Mr. H. challenged him, and the challenge was accepted. H. went to Benicia, expecting T. to follow, but the latter showed the "white feather," informed one of his friends of the affair, and the authorities interfered. The friends of the parties discussed the affair quite warmly, and for awhile it appeared that a half dozen duels would grow out of it. The matter, however, was neatly settled yesterday afternoon by Hopkins cowhiding Taylor in the streets. T. made no resistance. I think all is now settled.[37] Our Custom House is quite a belligerent institution.

Oct. 14th.

To day has been full of excitement owing to the departure of the Steamer North America. She left at 4 P.M., her first departure from this port, literally jammed with passengers.

15th. More excitement than ever this morning. The North America was compelled to return last night owing to mutiny among the crew. All being settled amicably, she departed at 9 A.M. The P. M. S. California sail'd at 6 A.M., likewise crowded with Passengers and carrying $1,600,000. At 4 P.M. the New Orleans also sailed. I have been very unwell all day and, in addition, have had the "blues" worse than at any time since I left home. By the mail I sent papers to J. B. and to mother. Letters to Mother, to Charley Hayback, and to L. C. H.[Louis C. Hopkins?] Weather still very Beautiful.

Oct. 17.

Arrived last night from San Juan del Sud Vanderbilt's Steamer Pacific in 12 days and 4 hours running time with dates from N. York to 12th

---

[37]Sheldon U. Hopkins, a former deputy customs collector in Philadelphia, arrived in California with Thomas Butler King in December 1850. He was, according to his cousin, Caspar T. Hopkins, "a creature of extremes . . . at times witty, sociable, charming and energetic; at other times morose, taciturn, averse to company or occupation." The cause of his quarrel with Samuel Taylor is obscure, but the correspondent of the *Sacramento Union* claimed that Taylor was "guilty of an act of base ingratitude" toward Hopkins. Hopkins, according to the *Alta California,* later "exonerated Mr. Taylor from acting a principal part in the insult offered to him." Soon afterwards, Hopkins cowhided another associate, Assistant Collector Green. Hopkins, "California Recollections," *CHSQ,* 25: 332; *Union,* October 15, 1851; *Alta,* October 30, 1851; June 12, 1865.

Sept. N. Orleans 13th do. The news brought is unusually tame, far different from that we have been led to expect through the news by the North America. All Californians, however, were exalted to learn of the victory of the Yacht America over our braggadocio relative John Bull.[38] I don't know when I have felt more like shouting "huzzah for the Universal Yankee Nation!" Also arrived this morning the P. M. S. *Tennessee* with large Mail from the Atlantic... No news of importance in our city. I noticed a paragraph in one of our papers early this week giving an account of a single cabbage head grown in California this year weighing 28 pounds. Whew!

Saturday, October 18th, 1851.

Huzzah for the Steamer Tennessee! I shall ever after this day hail her arrival from Panama with lively joy, and swelling hopes! She has bourne me in her huge bosom such treasures of delightful souvenirs from home! Only to contemplate the glorious fact, she has brought me a letter from Sister Angie, a long epistle from Sister Emma, a treasure of affection from my Mother, besides letters from my acquaintances, W. C. Poor[39] and Hugh Dugan. Also a Cincinnati Gazette of Sept. 4th, which contained several of *mine own* "lucid productions," which, indeed, were quite pleasing, and quite natural too, for one certainly has a partiality for one's own offspring. But huzzah for the Tennessee! say I, for her coming has brought me pleasure superior to any I have experienced for many a day.

Yet still am I somewhat disappointed. But is that *strange*, for was man ever satisfied? Oh I have such a Brobdignagian appetite for "letters," I could devour an hundred at a sitting and my appetite would not be sated. I did expect a remembrance of the past from_____. I felt assured

---

[38]On August 22 the yacht *America,* designed along clipper lines by Commodore John Cox Stevens of the New York Yacht Club, defeated fourteen British cutters and schooners in a 53 mile race around the Isle of Wight. The trophy awarded by the Royal Yacht Club became known as "America's Cup."

[39]William C. Poor, (d. 1878) the son of a Cincinnati merchant, set out overland for California in 1849 as a member of the "Experiment Club." He crossed the Sierra by pack mule in August, together with Silas Smith (see above, 55). Poor soon returned to Cincinnati where he was a wholesale grocer during the 1850s and '60s. *Cincinnati Daily Times,* October 23, 1849; Haskins, *Argonauts of California,* 406; *Republican,* April 23, 1849; Cincinnati city directories 1851-73; *"Old Woodward,"* 258; 1860 Census, Cincinnati, 14th ward, 707; 1870 Census, Cincinnati, 18th ward, 345.

[that Morris] Johnston would not forget me, and no less had reason
..[torn]... I would be the recipient of favors from Will Ludlow, Tom
Fould and Fran[k] Whetstone.[40] The De'il's in it. Who would have
thought that friends so full of warm protestations of friendship and
esteem would cool so quickly and content themselves with a formal
"Kindest Regards" on the envelope of another letter sent me... My
friends may visit the regions of darkness ere I shall trouble them again
without the[y] make amends for the past.

Sister Emma's letter is full of delightful as well as amusing gossip.
Perfectly natural and perfectly *womanly.* Women never did agree with
each other, and girls no less. They will allow their petty spite, jealousy,
and envyings to escape through some loop. Angie is more business like
and writes with a kind of good-natured air of wonderment. She says
Percy S. is a "perfect living curiosity." Both girls write with considerable
naiveté, perfectly innocent of having said anything to amuse, and perfectly natural, though "weary." Considerably careless. Angie thinks
she'll be "old" when she shall have numbered "nineteen years." Girls are
more aspiring than boys to be sure.

Sunday, October 19th, 1851.

On Board the Schooner Laura Bevan as Ins. of Customs.
Harbor of San Francisco, California.

My dear Sisters Emma and Angie:
My "Diary" for the year 1851, from the first of January to this date, is
finished. I now write my brief epilogue. I present the volume for you and
hope you may treasure it as a memorial of a brother's affection. I desire
too that you may fulfill my injunctions respecting its disposition. You
will naturally be proud of it as it is *my history* in California for ten
months, during which time I have been subject to many of the vicissi-
tudes of Life, meeting frequently with "ups and downs," most[ly] with
the latter, coping with difficulties, and struggling against the hard usages
of adversity, yet withal still keeping my banner aloft,... never forgetting
my dignity or honor as a man, and eternally desiring to gratify and

---

[40]Frank D. S. Whetstone (1828-75) a member of one of Cincinnati's leading linseed oil manufacturing firms, was characterized in his obituary as a "bold and enterprising businessman" noted
for "strict integrity." Wright, *Obituaries of Cincinnatians,* 62.

delight the hearts of far distant friends, of affectionate sisters, and a mother whose spirit has always guided, soothed, consoled, and urged me onward in the darkest hours, when fortune frowned or the sun of hope seemed about departing forever...

Epilogue

Although Bickham remained in California for over two years after closing his journal, relatively little is known of this period of his life. No diary for these years has yet emerged, and his letters to the *Cincinnati Gazette* for this period contain few autobiographical details.

He continued to serve as inspector of customs for the remainder of 1851, and was assigned to two further ships: the American barks *Anne Welch,* which arrived from Hong Kong on November 8, and *Isabella,* which arrived from Talcahauna, Chile, on December 4. He is not recorded as being assigned to any further vessels, and probably left the Customs Service at the end of the year.[1]

In 1852 Bickham reentered the field of journalism, working for several months for the *Evening Picayune,* which ceased publication in April of that year.[2] The following month he became co-editor and part proprietor of a new Whig newspaper, the *Daily Evening Journal,* together with Andrew M. Macy, a former co-editor of the *Picayune.*[3] The new paper elicited mixed opinions. The *Alta California* characterized it as "a small sheet, but very creditably printed," which threw "down the gauntlet quite fiercely to its democratic contemporaries."[4] F. D. May, a correspondent of the *Cincinnati Commercial,* denied that the *Evening Journal's* editorial columns indicated "anything very powerful,"[5] but the pro-Whig *Sacramento Daily Union* took a more favorable view of the *Journal* and its editors, characterizing Bickham as "a young man of fine

---

[1] BL: C-A 169, Part II, reel 11.
[2] *Union,* May 28, 1852.
[3] Ibid.; *Montgomery County History.* Book 3: 191.
[4] *Alta,* May 25, 1852.
[5] *Cincinnati Commercial,* July 1, 1852.

talents, great industry, and withal, a ready writer."⁶ Bickham remained
co-editor of the *Evening Journal* for much of 1852, but by January 1853,
both he and Macy had, for reasons which remain obscure, been
replaced.⁷ Sometime later in his San Francisco stay Bickham was,
according to the *Montgomery County History,* city editor of two other
newspapers, the *Evening Times* and the *Morning Ledger.*⁸ Late in 1853
he aided A. C. Russell in his attempt to reestablish the *Evening
Picayune,* serving as assistant editor of that paper.⁹ Throughout his
sojourn in San Francisco, Bickham also continued to send dispatches to
the *Cincinnati Gazette,* which, while they contained little about himself,
gave a lively account of events in San Francisco and the rest of Califor-
nia.¹⁰

Bickham involved himself in other San Francisco affairs. He continued to be active in the Young Men's Whig Club, serving on its executive
committee in early 1853.¹¹ Like other active San Franciscans, he joined
one of the city's volunteer fire-fighting associations, the Monumental
Engine Company.¹² In addition to fighting fires, these organizations
served as San Francisco's leading social clubs, and membership in one of
them was considered highly desirable for any man aspiring to prominence in the city.

More significant was Bickham's role in the Mercantile Library Association, which provided San Francisco with its first public library. Bickham was among the founding members of the Association, and served
on both the committee on its constitution and the committee to collect
subscriptions.¹³ He was appointed its first librarian and was entrusted
with fitting up its rooms on the second floor of the California Exchange.
"Our library," he wrote in a letter to the *Cincinnati Gazette,* "consists of

⁶*Union,* May 29, 1852.
⁷BL: Miscellaneous Newspapers: *Daily Evening Journal,* May 31, Sept. 1, 1852, Jan. 3, 1853.
⁸*History of Montgomery County,* Book 3: 191.
⁹*Cincinnati Daily Gazette,* January 3, 1854; San Francisco city directory, 1854.
¹⁰*Cincinnati Daily Gazette,* August 21, 27, 28, September 13, October 8, 13, 14, 24, 28, 1851,
February 7, June 10, 11, 19, 1852, August 16, September 2, 16, October 12, 13, 1853, January 10,
1854.
¹¹*Union,* January 22, 1853.
¹²Morgan, *Directory,* 77.
¹³Backus, "San Francisco Mercantile Library Association," 31.

1600 volumes of old (chiefly) standard works produced here, and will not, of course, be greatly enlarged until the treasury is in better condition."[14]

By July Bickham was forced to admit that the Association was "not in a very flourishing condition," a situation which he blamed on "the apathy or inattention of the community," and the "excitable character of the public mind," which rendered "it unfit for solid or regular reading."[15] At the end of August, Bickham claimed that the "prospects of the Association" were "brightening,"[16] but by the year's end its income had not increased and its membership was dropping off. It was not until after Bickham's departure the following March that the new librarian, Horace Davis, managed to save the Association by finding less expensive quarters, offering a cheaper grade of membership, and cataloguing the books.[17] Talented as he was as a journalist and writer, Bickham proved less successful as a librarian.

On March 1, 1854, almost exactly four years after his departure from Cincinnati, Bickham boarded the Panama-bound steamer *John L. Stephens,* for the first leg of his journey home.[18] The four years he had planned to stay in California had elapsed, and his longing for his family, friends, and boyhood home had probably increased. As the eldest male in the family he was, moreover, responsible for the support of his mother and siblings. Although active in San Francisco life, Bickham had neither put down roots nor established a career in the Bay City, and the failure of the revived *Picayune,* which was absorbed by another paper in January, 1854,[19] combined with the continuing problems of the Library Association, may have convinced him that his time in California had reached its proper end. Whatever his reasons, Bickham departed for Ohio in the spring of 1854, having played a small but active part in the story of early San Francisco.

Bickham's trip home proved almost as dramatic as his outward journey. On the evening of Tuesday, March 14, the *John L. Stephens* arrived

---

[14] *Cincinnati Daily Gazette,* August 16, 1853.
[15] Ibid.
[16] Ibid., October 12, 1853.
[17] Backus, "San Francisco Mercantile Library Association," 159-60.
[18] *Alta,* March 2, 1854.
[19] Kemble, *History of California Newspapers,* 116.

at Panama City,[20] and the following day Bickham and his fellow passengers set out across the Isthmus. The Panama Railroad by now extended from Aspinwall on the Atlantic side to within eighteen miles of Panama City, but it was still necessary to travel by mule as far as the Obispo railway depot. While riding through a narrow gorge, Bickham and Mrs. Andrews of Sacramento, a lady whom he was escorting, had fallen behind the rest of the mule train when Bickham, according to the *Aspinwall Courier*, "was suddenly startled by a fierce demand directly behind for his money." Turning in the saddle, he saw behind him a party of six or seven armed men. Drawing his single barreled pistol, Bickham aimed at the foremost bandit and pulled the trigger. The pistol misfired, and he was simultaneously fired on by one of the robbers. Although apparently not badly wounded, Bickham was hurled to the ground and found himself "surrounded by the party, who had several muskets leveled at him close to his body, and one fellow standing before him with a drawn *machete* at his breast." The bandits, having relieved Bickham of his portmonnaie, which contained between $200 and $250, his steamer ticket to New York, and a "small California gold ring," vanished into the chaparral. Mrs. Andrews had fallen from her mule and fled, but after a brief search, Bickham located her in a native hut about a quarter of a mile away, unhurt save for a cut in the head received during her fall.[21]

Despite this misadventure, Bickham managed to make his way to Cincinnati sometime in April, rich in experience if not in cash. As no newspaper work was then available he took employment as a brakeman on the Cincinnati, Hamilton and Dayton Railroad, of which family friend S. S. L'Hommedieu was now president. Bickham apparently performed his duties well, for within three months he was promoted to baggage master. It was not long, however, before he returned to the field of journalism, in which he would remain for the rest of his life. He was hired as a traveling correspondent by the *Cincinnati Daily Columbian*, and later held a similar position on the *Evening Times*. In 1856, while covering the state legislature for this paper, he was offered and accepted the position of city editor of the *Cincinnati Commercial*. In addition to his city editorship, Bickham served that paper until the outbreak of the

---

[20]*Daily Panama Star*, March 16, 1854.

[21]*Cincinnati Enquirer*, April 2, 1854 (quotation from *Aspinwall Courier*).

Civil War as its correspondent in the state and national capitals. During this period he made the acquaintance of such public figures as the future chief justice, Salmon P. Chase, and future presidents Rutherford B. Hayes and James A. Garfield.[22]

While covering county fairs during the mid 1850s, Bickham became acquainted with Abraham Strickle, a farmer of Swiss origin and the director of the Clinton County Fair. More importantly, Bickham also met Maria, one of Strickle's ten well-educated daughters, and in December 1855, he and Maria were married.[23] The following February, in a letter to his mother, Bickham, with characteristic fervor, referred to his young wife as "a priceless treasure," "one of the noblest creatures on God's footstool," and "an inestimably virtuous wife."[24] "I can recall," wrote Daniel Bickham, "nothing but blind affection for his wife, and devoted affection. She was the beginning and end of things for him."[25] William and Maria Bickham produced a total of seven sons, one of whom died in infancy, another of whom drowned at age seven. Three of the surviving sons, Abe, Daniel, and Charles, followed their father into journalism, while the eldest, William Strickle Bickham, moved to Spokane, Washington, where he dealt in real estate.[26]

The outbreak of the Civil War marked the beginning of another dramatic phase of Bickham's life, his two years as a war correspondent. The Civil War was the first war in history to be extensively covered by the news media, and Bickham, like many other journalists, found in this conflict an opportunity to advance his career. He was first attached to the army in western Virginia commanded by Ohio general William S. Rosecrans. Like several other Civil War correspondents, Bickham was appointed to a staff position, serving as Rosecrans' volunteer aide-de-camp with the rank of captain. In that capacity he took part in the battle of Carnifax Ferry on September 10, 1861, during which, according

[22]*History of Montgomery County.* Book 3: 191; DMCL Bickham Collection, "Biographical Notes."

[23]DMCL Bickham Collection, WDB-Personal, 3; WRHS Library: Bickham Family Papers, Container 1, folder 7.

[24]WRHS Library: Bickham Family Papers: Container 1, folder 1: Letter from WDB to mother from Columbus, Ohio, February 26, 1856.

[25]DMCL Bickham Collection. WDB-personal, 1.

[26]*Cincinnati Enquirer,* March 28, 1894; *Biographical Cyclopædia and Portrait Gallery . . . of the State of Ohio.* 5: 1,243.

to Rosecrans, "he staid by me when every other officer on my staff had become so perfectly exhausted that they could not go with me."[27] At the end of the long day of combat, Bickham and his equally weary fellow correspondent, Whitelaw Reid of the *Cincinnati Gazette*, had trouble finding a place to sleep. They were ordered away from one location by a sentry on the grounds of its being too dangerous, and from another by Rosecrans, himself, who claimed that they had chosen the likeliest spot for a Confederate attack. The two correspondents finally located a comfortable sleeping place in a stable which had been converted into a hospital, only to discover the following morning that they had been sleeping on a pile of horse manure.[28]

After the close of the West Virginia campaign, Bickham covered the campaigns of John C. Frémont in Missouri and of George Thomas in Kentucky. The following year he accompanied George B. McClellan's Army of the Potomac on the Peninsula Campaign, and was present during the Seven Days Battles of June 26 to July 2.[29] By the latter part of 1862, he was once more on the staff of General Rosecrans, now in command of the Army of the Cumberland in Tennessee. Service under this energetic commander proved neither safe nor dull. On December 26, when Rosecrans led a small party of staff officers, including Bickham, on a visit to a subordinate commander, the party got repeatedly lost both coming and going, narrowly escaped contact with a Confederate cavalry patrol, and strayed dangerously close to Rebel picket lines. Bickham and several of his fellows, having become separated from their general, arrived back at headquarters at 3:00 A.M., after sixteen hours in the saddle without food.[30] Five days later, during the battle of Stones River, Bickham once more found himself close to danger. As at Carnifax Ferry, he stayed close to his commander throughout the battle. This proved a far from safe position, as Rosecrans spent much of the day in the thick of combat, rallying his faltering troops, and was narrowly missed by a Rebel shell which decapitated his chief of staff. Rosecrans praised Bick-

---

[27]Quoted in DMCL Bickham Collection, WDB-Sketch, 4.

[28]Andrews, *The North Reports the Civil War*, 110-11.

[29]*History of Montgomery County*, Book 3: 191.

[30]Bickham, *Rosecrans' Campaign*, 157-63; *Cincinnati Commercial*, January 5, 1863.

ham's conduct in this action, and Bickham was rewarded with the rank of Major.[31]

Bickham's dispatches from these campaigns, which vividly describe battles, camp life, and the ravages of war, are of comparable interest to his California writings and enhanced his reputation as a journalist.[32] During the uneventful months which followed the Battle of Stones River, he used some of these dispatches, as well as the official army reports, as the basis of an account of the Stones River campaign, *Rosecrans' Campaign with the Fourteenth Army Corps*. This book proved successful, the first two editions sold out in May, and the third appeared on Cincinnati bookshelves on June 6.[33] *Rosecrans' Campaign*, although marred by strong pro-Union and pro-Rosecrans bias, presents lively portraits of the general and his staff and a swift narrative of the battle. Bickham greatly admired Rosecrans, whom he praised for "coolness, readiness, fertility of resource, celerity of thought, rapid decision, and comprehensive grasp of mind in the midst of the most trying situations of peril, personal and military."[34] Henry Villard, correspondent of the *New York Tribune*, who did not share Bickham's high regard for "Old Rosey," accused Bickham of being a "puffer," whose laudatory account of the general had been purchased with favors.[35] It was not uncommon for generals to befriend correspondents in the hope of good publicity, but Bickham's regard for Rosecrans appears to have been genuine and was not entirely undeserved. The Ohio general was an able administrator and strategist and a brave battle commander. Were it not for his disastrous defeat at Chickamauga later that year, his reputation in history would have risen far closer to Bickham's assessment.

As 1863 progressed with little action in the Tennessee theater, Bickham explored the possibility of returning to civilian journalism and of becoming editor and proprietor of his own paper. He had become weary of working for the *Commercial*, and frustrated in his hope of gaining an

[31]DMCL Bickham Collection, WDB-sketch, 4.
[32]Among Bickham's more interesting Civil War letters to the *Commercial* are those printed in the editions of November 5, 1861, December 12, 1862, and January 5, 1863.
[33]Hodgson, "William D. Bickham," 21.
[34]Bickham, *Rosecrans' Campaign*, 330.
[35]Henry Villard, *Memoirs*, 2: 67.

interest in the paper.[36] He was, moreover, anxious to move to a smaller city where he could spend more time with his family, and be independent of employers, but he lacked the means to establish his own paper, his only capital being, he claimed, "industry, energy, zeal, and experience."[37] He was, therefore, extremely interested when his editor, Murat Halstead, informed him that several prominent citizens of Dayton, Ohio, were offering him the post of editor and proprietor of the *Daily Journal*, the pro-Union newspaper in their small city.[38]

Dayton at this time was fiercely divided between Union supporters and the Peace Democrats, or "Copperheads," and riots and street fights were common. When, in early May 1863, General Ambrose Burnside, commander of the Department of the Ohio, arrested Congressman Clement Vallandigham, a Copperhead leader and Dayton resident, for sedition, the violence reached its peak, and on May 5 a Copperhead mob burned the *Journal* office to the ground. At the time of the fire or shortly thereafter, Bickham was in Dayton, negotiating the purchase of the paper. As he examined the ruins of the *Journal* office, he was approached by a menacing group of Copperheads who demanded to know if he was "that damned Bickham" who was planning "to start a new Union Paper." When Bickham replied in the affirmative, three men stepped forward, ordering him to leave town. Bickham, a skilled amateur boxer, knocked two of the men down, causing the third to back away. Reaching safety, Bickham wired his wife, "We go to Dayton to live."[39]

To meet the expenses of reestablishing the paper, several Dayton citizens raised $6,000 which they offered Bickham as a gift. This he declined, but accepted the money as a loan to be repaid in three years. On May 11 he took charge of publication, assuming the duties of business manager, reporter, and advertising solicitor in addition to those of editor and publisher. For the remainder of May and most of June, while the *Journal's* hoe press, which had been damaged in the fire, was being repaired, a four page newsletter was all that he was able to issue. By the

---

[36]WRHS Library. Bickham Family Papers. Container 1, Folder 4: Biography of William Strickle Bickham by his parents.

[37]DMCL Bickham Collection, WDB-Sketch, 3.

[38]Ibid.

[39]Ibid., 6-7; DMCL Bickham Collection. Newspaper clipping by Charlotte Reeve Conover (*News*, August 30, 1936).

end of June, however, the *Journal* had been relocated in offices protected by two loaded cannon, and on July 28 the first regular edition appeared.[40] During his early days at the *Journal,* Bickham continued to face local hostility and was, according to his son, Daniel, more than once fired on by snipers.[41] As the tide of war turned in the Union's favor, however, Copperhead influence began to decline. When Vallandigham, now living in exile in Canada, ran for governor of Ohio in the autumn of 1863, he was soundly defeated in his home city of Dayton, as well as in the rest of the state. Bickham, who had vigorously attacked Vallandigham in his paper, could claim a share in the Copperhead leader's defeat.[42]

By 1866 Bickham had repaid his loan and gained full ownership of the *Journal.* In time he was able to delegate some of his duties to subordinates, but he continued to serve as editor of all departments and to supervise several branches of the *Journal's* business, never allowing it to go into debt. He continued as editor and proprietor of the *Journal* for the remainder of his life and, as the animosities of the Civil War receded, he gained general respect as one of Dayton's leading citizens. Under his management, the *Journal* became known as "Bickham's paper," and was considered one of the state's leading newspapers outside of the major cities.[43]

Bickham remained involved in politics, although he refused to seek office for himself, and he displayed as much devotion to the Republican Party as he had to the Whigs in his youth. As a delegate to at least twenty state conventions, and every national one, he played an active role in constructing local, state and national tickets. He was believed in some quarters to have been largely responsible for the nomination of Rutherford B. Hayes for the presidency in 1876. There was, according to the *History of the Republican Party in Ohio,* "nothing half-way, luke-warm, or indifferent about his advocacy of Republican measures and Republican candidates," although "he never cherished personal animosities," and "after a protracted and peppery campaign, he would settle down to the

---

[40]*History of Montgomery County,* Book 2: 708-11; Hodgson, "William D. Bickham," 40-42; DMCL Bickham Collection, "High Spots."

[41]DMCL Bickham Collection, WDB personal, 5; address by Daniel D. Bickham, 6.

[42]Hodgson, "William D. Bickham," 45-77.

[43]*History of Montgomery County,* Book 2: 708-11; DMCL Bickham Collection, "High Spots;" White, "Western Journalism," *Harper's Magazine,* 1888, 77: 683.

enjoyment of a hard-earned victory or philosophize with good nature over a signal defeat, and figuratively shake hands all around with friend and foe."[44]

In 1882, when Bickham was at the peak of his editorial career, the *Montgomery County History* described him as follows:

> Major Bickham, although fifty-five years of age, is as vigorous as an ordinary man ten years younger, and has a large capacity for hard work. He owes his vitality to a powerful constitution and superior physical powers carefully cultivated in athletic exercises in his youth and earlier manhood. His habit now is to spend ten or twelve hours at work and walk six to eight miles daily for exercise. . . He is a blunt, plain man, yet kind and courteous to friend and stranger alike; and although his determined and vigorous partisan journalistic career has created enemies among his political opponents, his friends staunch and true may be counted by the hundreds.[45]

"He was," wrote another contemporary, "a figure often seen in the streets of Dayton and always an impressive figure. He had what they call a presence. There was a ruddy face, a little grey goatee, and behind it there was a man."[46]

Bickham's strong constitution, which enabled him to work long hours daily, held up until the winter of 1893-4, when he fell victim to a variety of ailments which caused his family to fear for his life. By March 1894, he had recovered sufficiently to be able to visit his office for a short time each day, although he was still unable to do much work. On Monday afternoon, March 26, he claimed to be feeling unwell, and feared that he would be forced to resume his sickbed. The following day, feeling much better, he ate midday dinner with his family, after which he and Maria retired to the library where, according to one account, "the Major chatted pleasantly and apparently was in better spirits than during the morning hours." At about 2:30 Maria left the room, and shortly afterwards Bickham started upstairs to take a nap, but as he reached the top of the staircase, he tottered and fell. Maria, hurrying to his side, found his face

---

[44]Joseph Smith, *Republican Party in Ohio*, 98-99.

[45]*History of Montgomery County*, Book 3: 191-92.

[46]DMCL Bickham Collection: Newspaper article by Charlotte Reeve Conover (*News*, August 30, 1936).

"suffused with blood," indicating an apoplectic seizure, and she called for their sons, Charles and Abe. As his sons carried Bickham to his bed, he gave a loud groan. A few moments later, he died.[47]

The news of Bickham's death, claimed one account, "as it swiftly traversed the city, caused profound sorrow. Like the felling of a huge oak amid its lesser surroundings, a strong man of superior mentality and attainments had suddenly disappeared from the ranks of his fellows."[48] An able journalist, and one of the liveliest witnesses of Gold Rush California had passed away.

[47]*Dayton Daily Journal,* March 28, 1894; *Cincinnati Enquirer,* March, 31, 1894.
[48]*Cincinnati Enquirer,* March 28, 1894.

Bibliography

Books and Articles:

Adams, W. Davenport. *Dictionary of English Literature.* 2nd edition. Cassell, Petter and Galpin. London, Paris and New York. (republished by Gale research Co. Book Tower, Detroit, 1966).

Ainsa, Joseph Y. *History of the Crabb Expedition into Northern Sonora.* Phoenix, 1951.

Allen, Michael. *Western Rivermen, 1763-1861: Ohio and Mississippi Boatmen and the Myth of the Alligator Horse.* Baton Rouge and London, 1900.

Allen, Walter C. (editor). *Society of California Pioneers Centennial Roster, Commemorative Edition.* 1948.

Andrews, J. Cutler. *The North Reports the Civil War.* Pittsburgh, 1955.

Angel, Myron. *History of Placer County.* Oakland, 1882.

Bancroft, Hubert Howe. *History of California.* 7 volumes. Reprint: Santa Barbara, California, 1963-70

_____ *History of Washington, Idaho and Montana.* San Francisco, 1890.

Barry, T. A. and B. A. Patten. *Men and Memories of San Francisco in 1850.* Oakland, 1947.

Bates, Mrs. D. B. *Incidents on Land and Water or Four Years on the Pacific Coast.* Boston, 1858.

Bell, Major Horace. *Reminiscences of a Ranger, or Early Times in Southern California.* Los Angeles, 1881.

Beiber, Ralph P. (editor). *Southern Trails to California in 1849.* Glendale, California, 1937.

Bickham, William Dennison. *From Ohio to the Rocky Mountains; Editorial Correspondence of the Dayton (Ohio) Journal by William D. Bickham.* Dayton, 1879.

_____. *Rosecrans' Campaign with the Fourteenth Army Corps; or the Army of the Cumberland.* Cincinnati, 1863.

Biggs, Donald C. *Conquer and Colonize, Stevenson's Regiment and California.* San Rafael, California, 1977.

The Biographical Cyclopædia and Portrait Gallery with an Historical Sketch of the State of Ohio. 6 vol. Cincinnati, 1883-95.

Biographical Directory of the American Congress, 1774-1949. United States Government Printing Office, 1950.

Bird, Isabella. *The Englishwoman in America.* London, 1856.

Bodley, Temple. *History of Kentucky, the Blue Grass State,* Vol. III, Chicago and Louisville, 1928.

Bordman, Gerald. *The Oxford Companion to American Theatre.* New York, 1984.

Brown, Charles H. *Agents of Manifest Destiny: The Lives and Times of the Filibusters.* Chapel Hill, 1980.

Bruff, J. Goldsborough. *Gold Rush: the Journals, Drawings and other papers of J. Goldsborough Bruff, April 2, 1849 - July 20, 1851.* Georgia Willis Read and Ruth Gaines, editors. New York, 1949.

Caldwell, Robert Granville. *The Lopez Expeditions to Cuba, 1848-1851.* Princeton, 1915.

Colcord, Roswell Keyes. "Reminiscences of Life in Territorial Nevada." *CHSQ,* vol. 7.

Conovor, Frank (editor). *Centennial Portrait and Biographical Record of the City of Dayton and Montgomery County.* A. W. Beven and Co., 1897.

Coy, Owen C. (compiler). *Guide to the County Archives of California.* Sacramento, 1919.

Crosby, Elisha Oscar. *Memoirs of Elisha Oscar Crosby.* Charles Albro Barker, editor. San Marino, California, 1945.

Dabble, Margaret (editor). *The Oxford Companion to English Literature.* 5th edition. Oxford, New York, Tokyo, Melbourne, 1985.

Daniell, L. E. *Types of Successful Men of Texas.* Austin, 1952.

Davies, J. Kenneth. *Mormon Gold: The Story of California's Mormon Argonauts.* Salt Lake City, 1984.

Davis, William Heath. *Seventy-five Years in California.* Harold A. Small, editor. San Francisco, 1967.

Davis, Winfield J. *History of Political Conventions in California, 1849-1892.* Sacramento, 1893.

Delano, Alonzo. *Pen-Knife Sketches, or Chips of the Old Block.* San Francisco, 1934.

Dickens, Charles. *American Notes: a Journey.* New York, 1985.

The Dictionary of American Biography. 22 vols. New York, 1958.

The Dictionary of National Biography. 63 vols. Leslie Stephen and Sidney Lee, editors. London, 1880-1901.

Drum, Stella M. (editor). "Glimpses of the Past: Recollections of a Septuagenarian by William Waldo of Texas." *Missouri Hist. Soc.* vol. V, nos. 4-6.

Estavan, Lawrence (editor). *San Francisco Theatre Research,* vol. 2. WPA Project 8386. San Francisco, 1938.

Foreman, Grant. *The Adventures of James Collier, First Collector of the Port of San Francisco.* Chicago, 1937.

Franklin, Benjamin. *Benjamin Franklin's Autobiography and Selected Writings.* New York, Chicago, San Francisco, 1964.

Gagey, Edmond M. *The San Francisco Stage: A History.* New York, 1950.

Gardiner, Howard C. *In Pursuit of the Golden Dream, Reminiscences of San Francisco and Southern Mines, 1849-1857.* Dale L. Morgan, editor. Stoughton, Mass., 1970.

Garrison, Winfred. *Religion Follows the Frontier.* New York and London, 1931.

Gerhard, Peter. *Pirates of the Pacific, 1575-1742.* Lincoln, Nebraska, and London, 1990.

Gilbert, F. T. *History of San Joaquin County.* Oakland, 1879.

Goodwin, Charles. *As I Remember Them.* Salt Lake City, 1913.

Graham, A. A. (compiler). *History of Richland County, Ohio.* Mansfield, Ohio, 1880.

Grant, F. J. (editor). *History of Seattle, Washington.* New York, 1891.

Greer, James Kimmins. *Colonel Jack Hays, Texas Frontier Leader and California Builder.* (Revised edition). College Station, Texas, 1987.

Greve, Charles Theodore. *Centennial History of Cincinnati and Representative Citizens.* 2 vols. Chicago, 1904.

Gudde, Erwin G. *California Gold Camps.* Berkeley, Los Angeles, London, 1975.

Hafen, LeRoy R. (editor). *The Mountain Men and the Fur Trade of the Far West.* 10 vols. Glendale, California, 1965-72.

Harker, George Mifflin. "Morgan Street to Old Dry Diggings." Stella M. Drum, editor. *Glimpses of the Past,* vol. I, Missouri Historical Society. St. Louis, 1939 (pp. 35-76).

Harlow, Alvin F. *The Serene Cincinnatians*. New York, 1950.

Haskins, C. W. *The Argonauts of California*. New York, 1890.

Heintz, William F. *San Francisco's Mayors, 1850-1880*. Woodside, California, 1975.

History of Hancock County, Ohio. Chicago, 1886.

The History of Montgomery County, Ohio. Chicago, 1882.

Hittell, Theodore H. *History of California*. 4 vols. San Francisco, 1885-97.

Hoover, Mildred Brooke; Hero Eugene Rensch, and Ethel Grace Rensch. *Historic Spots in California*. 3rd edition, revised by William N. Abeloe. Stanford, 1966.

Hopkins, Caspar T. "The California Recollections of Caspar T. Hopkins." *CHSQ*, vol. 25.

Howe, Octavius T. and Frederick C. Matthews. *American Clipper Ships, 1833-1859*. Volume I. Salem Massachusetts, 1926.

Hurt, Peyton. "The Rise and Fall of the 'Know Nothings' in California." *CHSQ*, Vol. 9.

Jackson, Donald Dale. *Gold Dust*. New York, 1980.

Johnson, Kenneth (editor). *San Francisco As It Is: Gleanings from the Picayune*. Georgetown, California, 1964.

Kelly, James Wells, (compiler). *First Directory of Nevada Territory*. San Francisco, 1861.

Kemble, Edward C. *A History of California Newspapers, 1846-1858*. Helen Harding Bretnor, editor. Los Gatos, California, 1962.

Kemble, John Haskell. *The Panama Route, 1848-1869*. Columbia, South Carolina, 1990.

Koon, Helene Wickham. *How Shakespeare Won the West; Players and Performances in America's Gold Rush, 1849-1865*. Jefferson, North Carolina, and London, 1989.

Lang, Herbert O. *A History of Tuolumne County, California*. San Francisco, 1882.

Lavender, David. *Nothing Seemed Impossible; William C. Ralston and Early San Francisco*. Palo Alto, California, 1975.

Lotchin, Roger W. *San Francisco, 1846-1856: From Hamlet to City*. Lincoln and London, 1979.

Lyell, Charles, esq. *Travels in North America in the Years 1841-42*. Vol. 2. New York, 1845.

Mack, Effie Mona. *Nevada; a history of the state from the earliest times through the Civil War.* Glendale, California, 1936.

Manarin, Louis H. (compiler). *North Carolina Troops 1861-65, a Roster. Vol. III, Infantry.* State department of Archives and History. Raleigh, North Carolina, 1971.

Marston, Anna Lee (editor). *Records of a California Family. Journals and Letters of Lewis C. Gunn and Elizabeth LeBreton Gunn.* San Diego, 1928.

Martzoleff, C. L. (collector and annotator). *Poems on Ohio.* 1911.

Massey, Ernest de. *A Frenchman in the Gold Rush, the Journal of Ernest de Massey, Argonaut of 1849.* Marguerite Eyer Wilbur, translator. San Francisco, 1927.

Melendy, Howard Brett, and Benjamin Franklin Gilbert. *The Governors of California from Peter H. Burnett to Edmond G. Brown.* Georgetown, California, 1965.

Merwin, Henry Childs. *The Life of Bret Harte.* Boston and New York, 1911.

Millard, Bailey. *History of the San Francisco Bay Region.* Vol. III. Chicago, San Francisco, New York, 1924.

Mullen, Kevin J. *Let Justice Be Done: Crime and Politics in Early San Francisco.* Reno and Las Vegas, 1989.

Myres, John. *San Francisco's Reign of Terror.* San Francisco, 1966.

Newell, Gordon. *Paddlewheel Pirate, the Life and Adventures of Captain Ned Wakeman.* New York, 1959.

Nugent, John "Scraps of Early History-VI." *The Argonaut,* vol. II, no. 14.

Oehler, Helen Irving (editor). "Nantucket to the Golden Gate in 1849." *CHSQ,* vol. 29.

Official Roster of the Soldiers of the State of Ohio in the War of the Rebellion 1861-1866. Akron, Cincinnati, Norwalk, 1883-95.

"Old Woodward" a Memorial relating to Woodward High School, 1831-1836, and Woodward College 1836-1851 in the City of Cincinnati. Cincinnati, 1884.

Phelps, Alonzo (compiler). *Contemporary Biography of California's Representative Men.* San Francisco, 1881.

Pisani, Donald J. "'Why Shouldn't California Have the Grandest Aqueduct in the World?' Alexis Von Schuidt's Lake Tahoe Scheme." *CHSQ,* vol. 53.

Rassmusen, Louis J. *San Francisco Ship Passenger Lists.* 4 volumes. Coloma, California, 1965 - 70.

Reinhardt, Richard (editor). "On the Brink of the Boom: Southern California in 1877, as witnessed by Mrs. Frank Leslie." *CHSQ,* vol. 52.

Remini, Robert V. *Henry Clay, Statesman for the Union.* New York, 1991.

Rocker, Willard R. *Marriage and Obituaries from the Macon Messenger 1881-1856.* Easly, South Carolina, 1988.

Rogers, Fred B. *Bear Flag Lieutenant, the Story of Henry L. Ford (1822-1860).* San Francisco, 1951.

Ruyssailh, Albert Bernard de. *Last Adventure, San Francisco in 1851.* Clarkson Crane, translator. San Francisco, 1931.

Schindler, Harold. *Orrin Porter Rockwell, Man of God, Son of Thunder.* Salt Lake City, 1966.

Scroggs, William O. *Filibusters and Financiers: The Story of William Walker and his Associates.* New York, 1916.

Secrest, William B. "The Rise and Fall of Thomas J. Henley in California." *Californians,* vol. 6, # 6.

Severson, Thor. *Sacramento, An Illustrated History: 1839 to 1874; from Sutter's Fort to Capital City.* San Francisco, 1973.

Shoemaker, Floyd Calvin (editor). *Missouri and Missourians.* Vol. IV, Chicago, 1943.

Shuck, Oscar Tully. *Bench and Bar in California: History, Anecdotes, Reminiscences.* 3 volumes. San Francisco, 1888-1889.

_____(editor). *History of the Bench and Bar in California . . . Los Angeles, 1901.*

Sioli, Paoli (compiler). *Historical Souvenir of El Dorado County.* Oakland, 1883.

Smith, Joseph (editor). *History of the Republican Party in Ohio.* Chicago, 1898.

Snowdon, Clinton A. *History of Washington. The Rise and Progress of an American State.* 5 vols. New York, 1909-1911.

Soulé, Frank, John H. Gihon and James Nisbet. *The Annals of San Francisco, together with the Continuation through 1855, compiled by Dorothy H. Huggins.* Palo Alto, California, 1966.

Steel, Edward M., Jr. *T. Butler King of Georgia.* Athens, Georgia, 1964.

Steele, R. J., James P. Ball and F. I. Houston (compilers and publishers). *Directory of the County of Placer for the year 1861.* San Francisco, 1861.

Stevens, George E. *The City of Cincinnati, a Summary of its Attractions, Advantages and Internal Improvements.* Cincinnati, 1869.

Stewart, George R. *Committee of Vigilance: Revolution in San Francisco, 1851.* Boston, 1964.

Stewart, W. F. *Pleasant Hours in an Eventful Life.* San Francisco, 1869.

Stowell, Levi. "Bound for the Land of Canaan, Ho!." Marco G. Thorne, editor. *CHSQ,* vol. 27.

Swasey, W. F. *The Early Days and Men of California.* Oakland, 1891.

Thrapp, Dan L. *Encyclopedia of Frontier Biography.* 3 vols. Glendale, California, 1988.

Truman, Benjamin Cummings. *The Field of Honor; being a complete and comprehensive history of dueling in all countries.* New York, 1884.

Van Nostrand, Jeanne. "Thomas A. Ayers, Artist-Argonaut in California." *CHSQ,* vol. 20.

Villard, Henry. *Memoires of Henry Villard, Journalist and Financier.* Boston and New York, 1904.

Walker, Franklin. *San Francisco's Literary Frontier.* Seattle and London, 1969.

The War of the Rebellion: a compilation of the official records of the Union and Confederate armies. 70 vols. Washington, D.C., 1880-1901.

Warner, Juan José, Judge Benjamin Hayes and Dr. J. P. Whitney. *A Historical Sketch of Los Angeles County, California.* Los Angeles, 1876.

Webb, Walter Prescott (editor). *Handbook of Texas.* Austin, 1952.

Wells, Laurenz. *History of Nevada County, California.* Oakland, 1880.

Wenzel, Caroline. "Historical Note on the Life of John Frederick Morse." in John Frederick Morse. *First History of Sacramento.* Sacramento, 1945.

Wheat, Carl I. (editor). "California's Bantam Cock, the Journals of Charles E. DeLong, 1854-1863." *CHSQ,* vol. 9.

White, Z. L. "Western Journalism." *Harper's Magazine,* Vol. 77: 678.

Williams, Mary Floyd. *History of the San Francisco Committee of Vigilance of 1851.* New York, 1969.

_____ (editor). *Papers of the San Francisco Committee of Vigilance of 1851.* Berkeley, 1919.

Wiltsee, Earnest A. *Gold Rush Steamers of the Pacific.* San Francisco, 1938.

Withington, Mary C. *A Catalogue of Manuscripts in the Collection of Western Americana founded by William Robertson Coe. Yale University Library.* New Haven, 1952.

Wright, George F. (editor). *History of Sacramento County, California.* Oakland, 1880.

Manuscripts and Public Records:

DMCL: Bickham Collection.

BL: C-A 169: U.S. Custom House Records: San Francisco.

BL: C-B 383.2: Records of El Dorado County Clerk.

BL: C-D 198: "Statement of George E. Schenck."

BL: C-D 94: Alfred E. Green, "Adventure of a '47er."

BL: C-D 196: "Statement of Gerritt W. Ryckman."

BL: PB 9- v. 1: Elwood Evans, "Northwest Coast History - interview."

California Census of 1852, DAR typescript.

CSL: Pioneer Card File: Thomas A. Morrow.

CSL: Biographical Information Files: John Love.

CSL: Information Card Catalogue sub "Pollock, Lewis," "Wood, Robert N."

Great Register of Placer County, 1867.

Great Register of San Francisco, 1867.

Journals of the Legislature of the State of California at its second session. Eugene Casserly, State Printer, 1851.

Journal of the Third Session of the Legislature of the State of California, San Francisco, 1852.

U.S. Census: 1850, 1860, 1870, 1880.

MHS: W. H. Dulany papers.

WRHS: Bickham Family papers.

Unpublished Theses and Dissertations:

Backus, Joyce. "A History of the San Francisco Mercantile Library Association." MA Thesis. University of California, 1920

Hodgson, Ila Draper. "William D. Bickham: Civil War Reporter and Editor." MA Thesis. Wright State University, 1971.

Kennedy, Chester Barrett. "Newspapers of the California Northern Mines 1850-1860: a Record of Life, Letters and Culture." Ph.D. Dissertation. Stanford University, 1949.

Newspapers:

Alta California.

Cincinnati Commercial.

Cincinnati Enquirer.

Cincinnati Daily Gazette.

Cincinnati Daily Times (Cincinnati Historical Society microfilm).

Cincinnati Tri-weekly Gazette.

Dayton Daily Journal.

Los Angeles Herald.

New Orleans Daily Picayune.

New York Times.

New York Daily Tribune.

Panama Star. 1854

Placerville Mountain Democrat.

Sacramento Bee.

Sacramento Placer Times.

Sacramento Transcript.

Sacramento Daily Union.

Saint Joseph Gazette.

St. Louis Missouri Republican.

San Francisco Daily Evening Journal.

San Francisco Daily Evening Bulletin.

San Francisco Call.

San Francisco Chronicle.

San Francisco Daily Herald.

San Francisco Daily Evening Picayune.

San José Pioneer.

Scrapbooks of Newspaper Clippings.

Dagget, John. *A Scrapbook of California Biography: Newspaper Clippings Relating to California Pioneers.* California State Library, Sacramento.

Newspaper Clippings on Cincinnati 1921-50. (compiled by Reference department of Public Library of Cincinnati).

Wright, Smithson (compiler). *Obituaries of Cincinnatians.* Cincinnati Historical Society Library.

City Directories.

Bogardus, J. P. *Bogardus' San Francisco, Sacramento City and Marysville Business Directory*. San Francisco, 1850.

Kimball, Charles Proctor. *The San Francisco City Directory. September 1, 1850*. San Francisco, 1850.

Morgan, A. W. *A. W. Morgan & Co.'s San Francisco City Directory. September, 1852*. San Francisco, 1852.

Parker, James M. *The San Francisco Directory for the Year 1852-3*. San Francisco, 1852.

Chicago: 1879-1901.

Cincinnati: 1825, 1836-7, 1840, 1843, 1846, 1849-95.

Columbus, Ohio: 1866-1911.

Evansville, Indiana: 1872-83.

New Orleans: 1842, 1849.

New York City: 1894-1905.

Portland, Oregon: 1869-95.

Sacramento: 1851, 1853-81.

San Francisco: 1850-95.

Washington, D.C.: 1862-86.

Index